ATTP 3-21.90 (FM 7-90)/MCWP 3-15.2

Tactical Employment of Mortars

April 2011

Headquarters, Department of the Army

DISTRIBUTION RESTRICTION: Approved for public release; distribution is unlimited.

PCN: 143 000092 00

Published by Books Express Publishing
Books Express Publishing, 2011
ISBN 978-1-78039-959-1

Books Express publications are available from all good retail and online booksellers. For
publishing proposals and direct ordering please contact us at: info@books-express.com

*ATTP 3-21.90 (FM 7-90)/MCWP 3-15.2

Army Tactics, Techniques, and Procedures
No. 3-21.90 (FM 7-90)

Headquarters
Department of the Army
Washington, DC

Marine Corps Warfighting Publication
No. 3-15.2

Marine Corps Combat Development Command
Quantico, VA

4 April 2011

Tactical Employment of Mortars

Contents

Distribution Restriction: Approved for public release; distribution is unlimited.

*This manual supersedes FM 7-90, 9 October 1992.

PCN: 143 000092 00

Figures

Tables

Preface

This Army and Marine Corps multiservice publication serves as doctrinal reference for the employment of mortar squads, sections, and platoons. It contains guidance on tactics and techniques that mortar units use to execute their part of combat operations described in battalion-, squadron-, troop-, and company-level manuals. This publication also contains guidance on how a mortar unit's fires and displacement are best planned and employed to sustain a commander's intent for fire support.

The target audience of this publication includes mortar squad, section, and platoon leaders, company and battalion commanders, battalion staff officers, and all others responsible for controlling and coordinating fire support during combined arms operations. Training developers also use this manual as a source document for combat critical tasks. Combat developers use this manual when refining and revising operational concepts for Infantry and reconnaissance mortar organizations. This publication serves as the primary reference for both resident and nonresident mortar tactical employment instruction.

This publication is not intended to be used alone. It is part of a set of doctrinal and training publications that together provide the depth and detail necessary to train and employ mortar units. Users must be familiar with appropriate company- and battalion-level maneuver manuals as well as mortar-related drills and collective tasks.

When employing mortars, Army and Marine Corps units use similar tactics and techniques. However, the differences are few at the battalion command level and below. Differences between the services' terms and definitions are more apparent when introducing or discussing general subjects, such as warfighting functions, tactical operations, and unit organizations. Detailed explanations of these differences are beyond the scope of this manual. They are, however, identified where appropriate and different terms are combined when possible. For example, sustainment/logistics is used to identify the Army's sustainment and the Marine Corps' logistic functions. Readers should refer to their own service's manuals for more detailed explanations.

Some common Army and Marine Corps terms have slightly different acronyms and, where needed, have been combined. For example, this manual uses FIST/FiST to represent a fire support team when addressing both services. Wherever possible, the use of acronyms has been minimized in this manual.

This publication applies to the Active Army, the Army National Guard (ARNG)/Army National Guard of the United States (ARNGUS), United States Army Reserve (USAR), Marine Corps, and Marine Corps Reserve unless otherwise stated.

The proponent of this publication is the United States Army Training and Doctrine Command (TRADOC). The preparing agency is the U.S. Army Maneuver Center of Excellence (MCoE). Comments and recommendations may be sent by any means—U.S. mail, e-mail, fax, or telephone—using or following the format of DA Form 2028, *Recommended Changes to Publications and Blank Forms*.

E-mail:	BENN.CATD.DOCTRINE@CONUS.ARMY.MIL
Phone:	COM 706-545-7114 or DSN 835-7114
Fax:	COM 706-545-8511 or DSN 835-8511
U.S. Mail:	Commanding General
	Maneuver Center of Excellence
	Doctrine and Collective Training Division
	Directorate of Training and Doctrine (DOTD)
	ATTN: ATZB-TDD
	Fort Benning, GA 31905-5410

Marines can send their comments to the above address or to—

U.S. Mail: Capabilities Development Directorate
Attn: Director, Fires and Maneuver Integration Division
Marine Corps Combat Development Command
3300 Russell Road
Quantico, VA 22134

Unless otherwise stated in this publication, masculine nouns and pronouns refer to both men and women.

Summary of Changes

- Redesignated the manual as a multi-service publication (U.S. Army and U.S. Marine Corps).
- Deleted references to the obsolete M30 107-mm and the M29A1 81-mm mortars and added references to the newly-fielded M121 and the RMSL-6 versions of the 120-mm mortar.
- Added discussions of the effects of newly fielded automated mortar fire direction control systems.
- Combined discussions of offense, defense, stability, and civil support operations into a single chapter.
- Incorporated lessons learned from combat operations in Iraq and Afghanistan:
  - Expanded discussion of the employment of mortar units by squad and section.
  - Discussed responsibilities of mortar unit leaders during noncontiguous operations.
  - Expanded discussions of the employment of light mortars.
  - Expanded and updated discussions of mortar ammunition supply rates.
  - Added discussions of the echeloning of fires and risk-estimate distance.
  - Added a discussion of a mortar leader's role in defending against stand-off attacks.
  - Updated discussions of mortar fire planning, lethality, and fuze/round selection.
  - Expanded discussions of mortar illumination and smoke missions.
  - Added discussions on massing mortar fires and time-on-target missions.
  - Updated the discussion of helicopter operations.
  - Added a discussion of the employment of mortars during operations in mountains.
  - Updated discussions of mortar employment during urban combat.
- Expanded discussions on the construction of mortar firing positions:
  - Established standards for mortar positions rather than mandating a specific design.
  - Added discussion of prefabricated construction materials.
  - Increased discussion of built-up mortar firing positions vice dug-in positions.
  - Validated construction standards for protection against common enemy weapons and munitions.
- Incorporated terminology and organizational changes based on FM 3-0, *Operations*, and other keystone doctrine:
  - Deleted references to Airland Battle but retained discussion of key mortar unit attributes.
  - Updated information on current mortar units and equipment to include U.S. Marine Corps and U.S. Army modular brigade combat team organizations.
  - Deleted redundant discussions of standard maneuver and fire control graphics.
- Added section on standards and coordination with the Field Artillery:
  - Updated a discussion of target numbering and aligned it with Field Artillery doctrine.
  - Reduced unnecessary redundency between Field Artillery manuals.
  - Updated discussions of command and support relationships.
  - Updated discussions of the role of Field Artillery fire support officers and fire support coordination.
- Expanded guidance on the development of a mortar unit's tactical standing operating procedures.

This page intentionally left blank.

Chapter 1

Introduction to Mortar Units

While talking on the radio, I heard someone say, "Charlie Six." I looked up to see Specialist Tommy Freese, the only man in his platoon who was not a casualty. Bullets were flying all around. Tommy was standing in the open with a 60-mm mortar on one shoulder and a sack of ammunition on the other. "Sir," he said, "the Fourth Platoon is ready. Where do you want me to shoot?"

Company Commander
First Infantry Division
Binh Duong Province, RVN
25 August 1966

Mortar platoons and sections provide commanders with organizationally responsive lethal indirect fires that all maneuver units in close combat need to defeat an enemy. Military history has repeatedly demonstrated the effectiveness of mortars in close combat. Their high-angle fires are invaluable against dug-in enemy troops and targets in defilade, which are not vulnerable to attack by direct fires. Commanders coordinate mortar fires with direct fire weapons to defeat enemy forces. Mortar fires destroy an enemy, suppress their fire, reveal their movements, and obscure their ability to observe. Mortar units are not simply small artillery batteries, although they are part of a total fire support system. They play a unique and vital role on the battlefield. They provide fires that ease combat tasks of company, battalion, and brigade combat team (BCT)/regimental combat team (RCT) commanders by providing agility, mass, and depth to a tactical-level battlefield.

SECTION I – TEXT REFERENCES

1-1.   Within this manual, selected topics are briefly discussed and readers are referred to another publication for more detail. Mortar and other combat units use these tactics, techniques, and procedures in the same or similar manner and a detailed discussion in this manual would be redundant. However, they are as important as the subjects discussed in detail. Table 1-1 consolidates the references to additional information.

Table 1-1. Guide for subjects referenced in text

Subject	References
Operational environment	FM 3-0/MCDP 1-0
Army brigade role in fires and effects planning	FM 6-30
	FM 6-20-20
Marine Corps regimental role in fires and effects planning	MCWP 3-16
Forward observer team responsibilities	MCWP 3-16.6
Mortar systems	FM 3-22.90
Fire direction	FM 3-22.91

SECTION II – OPERATIONAL ENVIRONMENT

1-2.   U.S. forces engage in periods of prolonged confrontation among states, nonstates, and individuals willing to use violence to achieve their political and ideological ends. To be effective, a Soldier must understand the operational environment that shapes any conflict. (See FM 3-0/MCDP 1-0 for details.)

1-3.   An operational environment is a composite of the conditions, circumstances, and influences that affect the employment of mortar units and tactical decisions. It includes all enemy, adversary, friendly, and neutral systems across the spectrum of conflict. It also includes an understanding of the physical environment, state of governance, technology, local resources, and culture of the local population relevant to a specific operation.

THREATS

1-4.   Threats are nation-states, organizations, people, groups, conditions, or natural phenomena able to damage or destroy life, vital resources, or institutions. Of special concern for mortar units, is a threat's ability to—

- Deliver fires, especially its counter fire and counter mortar capability.
- Detect friendly mortar fire.

1-5.   The following are types of threats:

- **Traditional** threats have conventional military capabilities. U.S. forces defeat these forces primarily through offensive and defensive operations. Traditional threats are most likely to have a counter mortar detection and destruction capability and pose other direct threats to mortar units such as manned and un-manned aerial platforms.
- **Irregular** threats are those posed by an opponent employing asymmetric methods and means to counter traditional U.S. advantages. Their operations combine conventional, unconventional, and irregular tactics. They focus on creating conditions of instability, seek to alienate legitimate forces from the population, and employ global networks to expand local operations. Threats employ advanced information operations and are not bound by conventional limits on the use of violence. Conflicts often take place in areas in which people are concentrated and require U.S. security dominance to extend across the population. Irregular threats often use surprise, conduct hit and run attacks, defend positions only long enough to inflict casualties, and use the civilian population to protect themselves from U.S. firepower.

MISSION VARIABLES

1-6.   The operational environment for each major operation is different and evolves as each operation progresses. Army and Marine Corps forces use operational variables to understand and analyze the broad environment in which they conduct operations. They use mission variables to focus analysis on specific elements of the environment that apply to their mission. Leaders use mission variables to synthesize tactical information with local knowledge about conditions relevant to their mission. Upon receipt of a warning order (WARNO/WARNORD) or mission, leaders begin their initial mission analysis and start to visualize their desired end state.

1-7.   Variables commanders use for mission analysis at the tactical level are— mission, enemy, terrain and weather, troops, support available, time available, and civil considerations (METT-TC).

> *Note.* The Marine Corps equivalent of METT-TC variables are— mission, enemy, terrain and weather, troops, support available-time available (METT-T). This manual uses the term METT-TC/ METT-T to represent mission variables for both the Marine Corps and the Army.

SECTION III – THE ROLE OF MORTARS

1-8.   The primary role of mortar units is to provide a commander with immediately available, responsive, and both lethal and nonlethal indirect fires in support of company/troop and battalion/squadron maneuver. They also serve to reinforce direct fires during close combat. Mortar units are assigned to—

- Combined arms battalions.
- Stryker Brigade Combat Team (SBCT) Infantry battalions.
- Army and Marine Corps Infantry battalions.
- Marine Corps light armored reconnaissance battalions.
- Ranger battalions.
- Reconnaissance squadrons and troops.

- Army Infantry, SBCT, and Ranger companies.
- Marine Corps Infantry companies.

1-9. Mortar sections and platoons provide a commander with—
- Organic indirect fire capability that is always present and responsive to the maneuver commander regardless of the changing demands placed on any supporting field artillery.
- Supporting fire that is immediately at hand from units close to the company and battalion fight. Because a mortar unit is aware of the local situation, it is able to respond quickly without lengthy coordination.
- Plunging fires that complement the heavier fires of supporting field artillery, helicopter close combat attack, close air support (CAS), and naval gunfire.
- Weapons whose high rate of fire and lethality fill the gap between the time field artillery fires shift to deeper targets, and the assault elements close onto an objective.
- Base of fire upon which to anchor his maneuver to the critical point of enemy weakness.
- Dense and lethal defensive fires that suppress, disrupt, and destroy enemy attackers.
- For reconnaissance units, the ability to immediately suppress an enemy and allow a unit to disengage. Without revealing their locations, scouts can engage targets with indirect fire.

1-10. Army combined arms battalions, SBCT battalions, and Marine Corps light armored reconnaissance battalions use carriers from which to fire and to move cross-country at speeds compatible with their battalions. These tracked and wheeled units can also ground-mount their primary mortars (except Stryker carriers). If equipped, these units can also ground-mount their secondary mortars. Infantry forces use wheeled vehicles or hand-carry mortars into firing positions. Infantry, SBCT, and Ranger companies have light mortars that can be man-packed across all terrain.

PURPOSE OF MORTAR FIRES

1-11. Mortar fires are employed for the following purposes:
- **Close support fires** are targeted against enemy troops, weapons, or positions that are threatening or can threaten the friendly unit during either the attack or the defense. Providing close support fires is the most common mission given to the mortar platoon or section. Close support mortar fires are normally requested and adjusted by platoon-level forward observers (FOs), but they may be initiated and controlled by any leader within the chain of command. Examples of close support fires include illumination, screening, suppressive, marking, preparatory, and final protective fires (FPFs).
- **Counterfires** are used to attack an enemy's indirect fire weapons, their observation posts (OPs), and their ability to control their forces. Counterfire at long range is mainly the responsibility of the field artillery, but mortar units provide close counterfire, especially against enemy mortars and rockets. Mortar counterfire is an immediate action taken to restore the freedom of action to a maneuver commander, before more powerful counterfire weapons can be brought to bear. Mortar smoke rounds are used to obscure enemy observation, thereby reducing the effectiveness of enemy fire.
- **Interdiction fires** are used to divert, disrupt, delay, or destroy an enemy's surface military potential before it can be used effectively against friendly forces. Field artillery is responsible for most ground interdiction fires. Mortar sections and platoons fire limited, specific types of interdiction fires on likely or suspected enemy assault positions or assembly areas, especially those in defilade. Occasionally, unobserved mortar interdiction fires intended to harass an enemy may be used, although a commander must weigh the costs of ammunition expended and the increased danger of counterfire.
- **Harassment fires** are used to disturb the rest of the enemy troops, curtail movement, and lower morale by the threat of losses.
- **Deception fires** are used to deceive and confuse an enemy. Mortars can be used to fire false preparatory fires on enemy positions or landing zones. They can also be used to create deceptive smoke screens to focus an enemy in one location while friendly forces attack from another.

EFFECTS OF MORTAR FIRES

1-12. A battalion or company commander must decide, and then clearly state, what effects he wants to achieve with mortar fire on a particular target. The effects are—

- **Destruction** puts a target permanently out of action. Thirty percent casualties or material damage usually is required to destroy a target. Mortars can destroy soft targets, but the amount of ammunition required to destroy a target is usually very large.
- **Neutralization** temporarily renders the target ineffective or unusable. Normally a target is neutralized when it suffers 10 percent casualties or damage. Against hardened targets, it is difficult to achieve neutralization with mortar fire. However, neutralization with mortar fire can be achieved against softer targets, including dismounted Infantry or wheeled vehicles.
- **Suppression** limits or prevents an enemy from firing back, observing, or maneuvering. The effects of suppressive fires are immediate, but they last only as long as the fires continue. Suppression is the key to any successful Infantry assault. A mortar unit's high rate of fire and organizational responsiveness make it an excellent means to suppress enemy forces. Suppressive fires play a large role in generating combat power by Infantry forces. The suppressive fires of mortars, along with other weapons, allow the Infantry to maneuver and close for a final assault. The more effective the suppressive fires, the less dependent Infantrymen are on stealth, cover, and concealment. Mortar fires can continue to suppress the enemy until the assaulting forces are close enough to use their hand-carried weapons for suppression.
- **Obscuration** hampers an enemy's ability to observe and acquire targets and conceals friendly movement and activities. Obscuration fires do not neutralize or suppress an enemy, since they can still employ their weapons, but they reduce the effectiveness of enemy fire. Mortars can fire smoke rounds directly on an enemy position to both suppress and obscure, or they can fire smoke rounds between friendly forces and the enemy position to obscure observation. Mortar obscuration is effective for immediate response missions of limited scope and for short periods. The 81-mm and the 120-mm mortars have effective obscuration rounds.
- **Illumination** illuminates a designated area and is used for signaling. Mortars provide a flexible type of illumination round, including both visible and infrared (IR) light.

CHARACTERISTICS OF MORTAR OPERATIONS

1-13. Commanders of maneuver units attempt to dictate the terms of action throughout an operation. They focus on gaining and retaining the initiative to achieve decisive results. Commanders combine synchronization with agility and initiative. Synchronization produces maximum relative combat power at a decisive place and time. Mortar units support a commander's intent by contributing to initiative, synchronization, agility, and depth.

INITIATIVE

1-14. Mortars contribute to gaining the initiative from an enemy by providing immediate fires to destroy enemy forces and to disrupt their plans during both offensive and defensive combat. The speed and effectiveness of mortar fires prevent an enemy from gaining the initiative.

1-15. Mortars are often used to deliver on-call immediate suppressive fires against enemy positions. Mortar sections and platoons can respond quickly with area fire that destroys the weapon, obscures its field of fire, or suppresses its gunner. The friendly force thus retains the initiative to either close with an enemy and destroy them or to bypass and strike at another point. In the offense, mortar sections and platoons allow a commander to weight the main effort in a phase. A commander can use mortars to screen his movement or to designate targets on which to concentrate other fires. In the defense, immediate counterfire suppresses an enemy and frees the friendly unit to take its own actions.

1-16. Because each maneuver battalion has organic mortars, the BCT/RCT commander is free to mass his organic and supporting artillery at the critical time and place to maintain the initiative at his level. Mortars help regain the initiative during the defense by destroying or disrupting attacking forces, by screening and isolating enemy supporting elements, or by disclosing enemy movements. Mortar sections and platoons permit company and battalion commanders to continue to bring indirect fires to bear on an assaulting enemy even while artillery shifts to attack enemy follow-on forces at a greater range.

SYNCHRONIZATION

1-17. Because mortar sections and platoons are organic parts of the maneuver and company battalion, their fires are easily synchronized with the actions of the other members of the combined arms team to destroy an enemy. The synchronization of mortar fires with the direct fires from vehicles, close combat missiles, machine guns, and small arms of the rifle platoons produces a greater combined effect on an enemy than the simple total of these fires.

1-18. Mortar fires are a critical and irreplaceable element of the unit's maneuver. They defeat an enemy, suppress their fire, or screen their vision, thus allowing the assaulting riflemen to close and destroy them.

1-19. Mortar fires alone normally cannot destroy enemy armor, but they contribute to an enemy's destruction through synchronized action. High explosive (HE) fire forces enemy armor crews to close hatches and observe through viewing ports. This severely reduces a crew's ability to observe and makes them vulnerable to direct antitank fires. High explosive and smoke can also separate armor vehicles from their dismounted Infantry support, leaving them isolated and vulnerable to mobile gun systems, tank main guns, and antitank guided missiles (ATGMs).

1-20. Mortar illumination can reveal enemy armored or ground forces during darkness for synchronized friendly attacks using ground-mounted antitank weapons, artillery, and attack helicopters. Mortars also contribute to synchronization by providing marking rounds for CAS and attack helicopters. They also illuminate and suppress enemy defenders who can then be destroyed by direct fires and close assault forces.

1-21. After the maneuver unit wins the antiarmor battle, or is still fighting around key engagement areas, friendly units may face dismounted attacks by enemy infantry, day and night. A maneuver commander uses mortar fires to dominate and destroy this enemy, while protecting and conserving the friendly force.

AGILITY

1-22. Agility is the ability to move and adjust quickly and easily. Mortar sections and platoons exemplify organizational and physical agility. Their high angle of fire, mobility, ability to rapidly shift fires, and available shell/fuze combinations allow a commander to move forces quickly about the battlefield without losing responsive and effective fires. The mortar's lightweight and simplicity allow Infantrymen to move them rapidly and to engage targets quickly with a high volume of fire. Dismounted forces can carry medium and light mortars over all terrain, and light vehicles and helicopters can move heavy mortars. Mortars can fire from almost any ground upon which a man can stand. Mortar platoons can shift quickly from engaging multiple targets to massing their fires on a single enemy location. In addition, Infantry battalions fighting on restrictive terrain can use the inherent agility of mortars to increase the offensive and defensive power of small, dispersed units.

DEPTH

1-23. Mortars add depth to the battlefield. They not only out-range most direct fire weapons, but also reach enemy forces sheltered in defilade and within field fortifications. The high angle of mortar fires make them effective against enemy forces hidden in wadis, ravines, reverse slopes, thick jungle, narrow streets, or alleyways.

1-24. At night, mortars extend the battlefield beyond the depth of normal vision. They can deliver planned fires to destroy an enemy or they may illuminate the enemy for other weapons to engage. Mortar obscuration rounds limit the enemy's view of the battlefield and disrupt their coordinated actions. Mortars also add depth to the battlefield by isolating a portion of an enemy's force, allowing their defeat in detail before other units can provide aid.

1-25. A mortar's ability to deliver fires in any direction at short ranges provides responsive fire support throughout the depth of the friendly area of operations (AO). Suppressive fires from mortars allow assaulting Infantrymen to advance close to their objective before these fires must be lifted or shifted. This not only conserves friendly combat power, but also allows the field artillery to shift and attack enemy supporting weapons or formations deeper to the rear. Units can also conduct raids to destroy targets deep in an enemy's AO by moving mortar units by air, ground transportation, or while dismounted.

MORTAR TASKS

1-26. Mortar units provide lethal and nonlethal fires that are vital for close combat in both the offense and defense. During stability and civil support operations, restrictions on lethal force laid out in the unit's rules of engagement (ROE) may limit the use of mortar fires. The following are some of the primary battlefield tasks for mortar units.

- In the offense, mortar units are used to—
  - Establish a base of fire (along with other weapons) on which the unit can maneuver.
  - Destroy or neutralize enemy units.
  - Suppress an enemy's observation and fire.
  - Fix an enemy.
  - Provide close supporting fires for the assault.
- In the defense, mortar units are used to—
  - Suppress or destroy enemy supporting weapons.
  - Disrupt enemy troop concentrations.
  - Destroy an enemy conducting close dismounted assaults.
  - Regain the initiative.
- In stability and civil support operations, mortar units are used to—
  - Support forces in contact.
  - Protect friendly bases from attack.
  - Destroy enemy indirect fire capability.
  - Provide illumination.
  - Perform Infantry-common tasks, such as conducting patrols.

MORTARS IN COMPANY- AND BATTALION-LEVEL BATTLE

1-27. At company- and battalion-level battle, mortar fire destroys enemy forces and enhances friendly mobility. They destroy, neutralize, or suppress an enemy, allowing friendly forces to close with and seize objectives.

1-28. Mortar units are organic fire support to battalions and companies and are available to a commander when other indirect fire support may not be available. Field artillery assets at all levels are limited. For BCT/RCT and division commanders to concentrate offensive combat power at the critical point, they must accept risk elsewhere. Some maneuver units have less artillery support than others. At battalion and company level, mortar units—

- Destroy or neutralize enemy forces.
- Suppress and isolate enemy forces.
- Support the destruction of enemy armor by forcing them to close hatches and observe through viewing ports, reducing their ability to employ supporting fires, and separating their dismounted infantry from their carriers and accompanying tanks. The battalion's direct antiarmor fires are then more effective against an isolated enemy with limited visibility and supporting fires.
- Penetrate buildings and destroy enemy field fortifications, preparing the way for dismounted assault.
- Enable battalion and company commanders to cover friendly obstacles with planned indirect fire.
- Attack enemy assault units and bases of fire.
- Integrate into a unit's FPFs to repulse an enemy's dismounted assault.
- Utilize the protection of prepared positions in defilade to continue indirect fire support, even when subjected to counterfire.
- Maneuver with and fire directly overhead of friendly troops from close behind the forward elements, concentrating and synchronizing combat power.

1-29. Commanders need to ensure the security of mortar units. Mortar units have a limited ability to provide their own security and are not as efficient if they are required to do so. This is especially true for light mortars because of their small crews and proximity to the fight. Based on a METT-TC/METT-T analysis, commanders may require mortar units to collocate with other elements, such as the headquarters (HQ) or reserve, or may attach Infantry to mortar units to provide security.

1-30. Fire support planning at the battalion and company level is the same for both the Army and Marine Corps. However, fire support organizations at the battalion and company level for the two services are slightly different.

BATTALION AND COMPANY FIRE SUPPORT PLANNING

1-31. Planning and conduct of battalion and company mortar fires is not done in a vacuum. Actions of mortar platoons and sections are part of a plan to support a commander's intent. Although they are organic to battalions and companies, mortar units adhere to the overall BCT/RCT fire support plan as refined by subordinate unit fire support plans. They execute their fires to accomplish the tasks, purpose, and effects identified by a commander.

BRIGADE AND REGIMENTAL COMBAT TEAM ROLES IN FIRES AND EFFECTS PLANNING

1-32. All fire support organizations within the BCT and RCT are subordinate to the fires cell. This cell plays a vital role in the battalion and company's fires planning and execution. The top-down plan developed and refined during the military decision-making process and preparation phase should incorporate fire support tasks supporting the BCT/RCT, battalion, and company schemes of maneuver. (See FM 6-30/MCWP 3-16.6 and FM 6-20-20/MCWP 3-16 for details.)

BATTALION'S ROLE IN FIRE SUPPORT PLANNING

1-33. Key to successful battalion fire support is the synchronization of mortar fires with the scheme of maneuver, the integration of the mortars into the scheme of fires, and planning their movement with the scheme of maneuver. A battalion develops a scheme of fires to support both tasks assigned by the BCT/RCT and targets developed by the battalion. It then issues the fire support plan to its subordinates and incorporates bottom-up refinement to support the commander's scheme of maneuver. Finally, a battalion forwards its fires and target refinements to the BCT/RCT and ensures the plan is clearly understood through rehearsals. A battalion must—

- Understand the integration of the BCT/RCT scheme of fires and maneuver.
- Understand a BCT/RCT commander's intent for fires and a battalion's role in the scheme of fires and maneuver.
- Develop a battalion concept and scheme of fires and effects.
- Understand the current ROE and clearance of fires procedures.
- Integrate company mortars (if any) into a battalion scheme of maneuver and fires.
- Integrate and refine BCT/RCT targets for the close fight.
- Plan for the synchronization of battalion mortars with the scheme of fires and effects and their movement with the scheme of maneuver.
- Ensure risk management is incorporated into fire support planning and execution.
- Incorporate bottom-up refinement from companies.
- Forward the battalion scheme of fires and effects and target refinements to BCT/RCT.
- Conduct rehearsals with maneuver and fires elements.
- Execute a battalion's portion of the scheme of fires.

COMPANY'S ROLE IN FIRE SUPPORT TARGET REFINEMENT

1-34. A company commander is responsible for the employment of indirect fires in his AO. He makes necessary changes to the fire support plan to ensure that targets accomplish their intended purpose. A company commander's fire support officer (FSO)/fire support coordinator (FSC) must be ready to adjust existing targets or to nominate new targets that allow engagement of specific enemy forces or to change the desired effect.

> *Note.* Fire support officers lead Army fires cells and fire support teams (FISTs) at the battalion and company level, respectively. Marine Corps FSCs lead equivalent fire support coordination centers (FSCCs), and fire support teams (FiSTs). This manual uses the term FSO/FSC to identify these personnel.

1-35. Necessary refinements usually emerge when a company commander war-games as part of the "complete the plan" step of the troop-leading procedures (TLPs). The war-gaming process allows him to identify required additions, deletions, and adjustments to the battalion fire support plan.

1-36. As a specific requirement in defensive planning, a company commander must focus on target refinement for the ground he will own during the operation. This includes the planning for engagement areas. The commander makes appropriate adjustments to the targets based on refinements to the situation template, such as the actual positions of obstacles and the anticipated positions of enemy direct fire systems.

BATTALION AND COMPANY FIRE SUPPORT ORGANIZATIONS

1-37. Both the Army and Marine Corps have fire support organizations at the maneuver battalion and company levels.

ARMY ORGANIZATION

1-38. Within BCTs, fires cells are organic to each maneuver battalion and the reconnaissance squadron. Fire support teams organic in the HQ company/troop are allocated by the battalion/squadron commander to the subordinate companies/troops or may be retained under battalion control. Infantry FISTs also have a sufficient number of FO teams to provide a team for each rifle platoon. Each FO team consists of an FO and a radiotelephone operator (except SBCT units that just have an observer).

Fires Cell

1-39. A fires cell provides each maneuver battalion with an organic fire support coordination capability. A battalion FSO is in charge of the cell and is the principal advisor to a commander on fire support matters (Table 1-2). In combined arms battalions, SBCT battalions, and reconnaissance squadrons, the fires cell is equipped with a fire support vehicle with radios that allow communications by both voice and digital transmissions.

Table 1-2. Army battalion fires cell personnel

Title	Rank	Quantity
FSO	CPT	1
Assistant FSO (plans)	ILT	1
Fire support sergeant	SFC	1
Fire support sergeant	SSG	1
Fire support specialist	SPC	2

Fire Support Team

1-40. Each Infantry company, mechanized company, armor company, and reconnaissance troop normally has an attached FIST (Table 1-3). In armor, mechanized, and SBCT companies, the FIST has an armored personnel carrier/Stryker variant with a laser rangefinder/designator, an FO system computer, and a suite of radios that are removable for dismounted operations. The FIST is led by a field artillery officer and the company FSO, and has two or three two-man FO teams for each mechanized and Infantry company. In tank companies and reconnaissance troops, leaders within the platoons perform the FO's functions and the FIST consists only of the FIST HQ with no FO teams. An SBCT Infantry rifle company also has a FIST HQ and three FOs, one for each rifle platoon. All FO teams and SBCT FOs are equipped with radios that can be man-packed. In Infantry and Ranger battalions, the FIST may have a wheeled vehicle or may operate dismounted.

Table 1-3. Army fire support team

Title	Rank	Quantity
FSO	ILT	1
Fire support sergeant	SSG	1
Fire support specialist	SPC	1
FO	SGT	3*
Radio/telephone operator	PFC	4*
*One FO and one radio/telephone operator for each rifle platoon, except just the FO for SBCT platoons.		

Forward Observer

1-41. An FO, with or without an RTO, is normally attached to each rifle platoon. However, he can be employed in other ways, such as tasked to observe a specific AO or named area of interest. As the maneuver platoon's fire support representative, the primary duty of the FO is to locate targets and to call for and adjust indirect fire support. The FO must also be able to—

- Submit key targets for inclusion in the company fire plan (limited fire planning).
- Prepare, maintain, and use situation maps.
- Establish and maintain communications with the company FIST.
- Advise the platoon leader regarding the capabilities and limitations of available indirect fire support.
- Report battlefield intelligence.
- Provide targeting information for helicopter close combat attack and CAS execution with nonjoint terminal attack controller personnel (emergency CAS) as required.

Other Organizations

1-42. Other organizations may be placed under the operational control (OPCON) of the battalion. An Air Force tactical air control party may be provided to advise a commander and to control CAS. The following units can be placed under the OPCON of the battalion and are able to call for and adjust fires:

- Combat observation and lasing team.
- Supporting arms liaison team from the air and naval gunfire liaison company.

MARINE CORPS ORGANIZATION

1-43. Within the Marine Corps, an FSCC is assigned to each Infantry battalion, regiment, and division. At company level, there is a FiST with an FO team from the artillery and, based on a commander's task organization, FOs from the battalion mortar platoon.

Note. The Marine Corps uses the acronym FiST for their fire support teams. This manual uses the term FIST/FiST to represent fire support teams when referring to both services.

Marine Corps Fire Support Coordination Center

1-44. Each Marine Corps Infantry battalion has an FSCC. Separate battalions operating as maneuver elements also establish FSCCs, such as a light armored reconnaissance or tank battalions. The FSCC is a single location in which there are centralized communications facilities and personnel to coordinate all forms of fire support. This includes—

- Field artillery.
- Battalion mortars.
- CAS.
- Naval gunfire.

1-45. A battalion FSCC performs fire support coordination in terms of closely integrating multiple supporting arms with maneuver (Table 1-4). It monitors and receives all fire support requests originating within the battalion. A battalion FSCC ensures that supporting arms are integrated with the scheme of maneuver and that friendly forces are not endangered. It may also coordinate missions for observers to attack targets outside the battalion's zone of action.

Table 1-4. Marine Corps battalion fires cell

Title/Component	Title/Size (Officer/NCO/EM)
Fire support coordinator	Weapons company
Artillery liaison section	1/2/3
Shore fire control party	2/3/5
Tactical air control party	3/12
Battalion mortar representative	0/1/3

Fire Support Coordinator

1-46. The Infantry battalion weapons company commander is the FSC and is in charge of the FSCC.

Artillery Liaison Section

1-47. An artillery liaison section is organic to a firing battery of the supporting artillery battalion. It consists of four officers: an observer liaison chief, four observer liaison men, and nine field radio operators. The senior officer is the artillery liaison officer in the battalion FSCC. The remaining three officers are FOs and each heads an FO team to support a company. The FO team plans company artillery fires and can coordinate all fire support (mortars, artillery, air, and naval gunfire) at that level. (See MCWP 3-16.6 for details.) The team may be divided into two elements, each capable of independent operations for a limited period. Each FO team consists of—

- FO.
- Fire support man.
- Two radio/telephone operators.

Shore Fire Control Party

1-48. A battalion shore fire control party is from the HQ battery of the supporting artillery battalion. It includes a battalion naval gunfire liaison team and a naval gunfire spot team. A liaison team consists of a naval gunfire liaison officer, a naval gunfire chief, and three field radio operators. It performs liaison and coordination functions in the battalion FSCC. Spot teams call for and adjust naval gunfire. A team is normally employed with a company of the battalion. However, it may be divided into two elements, each capable of independent operations for a limited period. A spot team consists of—

- A naval gunfire spotter (Marine lieutenant).
- Two shore fire control party men.
- Two radio/telephone operators.

Tactical Air Control Party

1-49. A tactical air control party is organic to the battalion. It consists of three aviators and 12 field radio operators. A senior aviator acts in a dual capacity as battalion air officer, a special staff officer to the battalion commander concerning all aviation matters, and is in charge of the battalion tactical air control party. As the officer in charge, he works within the FSCC as the air representative. Each of the other two aviators is the leader of a forward air control party with four communicators each. A forward air control party requests and provides terminal control of CAS. The tactical air control party also provides input to the company fire plan.

81-mm Mortar Platoon Representative

1-50. A battalion's organic 81-mm mortar platoon provides a mortar liaison party to the battalion FSCC and four FO teams to support the companies and to occupy OPs. A mortar liaison party consists of a mortar representative, two field radio operators, and a wireman. An FO team consists of—

- FO.
- Two radio/telephone operators.
- One wireman.

Company Fire Support Team

1-51. A FiST is responsible for the development and execution of fires in support of a company commander's scheme of maneuver. A FiST is the integral element in the combined arms fight. It is through the FiST that air-to-surface and surface-to-surface fires, as well as maneuver, are integrated and deconflicted to achieve the maximum effects on the enemy in support of the company commander's scheme of maneuver. (See Table 1-5 for details on the organization of the FiST.)

Table 1-5. Marine Corps fire support team

Title	Rank	Quantity
FiST leader	1st Lt	1
Forward air control team		
Forward air controller	Capt	1
RTO	Cpl/LCpl	2
Artillery FO team *		
FO	2nd Lt	1
Fire support man	Sgt	1
RTO	Cpl/LCpl	2
Mortar FO team*		
FO	Cpl	1
*Attached from battalion		

1-52. A company FSO—

- Serves as company FSC.
- Develops the company fire support plan in support of the company commander's scheme of maneuver.
- Directs FiST members in the execution of fires in support of the company.
- Approves all indirect missions and CAS.
- Maintains updated friendly and enemy situation.
- Ensures coordination and deconfliction of maneuver and supporting arms under the FiST's control.

SECTION V – MORTAR UNIT COMPOSITION AND EQUIPMENT

1-53. The accurate and rapid delivery of indirect fires is a team effort. Effective communication is vital to the successful coordination of an indirect fire team's efforts. When mortars are fired, an indirect fire team determines and applies the required data, and coordinates the fires with the concept of the operation. This team consists of an FSO/FSC, the mortar squads, the fire direction center (FDC), and the FO. This section discusses mortar systems, Army and Marine Corps mortar unit organizations, their equipment, and target acquisition assets.

MORTAR SYSTEMS

1-54. Simplicity, ruggedness, maneuverability, and effectiveness are the principle characteristics of mortars. The following discusses the specific characteristics and capabilities of U.S. mortars and current organization of these weapons into squads, sections, and platoons.

COMMON CHARACTERISTICS

1-55. All U.S. mortars are smooth bore and fire fin-stabilized projectiles. (See Table 1-6 for general characteristics and FM 3-22.90 and the applicable mortar technical manuals for more detailed technical information.)

Table 1-6. U.S. mortar characteristics*

Type	Crew	Weight (Lbs)	Range† (Meters) Min	Range† (Meters) Max	Rates of Fire Round/Min.	Projectiles	Fuzes
M224 60-mm Conventional Mode	3	47	70	3,520	Maximum 30/4 Sustained 20/1	HE Smoke, WP ILLUM IR ILLUM	Multioption (prox, PD, NSB, Delay) Point Detonating Time Mechanical Time Superquick
M224 60-mm Hand-Held Mode	3	18	75	1,340	No Limit at charge 0 or 1	Same as Conventional	Same as Conventional
M252 81-mm	4 (Army) 6 (USMC)	93	83	5,792	Maximum 30/2 Sustained 15/1	HE Smoke, WP Smoke, RP ILLUM IR ILLUM	Multioption (prox, PD, NSB, Delay) Point Detonating Time Mechanical Time Superquick
M120/121 120-mm	4	320	200	7,200	Maximum 16/1 Sustained 4/1	HE Smoke, WP Smoke, RP ILLUM IR ILLUM	Multioption (prox, PD, NSB, Delay) Point Detonating Time Mechanical Time Superquick
RMSL-6 120-mm	5	1,466	180	6,700	Same as M120/121	Same as M120/121	Same as M120/121

Legend

ILLUM: illumination
IR: infrared
NSB: near surface burst

PD: point detonating (surface burst)
prox: proximity
superquick: point detonating (surface burst)

*Mortar characteristics are taken from the tabulated data for each mortar system in FM 3-22.90.
† Range is a function of the ammunition and charge used. Refer to the mortar system's firing table for more information.

LIGHT MORTAR

1-56. The 60-mm mortar, M224, provides Infantry, SBCT, Ranger, and Marine Corps rifle companies with an effective, efficient, and flexible weapon. Careful planning and a thorough knowledge of its capabilities can maximize its advantages, such as its light weight and its small crew, while minimizing its limitations, such as its short-range and small-explosive charge. The M224 can be employed in two configurations. The hand-held mode weighs about 18 pounds and consists of the mortar tube and the M8 baseplate that permits limited traverse. The conventional mode weighs about 45 pounds and consists of the complete mortar with bipod, sight, and M7 baseplate that permits 6400 mil traverse. Each round weighs about 4 pounds.

MEDIUM MORTAR

1-57. The 81-mm mortar, M252, is the current U.S. medium mortar. The M252 offers a compromise between the light and heavy mortars. Its range and explosive power are greater than the M224, yet it is still light enough to be man-packed over long distances. The M252 weighs about 93 pounds, and can be broken down into several smaller loads for easier carrying. Rounds for this mortar weigh about 15 pounds each.

HEAVY MORTAR

1-58. The 120-mm mortar is the current U.S. heavy mortar. The three versions of the 120-mm mortar are—
- Towed M120.
- Tracked vehicle-mounted M121.
- Stryker-mounted recoil mortar system, RMS6-L.

1-59. All three have the same cannon assembly. Although heavy mortars require trucks or tracked mortar carriers to move them, they are still much lighter than field artillery pieces. They outrange light and medium mortars and their explosive power is much greater. The M120 weighs about 320 pounds. Rounds for the 120-mm mortar weigh almost 33 pounds each.

MORTAR UNIT ORGANIZATION

1-60. The organization and equipment of mortar sections and platoons is based on approved or modified tables of organization and equipment. (See Table 1-7 and Figure 1-1 through Figure 1-5 for details.)

Table 1-7. Number and type of mortars in Army and Marine Corps units

	Maneuver Battalion			Rifle Company			Reconnaissance Troop		
Army	Heavy	Medium	Light	Heavy	Medium	Light	Heavy	Medium	Light
IBCT	4	4				2	2*		2*
HBCT	4						2		
SBCT	4	4		2		2	2		
Ranger	4	4	12						
Marines	Heavy	Medium	Light	Heavy	Medium	Light	Heavy	Medium	Light
Infantry		8				3			
LAR								2	
Legend									

Legend
HBCT: heavy brigade combat team   LAR: light-armored reconnaissance
IBCT: Infantry brigade combat team   SBCT: Stryker brigade combat team
* Mounted reconnaissance troops have two heavy mortars and the dismounted troop has two light mortars.

ARMY MORTAR UNITS

1-61. Army mortar units are organized into squads, sections, and platoons. The basic unit is a squad with one mortar. Each mortar section has two squads and each mortar platoon has two sections. All Infantry companies and reconnaissance troops have mortar sections. All Infantry battalions and combined arms battalions have mortar platoons. Ranger units have all of their mortars located at the battalion level with mortar elements habitually assigned to companies. Some sections and platoons can also operate another type of mortar depending on the mission. All mortar units can be attached to subordinate or other units. Their fires can then be integrated into the unit's fire control system.

1-62. Mortar platoons are located in the battalion's HQ and HQ's company. A junior commissioned officer leads mortar platoons and staff sergeants lead sections. All mortar platoons have an FDC section with personnel designated to man the FDC. Mortar sections in the Infantry, SBCT, and Ranger companies and in the reconnaissance troops do not have designated FDC personnel and a senior squad leader performs the FDC functions.

1-63. A combined arms battalion mortar platoon is equipped with four M121 120-mm mortars (Figure 1-1). Both mortar squad and FDC personnel operate from tracked carriers, which offer protection from small-arms fire and shell fragments. There are no organic mortar sections in a mechanized company.

1-64. An SBCT Infantry battalion mortar platoon has four recoil mortar system-light 120-mm mortars carried and fired from the Stryker mortar carrier vehicle (Figure 1-2). The FDC section uses a wheeled vehicle, as does the mortar section leader. Each SBCT rifle company also has a section of heavy mortars. For dismounted operations, SBCT mortar units use the arms room concept with battalion mortars platoon carrying additional medium mortars and the company mortars section carrying additional light mortars. Both mortar squad and FDC personnel operate from Stryker mortar carrier vehicles, which offer protection from medium caliber fire and shell fragments. Stryker has additional armor kits such as slat armor for rocket-propelled grenade (RPG) protection and Stryker reactive armor tiles for RPG/ATGM protection.

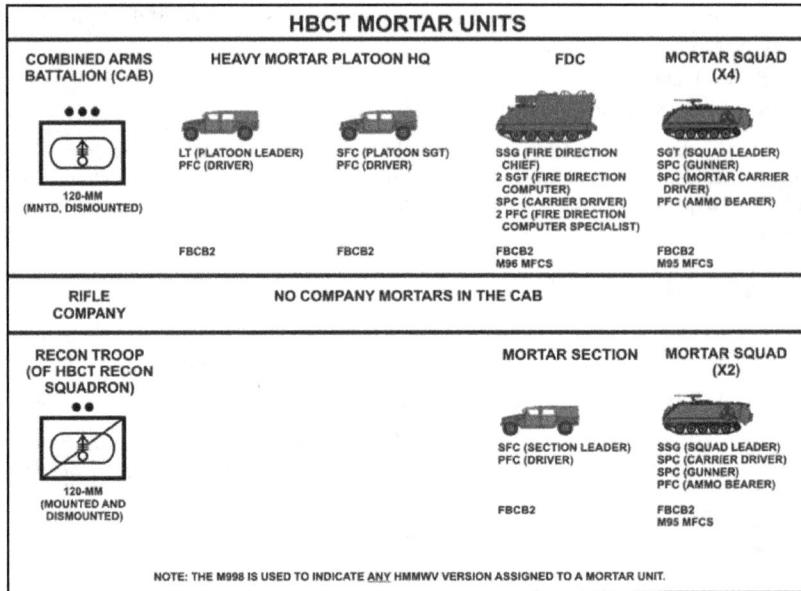

Figure 1-1. Army combined arms battalion and reconnaissance troop mortar units

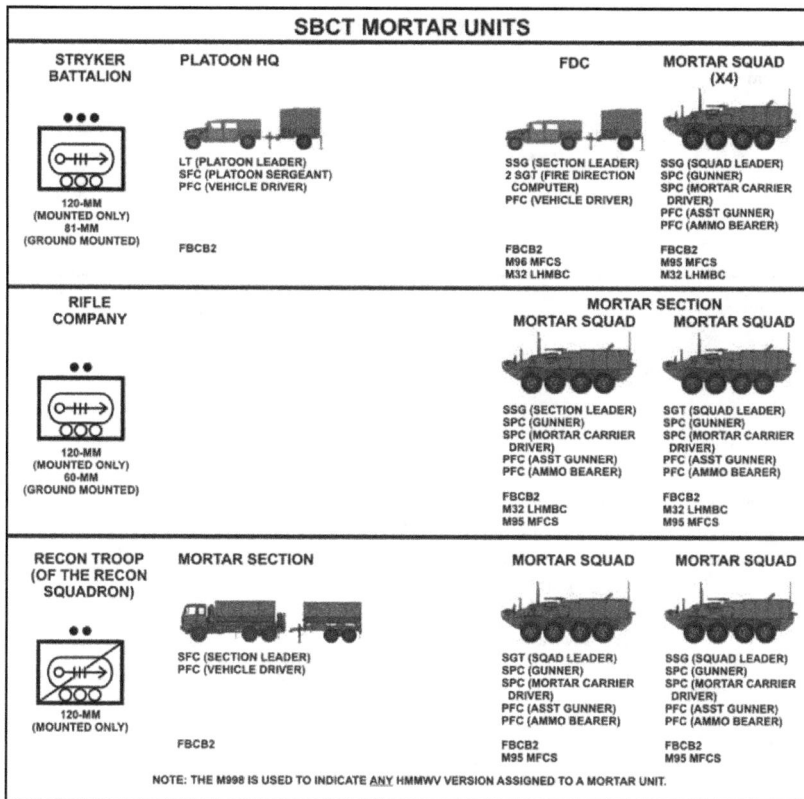

Figure 1-2. Army SBCT Infantry battalion and reconnaissance troop mortar units

1-65. Army Infantry battalions have mortar platoons at battalion level, equipped with four M120 120-mm mortars, and mortar sections at company level, equipped with two light mortars (Figure 1-3). Battalion mortar platoons also carry four medium mortars for dismounted operations. Battalion mortar platoons are equipped with trucks and trailers to carry mortars, while a company's light mortars are hand-carried.

1-66. A Ranger battalion mortar platoon has four M120 heavy, four medium, and 12 light mortar systems (Figure 1-4). These are carried on trucks and trailers, and are man-packed. Depending on the mission, light mortar systems are assigned to each rifle company. Each mortar squad is habitually assigned to specific Ranger rifle platoons.

1-67. Mounted ground reconnaissance troops have heavy mortar sections equipped with vehicle-mounted heavy mortar. A dismounted reconnaissance troop of the Infantry BCT has two light mortars. Reconnaissance mortar sections do not have dedicated FDC personnel.

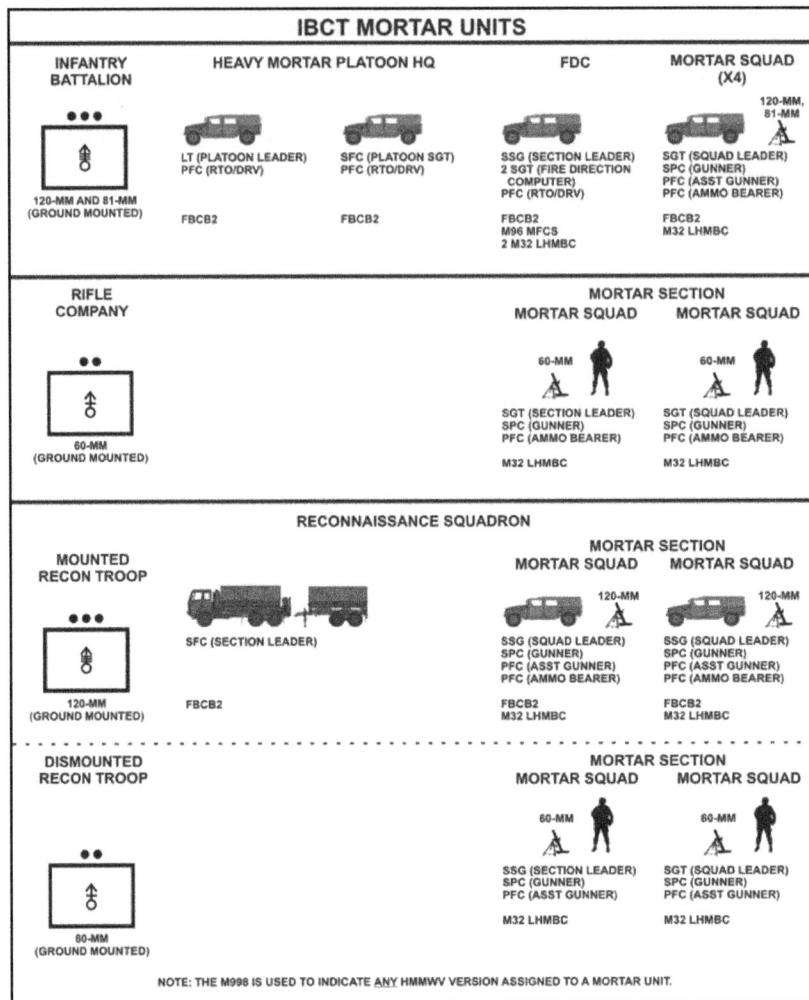

Figure 1-3. Army Infantry battalion and reconnaissance troop mortar units

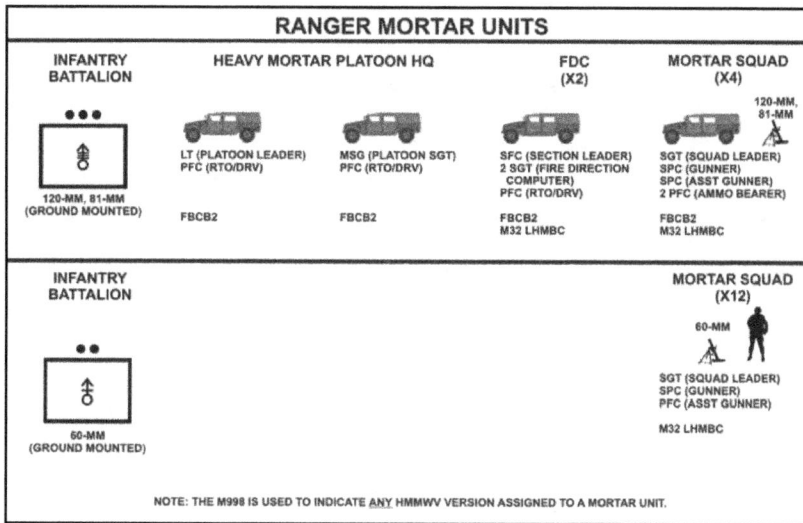

Figure 1-4. Army Ranger battalion mortar units

MARINE CORPS MORTAR UNITS

1-68. Marine Corps 81-mm and 60-mm mortar units are also organized into squads, sections, and platoons. Marine Corps 120-mm mortars are artillery assets. Figure 1-5 displays Infantry battalion, company, and light armored reconnaissance battalion mortar units. Each mortar squad operates one mortar. Each Marine Corps Infantry company has, as part of the weapons platoon, a mortar section of three squads. Each Marine Corps Infantry battalion has, as part of the weapons company, a mortar platoon with two FDCs and two sections each with four mortar squads, for a total of eight M252 81-mm mortars. A mortar platoon can therefore operate from two locations, each with a complete FDC and a four-mortar section.

1-69. 81-mm mortar platoons are located in the battalion's weapons company. Besides a platoon commander and a platoon sergeant, a Marine Corps mortar platoon HQ has one ammunition technician and two ammunition men. A platoon consists of two FDCs and two mortar sections, each with four mortar squads.

1-70. Each FDC is led by a sergeant, who is the plotter, and consists of two other FDC personnel and two FOs. Battalion mortar squads, led by a sergeant, operate the medium mortar.

1-71. Mortar sections are located in the Infantry company's weapons platoon. They consist of a section leader with the rank of staff sergeant and three mortar squads manning a light mortar. Mortar squads are led by a corporal, who is also a gunner, and have two other crewmen.

1-72. Light armored reconnaissance battalions normally have 81-mm mortars in the company. Each of the five line companies in the light armored reconnaissance battalion has a two-gun mortar section. They are equipped with two light armored vehicles mortar variants, each mounting an M252 81-mm mortar capable of firing from the vehicle or being ground-mounted.

USMC MORTAR UNITS

INFANTRY BATTALION
81-MM (GROUND MOUNTED)

MORTAR PLATOON HQ
LT (PLATOON CDR)
GYSGT (PLATOON SGT)
LCPL (AMMO TECH)
PVT (AMMO MAN)
PVT (AMMO MAN/DRIVER)
FBCB2

MORTAR SECTION (X2)
SSGT (SECTION LEADER)
CPL (DRIVER/AMMO MAN)
PVT (AMMO MAN)
FBCB2

FDC (X2)
SGT (PLOTTER)
CPL (PLOTTER/RECORDER)
LCPL (RECORDER/DRV)
2 CPL (FO)
FBCB2

MORTAR SQUAD (X8)
81-MM
SGT (SQUAD LEADER)
CPL (GUNNER)
LCPL (ASST GUNNER)
2 PVT (AMMO MAN)
PVT (AMMO MAN/DRIVER)
FBCB2
M32 LHMBC

RIFLE COMPANY
60-MM (GROUND MOUNTED)

SSGT (SECTION LEADER)

MORTAR SQUAD
60-MM
CPL (SQUAD LEADER/GNR)
LCPL (ASST GUNNER)
PVT (AMMO MAN)
M32 LHMBC

MORTAR SQUAD
60-MM
CPL (SQUAD LEADER/GNR)
LCPL (ASST GUNNER)
PVT (AMMO MAN)
M32 LHMBC

MORTAR SQUAD
60-MM
CPL (SQUAD LEADER/GNR)
LCPL (ASST GUNNER)
PVT (AMMO MAN)
M32 LHMBC

LIGHT ARMORED RECONNAISSANCE COMPANY
81-MM (MOUNTED AND DISMOUNTED)

MORTAR SECTION

MORTAR SQUAD
SSGT (SECTION LEADER)
SGT (GUNNER)
LCPL (ASST GUNNER)
PFC (LOADER/AMMO MAN)
LCPL (DRIVER)
FBCB2
M32 LHMBC

MORTAR SQUAD
SGT (SQUAD LEADER)
SGT (GUNNER)
LCPL (ASST GUNNER)
PFC (LOADER/AMMO MAN)
LCPL (DRIVER)
SGT (MORTAR/FDC MAN)
FBCB2
M32 LHMBC

NOTE: THE M998 IS USED TO INDICATE ANY HMMWV VERSION ASSIGNED TO A MORTAR UNIT.

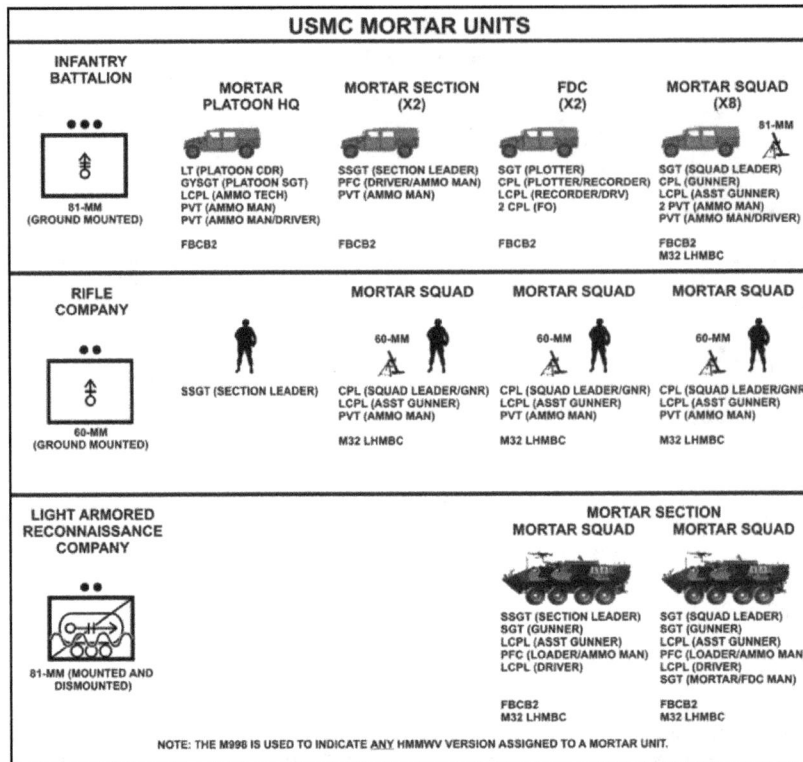

Figure 1-5. Marine Corps Infantry battalion, company, and light armored reconnaissance battalion mortar units

FIRE DIRECTION

1-73. An FDC is the element of an indirect fire team that receives the call for fire from an FO, company FSO/FSC, or higher HQ; determines firing data; and announces fire commands to firing section(s). An FDC also determines and applies corrections to chart data and to standard firing table values to achieve accuracy in firing. An FDC normally produces firing data, but a firing unit operating as a mortar/FDC, if an FDC is unavailable or not assigned, may produce this data. (See FM 3-22.91 for more details.)

ARMY FIRE DIRECTION PERSONNEL

1-74. Army mortar platoons have an FDC section while a section leader performs FDC duties for a company mortar section. An FDC of a battalion mortar platoon consists of the following personnel—

- Section leader.
- A chief computer and a check computer.
- Driver/radio/telephone operator.

1-75. An FDC uses a mortar fire control system (MFCS) or a light hand-held mortar ballistic computer (LHMBC) to convert observer data into fire commands. These commands are then reported to the firing section. Under other circumstances, FDC personnel might use the M16 (alternate means of fire control for all mortars) or M19 (alternate means of fire control for 60-mm mortar sections) plotting board.

MARINE CORPS FIRE DIRECTION PERSONNEL

1-76. Marine Corps mortar platoons have FDC sections while a section leader performs a company section's FDC duties. FDC personnel cross-train in computer skills to allow rotation for round-the-clock operations.

1-77. At a battalion, there are two FDCs in the mortar platoon, each led by a sergeant, who is the plotter, and consists of—

- Plotter.
- Plotter/recorder.
- Recorder/driver.
- Two FOs.

1-78. In a company, a staff sergeant mortar section leader reports to a weapons platoon commander. He is responsible for tactical employment, fire discipline, and fire control of the mortar section.

FIRE CONTROL SYSTEMS

1-79. Fire direction center personnel use fire control systems to convert data received from an FO in a call for fire into firing data that can be applied to the mortar and ammunition. With the exception of a manual M16 and M19 plotting board, each system has capabilities that are constantly being upgraded. Fire control systems include the following:

M16 AND M19 PLOTTING BOARDS

1-80. M16 and M19 plotting boards are usually the secondary, but may be the primary means of mortar fire control. Using these tools, a computer manually determines deflections, azimuths, and ranges. An M16 plotting board is the manual backup fire control system for combined arms battalion, SBCT, and Infantry battalion mortar platoons and SBCT rifle company mortar sections. An M19 plotting board is the manual backup fire control system for Infantry mortar sections.

1-81. Plotting boards are invaluable in showing the location of targets in relation to a firing unit and FOs. They also show the overall plan of fires by graphically displaying friendly units, target reference points, as well as maneuver and fire support coordinating measures (FSCMs).

MORTAR FIRE CONTROL SYSTEM

1-82. An MFCS is an automated system designed to improve command and control of mortar fires and speed of employment, accuracy, and survivability of mortars. An MFCS-M is used for mounted mechanized and SBCT mortar units. An M95 MFCS-M is mounted on combined arms battalion, Stryker, and reconnaissance mortar carriers and the M96 MFCS-M is used by combined arms battalion and SBCT FDCs. An MFCS-D is used for ground-mounted Infantry, Ranger, and Reconnaissance mortar units. An M150 MFCS-D is used by towed 120-mm units in Infantry, Ranger, and reconnaissance units and an M151 MFCS-D is used by Infantry and Ranger FDCs. A commander's interface/fire control computer manages computer activities, performs computations, and controls the interface with peripheral and external devices. A commander's interface/fire control computer operator enters data at the keypad and composes messages. Completed messages are then transmitted digitally or by radio. Should an FDC become disabled, each mortar crew can compute its own fire missions if an MFCS is configured in the gun/FDC or FDC role. System accuracy is increased through the use of a Global Positioning System (GPS), an onboard azimuth reference for the mortar, and digital meteorological updates. An MFCS enables self-surveying mortars, digital call for fire exchange, and automated ballistic solutions.

LIGHT HAND-HELD MORTAR BALLISTIC COMPUTER

1-83. An LHMBC is a ruggedized personal digital assistant. It provides the essential functions of an MFCS with similar software in a man-portable package and allows an operator to quickly calculate accurate ballistic solutions for all current Army mortar cartridges. An M32 LHMBC is the primary fire control systems for all ground-mounted mortar units. The basic model of an LHMBC can be expanded to include GPS and digital communications. LHMBC software can be easily upgraded or reinstalled from either a secure digital card or the onboard system read-only memory. System accuracy can be increased through the use of a GPS and digital meteorological messages. LHMBC allows for self-surveying mortars, digital call for fire exchange, and automated ballistic solutions.

TARGET ACQUISITION

1-84. Target acquisition is the detection, identification, and location of a target in sufficient detail to permit effective employment of weapons (FM 1-02). Mortar units use targeting information from many different sources. Their primary sources of targeting information are FOs, FIST/FiST, small unit leaders, Soldiers, and Marines who aggressively report targeting information. These observers acquire targets for an entire fire support system by observing the battlefield to detect, identify, and locate targets. Other target acquisition assets for the battalion task force and below include the following:

- Combat observation and lasing teams.
- Striker teams.
- Manned and unmanned aircraft systems (UASs).
- Weapons locating radars.
- Ground surveillance radar.
- Remotely employed sensors.
- Enemy prisoners of war.
- Battle damage assessment reports.
- Local populace and refugees.

Chapter 2

Command and Control

Command and control is the exercise of authority and direction by leaders over assigned and attached forces in the accomplishment of a mission. This chapter discusses the responsibilities of mortar section and platoon leaders and other key personnel, troop-leading procedures, and tactical standing operating procedures (TACSOPs). A mortar leader's primary duty is mission accomplishment. He influences and directs his men to gain their confidence, respect, cooperation, and obedience in combat operations. His leadership involves an understanding of human behavior, organizational functions, and mortar unit tactics. A mortar unit leader leads from a position where he can control mortar fire, making decisions within his authority and executing command decisions.

SECTION I – TEXT REFERENCES

2-1.   Within this manual, selected topics are only briefly discussed and readers are referred to another publication for more detail. Mortar and other combat units use these tactics, techniques, and procedures in the same or very similar manner and a detailed discussion in this manual would be redundant. However, they are as important as the subjects discussed in detail. Table 2-1 consolidates the references to additional information.

Table 2-1. Guide for subjects referenced in text

Subject	References
Troop-leading procedures	FM 5-0/MCWP 5-1
Pre-combat inspections	FM 3-21.8/MCWP 3-11.1/MCWP 3-11.2
Fire Direction Center terminology	FM 3-22.91
Orders	FM 5-0/MCWP 5-1

SECTION II – COMMAND

2-2.   Command is the authority that a leader lawfully exercises over subordinates. Command includes authority and responsibility for effectively using available resources for planning the employment of, organizing, directing, coordinating, and controlling military forces for the accomplishment of assigned missions (FM 1-02).

RESPONSIBILITIES OF KEY PERSONNEL

2-3.   This section discusses the responsibilities of key personnel that directly affect the performance of mortar sections and platoons. It does not discuss the common responsibilities of a leader or staff personnel.

> *Note.* Where necessary, personnel responsibilities are divided into categories based on warfighting functions. When there is a difference in terminology between Army and Marine Corps warfighting functions, both service's terms are used. For example, the Army uses sustainment and the Marine Corps uses logistics, which will be represented as sustainment/logistics.

BATTALION AND SQUADRON COMMANDER

2-4.   A battalion (or squadron) commander is responsible for the tactical employment of his mortar platoon. He cannot delegate this responsibility. The final responsibility for the tactical employment of a mortar unit, just as with all other elements, rests with the commander. For his mortar unit to be effective, a commander must provide a clear idea of what he wants his mortar unit's fires to do and how he wants them to support his maneuver. He must know the capabilities, limitations, and characteristics of mortars. Specific areas of his responsibility concerning the mortar unit include—

- Tactical employment, to include missions, priority of fires, general locations, security, and final approval of fire plans.
- Task organization, to include attachments and detachments, command and support relationships, and communications.
- Logistical support, to include basic loads, types and mix of ammunition, priority of transportation, maintenance, and other support.

2-5. In the Army, a maneuver battalion commander directly controls his mortar platoon, attaches elements to subordinate commanders, or exercises command through his HQ and HQ company commander. In the Marine Corps, a battalion commander exercises command of his mortar platoon through his weapons company commander or attaches elements to subordinate commanders.

COMPANY COMMANDER

2-6. A company/troop commander is responsible for the tactical employment of his mortar section. He exercises command through subordinate leaders and employs his company to accomplish its mission according to the battalion commander's intent and concept. He also ensures that a mortar unit has adequate security. A SBCT and Infantry rifle company commander directly controls his mortar section or attaches one or more squads to a platoon. A Marine Corps rifle company commander commands his mortar section directly, through his weapons platoon commander, or attaches one or more squads to a rifle platoon.

OPERATIONS OFFICER

2-7. A battalion (or squadron) operations officer is a commander's principal staff officer in matters concerning combat operations, plans, organization, and training. The nature of an operations officer's responsibilities requires a high degree of coordination with the mortar unit leader. An operations officer does not exercise command authority over the mortar unit. However, he does exercise a degree of control over a mortar unit's actions. He has the authority to direct a unit to accomplish specific missions or tasks within the framework of a battalion or squadron commander's intent. He does not exercise administrative control. Concerning a mortar unit, an operations officer—

- Prepares, coordinates, authenticates, and publishes operations plans and orders, incorporating the mortar unit leader's input to these plans and orders while they are being prepared.
- Recommends priorities for critical resources, to include establishing mortar ammunition basic loads by type and number of rounds and the required and controlled mortar ammunition supply rate.
- Recommends task organization to the commander and assigns specific missions to the mortar unit.
- Considers additional security measures when the mortar platoon is dispersed.
- Advises the commander and coordinates fires and displacement of the mortar unit with the actions of other units.
- Prepares, authenticates, and publishes the battalion TACSOP.

FIRE SUPPORT OFFICER/FIRE SUPPORT COORDINATOR

2-8. A battalion FSO/FSC and company FSOs are charged with planning and coordination to execute the fire support plan and support a commander's intent. A mortar unit leader and a battalion FSO/FSC or company FSO have a close relationship. They must both understand a battalion or company commander's intent for fires, and they must work closely to ensure it is properly executed. An FSO/FSC or FSO must know a mortar unit's capabilities, limitations, and technical aspects. An FSO/FSC or FSO also—

- Recommends to the operations officer the appropriate unit to fire on each planned target.
- Integrates all available fire support into the commander's concept of the operation.
- Anticipates requirements and passes information and instructions to the mortar unit during the battle.

MORTAR PLATOON LEADER

2-9. A mortar platoon leader is primarily a combat leader. He is also principal advisor to the battalion commander and battalion FSO/FSC on the tactical employment of mortars. He and a platoon sergeant work closely together to ensure their platoon is trained, prepared, and able to execute its mission. Even though some duties, such as training and ammunition management, are primarily the responsibility of the platoon sergeant, the platoon leader is ultimately responsible.

2-10. For tasks related to the warfighting functions of intelligence and mission command/command and control, a mortar platoon leader—

- Recommends task organization, employment techniques, and positioning of the mortars to support the scheme of maneuver.
- Informs the commander, operations staff officer, and FSO of all significant range or ammunition limitations.
- Maintains situational awareness (SA) of the actions of company mortar sections and operates in concert with them.
- Keeps abreast of the enemy situation and locations of friendly units to ensure the best use of ammunition and the safety of friendly troops.
- Assigns missions and issues instructions and orders to subordinate leaders.
- Supervises the execution of orders, ensures that priority targets are covered at all times, and establishes the amount and type of ammunition set aside for priority targets.
- Coordinates the fires and displacement of the mortar platoon with the action of other units; directs mortar section and platoon displacement.
- Commands and controls the execution of the mortar platoon portion of the battalion fire support plan and coordinates the fires and displacements of his mortar sections.
- Relays intelligence information, shelling reports, mortar bombing reports, and spot reports to the intelligence staff officer.
- Holds responsibility for the training of the platoon to ensure technical and tactical proficiency, to include ensuring sufficient soldiers are trained and certified in combat life saving, field sanitation, and other skills that are trained outside of the platoon and company.
- Holds responsibility for the cross training of personnel within the platoon on key tasks to ensure continuous operations.
- Establishes and maintains communications with supported companies and FISTs/FiSTs.
- Keeps abreast of all changes to the enemy countermortar capability.
- Provides input to the appropriate sections of the battalion TACSOP and establishes an internal unit TACSOP that adheres to the battalion's TACSOP, while addressing all issues of special concern to the unit.

2-11. For tasks related to the warfighting functions of fires and movement and maneuver, he—

- Exercises tactical fire control through the mortar section leaders and the FDC.
- Assists in developing the fire support plan in conjunction with the company or battalion FSO/FSC and determines the appropriate type and amount of mortar ammunition to fire.
- Designates reconnaissance and advance parties.
- Selects and reconnoiters new positions and routes for the platoon; controls the movements of all elements of the platoon not attached or under the OPCON of other units.
- Informs commander of any factors that may reduce his unit's capability.
- Lays mortars for firing and verifies the direction of fire selected by the FDC, when required.
- Performs map spot and hasty survey operations.
- Coordinates through the FSO/FSC with supporting artillery units for survey support, when required.
- Performs hasty crater analysis and reports the results.
- Coordinates radar registration, when appropriate.
- Trains the platoon on the proper execution of all firing and misfire reduction procedures.

2-12. For tasks related to the warfighting functions of protection and sustainment/logistics, he—

- Assists the operations officer in determining the mortar ammunition required supply rate (RSR). The platoon leader may need to recommend changes to the mortar platoon's mission based on the controlled supply rate (CSR).
- Analyzes risk from ground, air, and counter-mortar attack. As required, recommends actions to mitigate these risks, including any additional security measures.
- Ensures enforcement of security measures to increase the survivability of the platoon against the ground, air, and indirect fire attacks.
- Plans the platoon ground defense and maintains security while on the move or halted.
- Submits ammunition and platoon status reports.
- Anticipates needs and ensures submission of ammunition resupply, maintenance, and refuel requests to sustain combat operations.

COMPANY AND TROOP MORTAR SECTION LEADER

2-13. A company and troop mortar section leader is primarily a combat leader. He is also principal advisor to his company commander and company FSO on the tactical employment of mortars. A section leader also performs selected duties of the mortar platoon leader listed above. He also—

- Assists the company commander in planning the employment of the mortar section.
- Coordinates with the company FSO.
- Controls the section during tactical operations.
- Acts as the primary trainer for mortar systems.

MORTAR PLATOON SERGEANT

2-14. A mortar platoon sergeant is the principal assistant to a platoon leader and assists him in all matters pertaining to training and operation of the platoon, and with the platoon leader's duties as listed above. He assumes responsibilities of the platoon leader during his absence.

2-15. For tasks related to the warfighting functions of intelligence and mission command/command and control, a mortar platoon sergeant—

- Inspects and supervises to ensure execution of the platoon leader's orders.
- Leads the reconnaissance party and conducts reconnaissance of routes and positions, when required.
- Ensures maintenance of situation maps in the FDC.
- Ensures establishment of communication nets and proper use of radio/telephone operating procedures by personnel.
- Ensures platoon training of personnel in their primary job assignments and cross training to perform key functions within the FDC.
- Assists in the preparation of paragraph four of the platoon operation order (OPORD).

2-16. For tasks related to the warfighting functions of fires and movement and maneuver/maneuver, he—

- Supervises movements, as required. (When the platoon is operating in two sections, he normally directly supervises one.)
- Lays the mortars for firing, when required.
- Ensures application of available meteorological data to firing data, when appropriate.
- Conducts hasty crater analysis and submits shelling reports and mortar bombing reports.
- Performs responsibilities related to the FDC, mounted fire direction systems, and Force XXI battle command, brigade and below (FBCB2).

2-17. For tasks related to the warfighting functions of protection/force protection and sustainment/logistics, he—

- Supervises the preparation of the platoon ground defense.
- Supervises the test firing and zeroing of weapons and boresighting of mortars.
- Ensures that aiming circles are declinated properly.

- Supervises camouflage, field hygiene, and sanitation.
- Supervises the platoon's security and sleep plans.
- Ensures the availability of the required basic load for all weapons and platoon equipment.
- Monitors ammunition expenditures and ensures maintenance of ammunition records.
- Submits timely ammunition resupply requests.
- Supervises ammunition prestockage, when used.
- Ensures active supervision of maintenance by subordinate leaders.
- Coordinates and supervises petroleum, oils, and lubricants resupply and maintenance support.
- Coordinates and supervises vehicle recovery.
- Requests fortification materials.
- Coordinates resupply needs.
- Adjusts personnel as needed and cross-levels personnel within mortar squads to maintain maximum firepower.
- Ensures performance and recording of all necessary safety, borescope, and pullover gauge inspections.
- Coordinates casualty evacuation.

FIRE DIRECTION SECTION LEADER

2-18. A section leader assumes the duties of a platoon sergeant during his absence.

2-19. For tasks related to the warfighting functions of intelligence and mission command/command and control, a fire direction section leader—

- Leads the reconnaissance or advance party, when directed.
- Assists in vehicle placement.
- Establishes and maintains situation maps; marks all restrictive fire control measures on the map and ensures their addition to the automated fire direction system or onto the plotting board.
- Relays information to the battalion FSO/FSC and platoon leader.
- Issues the FDC order.
- Assumes control of a section during split-section operations.
- Supervises the laying of communications wire in the mortar position, when warranted.
- Ensures proper use of radiotelephone operating procedures by FDC personnel.
- Trains FDC personnel in FDC procedures; assists and trains squad leaders in FDC procedures.

2-20. For tasks related to the warfighting functions of fires and movement and maneuver/maneuver, he—

- Advises of necessary displacements because of range limitations.
- Controls FDC personnel; ensures use of safe procedures in computing firing data and validates the computer safety check before issuing the FDC order.
- Supervises all fire missions; examines target location relative to friendly units, fire control measures, and reference points. (Based on the nature of the target, ammunition available, and command guidance, he decides if the mission should be fired, the number of mortars to fire, and the amount and type of ammunition to expend.)
- Lays mortars for firing, when directed.
- Checks the accuracy of fire direction system operations, computer operators, and FDC records; ensures fires are correctly plotted.
- Recommends necessary conduction of re-registration.
- Determines and applies meteorological corrections for firing data.
- Ensures the accomplishment of the technical aspects related to the mortar fire direction systems and FBCB2.

2-21. For tasks related to the warfighting functions of protection/force protection and sustainment/logistics, he—

- Informs platoon leader and platoon sergeant of ammunition status and of changes in the tactical situation.
- Maintains ammunition records.
- Reports ammunition status.
- Supervises the FDC sleep plan to ensure 24-hour operation.
- Ensures understanding of FDC and mortar crew personnel roles in defending the platoon position.
- Ensures properly camouflaged FDC and section vehicles.
- Supervises the maintenance of vehicles and equipment.
- Consolidates and submits FBCB2 nuclear, biological, and chemical (NBC) reports 1, 3, and 4.
- Supervises section and FDC chemical, biological, radiological, and nuclear (CBRN) protective and decontamination measures.
- Designates and ensures alertness of the duty mortar crew during continuous operations.

MORTAR SQUAD LEADER

2-22. A mortar squad leader is a combat leader. He is responsible for what his squad does or fails to do.

2-23. For tasks related to the warfighting functions of intelligence and mission command/command and control, a mortar squad leader—

- Controls squad movement.
- Places squad into position.
- Briefs squad on the platoon or section leader's orders.
- Keeps squad aware of the current situation.
- Ensures communications are maintained with the FDC.
- Ensures proper use of radio/telephone operating procedures by the squad.

2-24. For tasks related to the warfighting functions of fires and movement and maneuver/maneuver, he—

- Ensures properly laid mortar.
- Checks mask and overhead clearance.
- Ensures indexing of proper deflection and elevation on the mortar sight.
- Conducts emergency fire missions without an FDC, when required.
- Plots fires and determines firing data when operating separately from the section.
- Fulfills responsibilities related to the fire direction systems and FBCB2.

2-25. For tasks related to the warfighting functions of protection/force protection and sustainment/logistics, he—

- Ensures camouflaged mortar position.
- Ensures proper preparation of ammunition for firing and reports any ammunition discrepancies to the FDC.
- Supervises the preparation and manning of squad fighting positions.
- Implements the squad sleep and security plans.
- Supervises the maintenance of personal weapons and squad equipment.
- Supervises weapons test firing and mortar boresighting.
- Ensures proper storage of ammunition and equipment.
- Informs FDC of any changes in ammunition status.
- Maintains responsibility for the training, welfare, and safety of squad members.
- Trains squad members in individual and crew-related skills and cross trains to maintain technical proficiency at all times.

- Submits FBCB2 NBC reports as appropriate.
- Supervises squad CBRN protective and decontamination measures.

TROOP-LEADING PROCEDURES

2-26. Troop-leading procedures provide small unit leaders a framework for planning and preparing for operations. Leaders of mortar platoons and sections use TLPs to develop plans and orders. Mortar units use the same TLPs as any other unit. The sequence of individual procedures is not rigid; it is modified to meet the mission, situation, and available time. Some steps are done concurrently, while others may go on continuously throughout the operation. The procedures save time. A leader uses them in the order that is most efficient. (See FM 5-0/MCWP 5-1 for more details.)

2-27. The Army and Marine Corps both use TLPs, but they have different numbers of steps and slightly different step names (Table 2-2). (Marine Corps TLPs begin after the WARNORD is issued.)

Table 2-2. Comparison of Army and Marine Corps troop-leading procedures steps

Army	Marine Corps
Receive the mission	
Issue a WARNO	
Make a tentative plan	Begin planning
Initiate movement	Arrange reconnaissance
Conduct reconnaissance	Make reconnaissance
Complete the plan	Complete the plan
Issue the order	Issue the order
Supervise	Supervise

2-28. TLP steps for mortar units are—

- **Receive the mission.** A mission for a mortar unit may be received in the form of a written or oral WARNO/WARNORD, OPORD, or fragmentary order (FRAGO). At times, a leader may deduce a change in mission, based on a change in the situation. A mortar platoon leader should attend the battalion OPORD. Once an upcoming mission is identified, a leader takes action to begin preparing the unit. He conducts an initial analysis, considering METT-TC/METT-T variables, to determine the requirements for his WARNO/WARNORD.

- **Issue a warning order.** A mortar unit leader issues the best WARNO/WARNORD possible with the information at hand and updates it as needed with additional WARNOs/WARNORDs. The WARNO/WARNORD allows units to prepare for combat as soon as possible after being alerted of an upcoming mission. This normally involves a number of standard actions that should be addressed by the TACSOP. The WARNO/WARNORD addresses items not covered in the TACSOP that are required to prepare for the mission. The specific contents for each WARNO/WARNORD will vary, based upon the unique tactical situation.

- **Make a tentative plan and begin planning.** Tentative plans are the basis for the OPORD. A leader uses the commander's visualization to analyze METT-TC/METT-T information, develop and analyze a course of action, compare courses of action, and make a decision that produces a tentative plan.

- **Initiate movement and arrange reconnaissance.** A subordinate leader moves the section or platoon to an assembly area or firing position. The instructions for this move can be given in the WARNO/WARNORD. A leader ensures that all movements are coordinated with his HQ and that security is maintained.

- **Conduct reconnaissance.** Reconnaissance is a continuous process during the procedures. The tentative plan should include time for reconnaissance. Reconnaissance is planned and conducted to confirm or adjust the tentative plan.

- **Complete the plan.** A leader must be prepared to adjust his tentative plan based on the results of the reconnaissance and other information. He may have to change courses of action if the situation has changed or it is not what he expected. Coordination continues with all supported agencies, company or battalion, and adjacent units.

- **Issue the order.** A leader issues the order while viewing the avenues of approach/objective area, and while making use of visual aids (sketches and terrain models) to make it more effective and increase the participants' understanding.

- **Supervise and refine.** Throughout TLPs, leaders monitor mission preparations, refine the plan, perform coordination with adjacent units, and supervise and assess preparations. Mortar leaders should confirm their missions and responsibilities with their FSO and confirm that the correct amounts and types of ammunition are available. Normally unit TACSOPs state individual responsibilities and the sequence of preparation activities. Leaders supervise subordinates and inspect their personnel and equipment to ensure the unit is ready for the mission. A crucial component of preparation is rehearsals, to include confirmation and back briefs, combined arms support, and battle drill or TACSOP rehearsals.

REHEARSALS

2-29. Leaders should conduct rehearsals. They are essential to ensure complete coordination and subordinate understanding. A mortar section or platoon must participate in the maneuver and fire support plan rehearsals held by the battalion. These rehearsals are critical to success. The WARNO/WARNORD should provide subordinate leaders sufficient detail for them to schedule and conduct rehearsals of drills/TACSOPs before receiving the OPORD. Rehearsals conducted after the OPORD can then focus on mission specific tasks. Alternative courses of action and contingencies should also be rehearsed if time is available.

PRECOMBAT INSPECTIONS

2-30. Precombat inspections are critical to combat mission success. They ensure that Soldiers are prepared to execute the required individual and collective tasks that support the mission. Checks and inspections are part of TLPs that protect against shortfalls that could endanger Soldiers' lives and jeopardize the successful execution of a mission. Units TACSOPs include precombat inspection checklists. When inspecting equipment, leaders should refer to the preventive maintenance checks and services section in the applicable technical manual. (See FM 3-21.8 for precombat checklists for Infantry personnel, equipment, and vehicles.) In addition to these, mortar leaders check and inspect their unit's mortar-specific knowledge, equipment, and supplies. These inspections can include, but are not limited to, the following:

PERSONNEL

2-31. Mortar unit personnel may be inspected for the following:

- Individual uniform and equipment, including weapons, protective mask and nerve-agent antidote, helmet, body armor, eye protection, earplugs, and dog tags.
- Contents of assault packs or personal equipment carried on the mission.
- Camouflage.
- Knowledge of the mission and individual responsibilities, such as the displacement and fire plan.
- Knowledge of radio nets, frequencies, and call signs.
- Knowledge of emergency signals, challenge and passwords, and code words.
- Reference cards and checklists, such as ROE and medical evacuation procedures.
- Leaders for personnel and equipment rosters and information.

EQUIPMENT

2-32. The following are examples of equipment that may be inspected:

- Mission-essential equipment, such as mortar sights, night lights, bulbs, CBRN equipment, aiming circle, compasses, aiming posts, boresight, and chemical lights.
- Number and serviceability of batteries.

- MFCSs, including preparation and setup, loading data and secure settings, precomputing firing data, and so forth.
- FDC equipment, including sufficient supplies of forms, complete and prepared plotting boards, and firing tables.
- Complete, operable, and serviced mortar.
- Weapons, including individual and crew-served weapons.
- Operable communications equipment, communication checks, and proper security data.

VEHICLES

2-33. The following are examples of vehicle-related items that may be inspected:
- Vehicle maintenance, camouflage, communications equipment, fuel and fluid levels, load plan, and tools.
- Complete and properly mounted communications equipment, and complete and mounted antennas.
- Equipment in vehicles according to vehicle load plans.
- Readily accessible emergency or maintenance equipment, such as tow bars/slings and basic issue items.
- FBCB2 function checks, deleted old messages, and properly configured system.
- Operable additional equipment, such as electronic countermeasure equipment.
- Operable and properly stowed spare equipment.
- Properly secured and stowed mortar equipment.
- Padded parts, such as tailgates, to reduce noise.

SUPPLIES

2-34. The following are examples of supplies that may be inspected:
- Ammunition, including amount, type, and storage.
- Class I supplies (water and rations).
- Batteries.
- Medical supplies, including combat lifesaver bags.

TACTICAL STANDING OPERATING PROCEDURE

2-35. A TACSOP is a set of instructions that establish unit tactical procedures for common and recurring actions. A unit may have other TACSOPs that cover administration, sustainment/logistics, and other procedures. TACSOPs standardize unit-level techniques and procedures to enhance effectiveness and flexibility. As the name implies, TACSOPs standardize routine or recurring actions not needing the commander's personal involvement. However, TACSOPs may also address rare or abnormal events that could cause mission failure.

PURPOSE

2-36. TACSOPs facilitate and expedite operations by—
- Reducing the number, length, and frequency of combat orders.
- Simplifying the preparation and transmission of combat orders.
- Establishing priorities in the absence of specific instructions.
- Reducing the time to prepare for operations.
- Promoting teamwork and understanding between the leaders and troops.
- Advising new arrivals or newly attached units of procedures.
- Reducing confusion and errors.

CONTENT

2-37. Higher unit TACSOPs need not be restated in platoon and squad TACSOPs unless more detail is needed for actions to be accomplished at those levels. A mortar platoon TACSOP must comply with all parts of the company and battalion's TACSOP. Virtually any item relating to the platoon can become a matter for the unit TACSOP. Many TACSOP items are derived from the personnel and equipment available to the organization. Other items are a function of good tactics and techniques. Leaders establish TACSOP items based on how they can operate most efficiently and best prepare their unit for combat. TACSOPs remain in effect unless modified by an order. If certain items continually need modification, they should not be a part of the TACSOP.

2-38. The following are some categories to be included in the platoon TACSOP:

- **Command and control**, including—
  - Chain of command.
  - Extracts from and in compliance with higher unit TACSOPs.
  - Routine and nonroutine reports.
  - Responsibilities of key personnel.
  - OPORD, WARNO/WARNORD, and FRAGO formats.
  - Communications.
- **Operations**, including—
  - Assembly area procedures.
  - Limited visibility operations.
  - Priority of work.
  - Occupation of firing positions.
  - Stand-to alert procedures.
  - Response to countermortar fires.
  - Actions on contact.
  - Conduct of FPF missions.
- **Preparation for operations**, including—
  - Organization for combat.
  - Prescribed uniforms and protective equipment.
- **Sustainment/logistics**, including—
  - Ammunition resupply, storage, and handling.
  - Handling of enemy prisoners of war.
  - Casualty reporting.
  - Safety precautions and hazard reporting.
  - First aid and field sanitation.
- **Protection/force protection**, including—
  - Construction of firing positions.
  - Air defense and air guards.
  - CBRN protective measures.
- **Movement**, including—
  - Advance party composition and duties.
  - Road marches and convoy operations.
  - Straggler control.

FIRE DIRECTION CENTER

2-39. An important area for standardization by TACSOP is in FDC operations and fire commands. A mortar platoon leader and FDC chief must establish a clear and detailed TACSOP for these areas. An FDC requires technical proficiency and highly disciplined procedures that emphasize both time and motion efficiency. Wasted motion, unnecessary talking, clutter, and duplication of effort all result in lost time and errors during fire missions. (See FM 3-22.91 for the specific terminology for FDC orders and fire commands that must be taught and used during every fire mission.) Cross-talk and the free flow of information must be encouraged in an FDC, but ambiguous talk and nonstandard terms detract from combat efficiency. Communications between an FDC and mortar squads, and within mortar squads, must be standardized. This saves time, prevents misunderstanding during periods of stress and confusion, and allows efficient personnel cross-leveling within a platoon.

MISSION EXECUTION

2-40. During mission execution, a leader continuously assesses the operation. He compares planned with actual events and makes necessary adjustments to ensure his actions are in line with his commander's intent. During execution, a mortar unit leader—

- Provides required fire support to accomplish the mission.
- Responds to orders.
- Anticipates requirements.
- Maintains SA by monitoring unit actions.

SECTION III – CONTROL

2-41. Control is the regulation of forces to accomplish the mission according to a commander's intent (FM 1-02). For mortar units, this includes the use of orders and overlays, and communications.

ORDERS

2-42. Orders are written, digital, or oral. Leaders use them to transmit information and instructions to subordinates. Orders expressed in standardized formats or containing essential elements ensures that a leader conveys his instructions clearly, concisely, and completely. The detail of an order varies with the amount of time a leader has to prepare it. TACSOPs complement orders, allowing a leader to refer to them rather than issue the same instructions for tasks and situations that occur often. (See FM 5-0/MCWP 5-1 for details.)

2-43. Three kinds of orders are warning, operation, and fragmentary.

Warning Order

2-44. A WARNO/WARNORD is a preliminary notice of an order or action that is to follow (FM 1-02). Leaders use WARNOs/WARNORDs to alert their units of an impending mission and to provide initial instructions so that subordinates have a maximum amount of time to prepare for its execution. There is no prescribed format for a WARNO/WARNORD, but by following the outline of the five-paragraph field order, leaders can simplify and standardize their orders. This helps when a leader is exhausted or under great stress. A WARNO/WARNORD must provide any specific instructions not included in tacos but which are important for preparation of the mission, such as changes to the composition of the on-board ammunition load. A platoon leader may issue it only to a platoon sergeant if time does not permit the gathering of other personnel.

Operation Order

2-45. An OPORD is a directive issued by a commander to subordinate commanders for the purpose of effecting the coordinated execution of an operation (FM 1-02). An OPORD supplies all-important information on *who*, *what*, *when*, *how*, and most importantly, the *why* of the mission. It outlines a commander's intent for fire support. A leader uses an OPORD to tell subordinates how he intends to fight the battle. Leaders use the standard OPORD format to organize their thoughts in a logical sequence. This ensures that a platoon, section, and squad know everything necessary to accomplish their mission. Consistent use of this standard format allows a leader to refine TACSOPs and to streamline his orders.

2-46. The majority of the information needed for a mortar unit's OPORD comes directly from a battalion OPORD. A unit leader can get additional information from an intelligence staff officer, battalion FSO/FSC, and logistics staff officer. Some information he must determine himself during the analysis of his mission.

Fragmentary Order

2-47. A FRAGO is an abbreviated form of an OPORD (verbal, written, or digital) that eliminates the need for restating information contained in a basic operation (FM 1-02). It is issued after an OPORD to change or modify that order. Since FRAGOs are normally used during the conduct of an operation, instructions should be brief and specific. FRAGOs include all five OPORD paragraph headings. After each heading, new information or no change should be stated.

OVERLAYS

2-48. An overlay is a printing or drawing on a transparent or semi-transparent medium at the same scale as a map, chart, and so on, to show details not appearing or requiring special emphasis on the original (FM 1-02). Digital overlays are also used to show detail. A mortar unit leader must ensure that digital overlays are provided to subordinates and information is accurately transferred onto the fire control system. An overlay or transference should be simple, neat, and accurately drawn. It should include all control measures used during an operation and all other information that can be depicted graphically.

2-49. An OPORD may include several overlays, but most important for a mortar unit leader are operations and fire support overlays. They show the location, size, and scheme of maneuver and fires of friendly forces involved in an operation.

COMMUNICATIONS

2-50. Effective communications is critical in the delivery of fires. A mortar platoon or section uses frequency modulation (FM) voice, digital, and wire. Mortar units also use routine and nonroutine reports to keep commanders and their staff aware of their unit's tactical, administrative, and logistical status.

2-51. Wire is the most secure communication means and cannot be detected by radio direction finding. It is primarily used internally within a mortar unit by linking the mortar squads to the FDC. In a semi-permanent position, it may also connect an FDC with a command group, subordinate units, and FOs. Wire takes time to lay, is of limited range, and, if not properly buried, subject to breakage from fire and vehicular traffic.

2-52. A platoon's most flexible, most frequently used, and one of the most secure means of communications is the radio. It can quickly transmit information over long distances with great accuracy. Current equipment provides a platoon with communications security against most enemy direction finding, interception, and jamming capabilities. Sophisticated direction finding equipment, however, can trace almost any radio signal. If available, satellite systems are more secure and are less subject to interference from terrain and structures, but can be affected by weather. Structures, such as those generating an electrical signal, and terrain interfere with direct line of sight FM communications.

2-53. Electronic protection is part of electronic warfare that involves actions taken to protect units from the effects of friendly or enemy use of the electromagnetic spectrum that degrade, neutralize, or destroy friendly combat capability. Mortar and other units accomplish this by minimizing radio transmissions, using correct radio transmission procedures, reducing their signal signature, and employing other techniques to protect electronic transmission. Recent operations in Iraq and Afghanistan have introduced the wide-spread use of jamming devices to counter-improvised explosive devices. Units operating these devices can interfere with friendly signals within and outside their AO. Their use should be coordinated and minimized to the extent possible. Sending information digitally is the preferred method for transmitting data. It transmits information at a high rate of speed and handles large amounts of information. Digital transmissions also greatly inhibit the enemy's ability to trace the signal.

2-54. An FDC is the net control station for a mortar platoon and section. The smooth functioning of this net enables accurate information to pass quickly to and from an FDC. An FDC net control station communicates with mortars, mortar leaders, and command elements when in either general support (GS) or direct support (DS). Direct support is a support relationship requiring a unit to support another specific unit and authorizing it to answer a supported force's request for assistance directly. General support is a support relationship requiring a unit to support a supported force as a whole and not to any particular division thereof. A mortar unit FDC establishes and maintains communications with—

- A commander, command post (CP), or FSO/FSC (based on commander's guidance and TACSOP).
- Units having priority of fires, priority targets, or units to which the mortar platoon is in DS.
- Mortar sections and mortars under its control.
- Any FOs directly controlling the unit's fires.
- Any fires unit in its DS or providing supporting fires.

2-55. In combat, reports give commanders and leaders information on which to base their plans and decisions. These reports must be accurate, timely, and complete. Standardized reporting procedures save time, promote completeness, and prevent confusion. Ways to transmit and safeguard reports vary and depend on the information transmitted, available equipment, local requirements, terrain, and electronic-warfare threat. Whatever the method of reporting, communications security must be enforced. Any report that contains information about friendly units will be either encoded or transmitted on secure communications means with approved codes.

2-56. FBCB2 greatly enhances the speed and accuracy of reports. It is the primary method to transmit reports. The system's standard reports include—

- Free text messages.
- Status reports.
- Log reports.
- NBC reports (NBC 1, 3, and 4; chemical downwind message; and effective downwind message).
- Battle damage assessment.
- Situation and spot reports.
- Medical evacuations (both combat and long form).
- Obstacle reports.

This page intentionally left blank.

Chapter 3

Fire Support Planning and Coordination

Mortar fire support planning is the continuous and concurrent process of analyzing, allocating, coordinating, and scheduling mortar fires. Integrating these fires with a maneuver plan optimizes a commander's organic fires. Mortar platoons and sections can be responsive and reliable only if their fires are planned, coordinated, and fully integrated into a scheme of maneuver.

SECTION I – TEXT REFERENCES

3-1. Within this manual, selected topics are only briefly discussed and readers are referred to another publication for more detail. Mortar and other combat units use these tactics, techniques, and procedures in the same or very similar manner and a detailed discussion in this manual would be redundant. However, they are as important as the subjects discussed in detail. Table 3-1 consolidates the references to additional information.

Table 3-1. Guide for subjects referenced in text

Subject	References
Command relationships	FM 5-0/MCWP 5-1
Graphical control measures	FM 1-02/MCRP 5-12A
Permissive fire support coordinating measures	FM 6-20-20/MCWP 3-16
Marine Corps battlefield coordination line	MCWP 3-16
Airspace coordination area	JP 3-09
Target symbols	FM 3-22.91
	FM 1-02/MCRP 5-12A
Consolidated target list	FM 3-22.90

SECTION II – STANDARDS AND COORDINATION WITH THE FIELD ARTILLERY

3-2. The conduct of fires and fire control has a standard set of procedures and techniques used by both mortars and field artillery. While FM 3-21.91 covers in detail the conduct of fires and fire control measures used by mortars, it is not sufficient for a mortar unit leader. He has to know and understand the procedures, techniques, and graphics used by an FSO/FSC to portray how mortars, field artillery, and other support assets support a commander. (See Table 3-2 for a list of FMs and MCRPs that Army and Marine mortar leaders need to understand to accomplish the mission effectively.)

Table 3-2. Essential references

Army/USMC Publications	Purpose
FM 1-02/MCRP 5-12A	Standard for military symbols for situation maps, and overlays
FM 3-09.31/MCRP 3-16C	Synchronization of fires with the scheme of maneuver
FM 6-20-20/MCWP 3-16	Fire support at battalion and company levels
FM 6-30/MCWP 3-16.6	Observed fire procedures
FM 3-09.32/MCRP 3-16.6A	Requesting fire support including coordination and planning procedures, communications, and weapons data
MCWP 3-16	Coordination and employment of fires with maneuver elements

SECTION III – PRIORITY OF FIRES

3-3. Priority of fires is the organization and employment of fire support means according to the importance of a supported unit's mission (FM 1-02). It is a key method for a commander to increase the combat power of one of his subordinate maneuver units and is normally given to the unit assigned the main effort for each phase. In the OPORD or FRAGO, mortar units are given the priority of fire and it becomes the basis for their fire support plan. A fires battalion supporting an operation, a mortar platoon, and a company mortar section may all have different priorities of fire. An order may assign a single unit as having the priority of fire or may designate the priorities of fire in descending order. For example, an order may assign the priorities of fire to A company, then C company, and then a reconnaissance platoon. Priorities of fire may also change with each phase of the operation. The important thing is that there is only one maneuver unit with the priority of fires at any one time.

3-4. A unit with priority of fires does not have exclusive use of these fires. It means that its call for fire has priority. For example, a mortar platoon may be firing a mission for A company when C company, who has priority of fires, requests fires. The mortar platoon ceases firing A company's mission and fires C company's mission. Once it completes C company's mission, it then continues to fire A company's mission.

3-5. A commander may shift the priority of fires to meet the threat, as required. He can assign priority of mortar fire to increase the effectiveness of direct fires. For example, the effectiveness of close-combat missiles can be increased by having mortar fire obscuring enemy overwatch elements, forcing enemy armor to close hatches, suppressing accompanying Infantry, and canalizing an enemy.

ASSIGNMENT

3-6. In both the offense and defense, priority of fire is normally assigned to a unit assigned the main effort of a phase. In the offense, a unit assigned the main effort may be different for each phase of the operation. A mortar unit must in position to support the unit with the priority of fire. This may include establishing decentralized or predesignated control methods for FOs and a mortar leader monitoring the unit's command net.

3-7. In the defense, priority of fires is normally given first to a company or platoon that can best place effective long-range fires on the enemy. As an enemy continues to advance, priority of fires may be shifted to the company responsible for defending the most dangerous avenues of approach into the unit's AO or battle position. If more than one unit is positioned to cover the same avenue of approach, such as around an engagement area, priority of fires should be given to the company or platoon that can best observe and place effective fire on enemy forces that pose the greatest threat. A commander may also assign priority of fires to the—

- Forward security force, either a reconnaissance platoon or another maneuver force given a security or counter reconnaissance mission.
- Counterattacking force upon initiation of a counterattack.

3-8. To ensure that the most threatening enemy forces are fired on first, a commander must prioritize anticipated demands, but may modify his guidance. A mortar unit leader must therefore stay in contact with the CP and the battalion FSO/FSC or company FIST/FiST to quickly change priorities of fires when needed.

CONFLICTS

3-9. A mortar unit FDC should have clear and unambiguous instructions on the priority of missions to fire. Careful analysis of the mission and a unit's support relationships allows leaders to identify and resolve potential conflicts. Potential conflicts related to priorities of fire should be identified and resolved prior to the mission.

SECTION IV – COMMAND AND SUPPORT RELATIONSHIPS

3-10. Mortar command and support relationships are the means by which commanders at battalion and company levels establish the framework within which they want mortar platoon or section to operate. Commanders choose and convey to all concerned command and support relationships that best support their plan of fire support. Since mortars are organic to the battalion and company, a commander normally retains control at that level. He has the option to attach or place mortars under the OPCON of a subordinate unit. The Army and Marine Corps have the same command relationships, but support relationships are different and, therefore, discussed separately.

COMMAND RELATIONSHIPS

3-11. Situations may occur when a mortar unit cannot support an entire battalion or company/troop while remaining under direct control as an organic element, such as when a company/troop or platoon is given a mission that separates it from its parent unit, to include—

- Raid or ambush.
- Advance, flank, or rear guard.
- Screen.
- Detachment left in contact.

3-12. In these situations, a commander may specify command relationships for mortars by placing a mortar platoon or section under the control of a maneuver element. These command relationships carry inherent responsibilities that everyone involved in fire support must know. When a standard command relationship does not adequately support a commander's intent, a nonstandard one may be assigned. This is accomplished by issuing a separate mortar platoon or section mission statement with explicit instructions on the command relationship desired.

OPERATIONAL CONTROL

3-13. OPCON is the authority delegated to a commander to direct forces provided him to accomplish specific missions, usually limited by function, time, or location. (See FM 5-0/MCWP 5-1 for details.)

3-14. A commander who has OPCON controls the tactical employment, movement, and missions of the mortar unit. He plans and controls its fires. He is not responsible for sustainment/logistics or administrative support. OPCON of the mortar unit is given for a limited time or for a certain mission. Once the mission is accomplished, a mortar unit reverts to its parent unit's control.

3-15. A mortar platoon or section that is under the control of a company or troop establishes direct communications with that HQ. Fire missions are passed on the battalion mortar fire direction net or on another net designated by the controlling HQ. A company or platoon that has OPCON of the mortar platoon plans the platoon's fires and can further assign priority of fires and priority targets.

ATTACHMENT

3-16. Attachment is the temporary placement of units or personnel in an organization (FM 1-02). Subject to any limitations imposed by an attaching commander, a commander receiving the attachment exercises the same degree of authority as he does over units organic to his command. (See FM 5-0/MCWP 5-1 for details.)

3-17. A commander who has mortars attached is responsible for planning and employing their fires, as well as providing all classes of supply, medical evacuation, vehicle recovery, and administrative support. He specifies the general mortar firing location and directs displacement. A commander also integrates the attached mortar unit into his unit's security plan.

3-18. Attachment is a restrictive command relationship. It ensures that mortar fires are immediately responsive to the new HQ. However, it hinders the mortar platoon or sections in providing responsive fires to any other element of the battalion or squadron. It places a logistics burden on the HQ receiving mortars as attachments. A commander with mortars attached must designate the priority of fires and priority targets.

3-19. Attachment of mortar platoons and sections is not a normal command relationship. Examples of when the attachment of mortars is appropriate are during—
- Unit movement over great distances or along multiple routes.
- Infiltrations over compartmentalized terrain.
- Widely dispersed and noncontiguous operations.
- Company or platoon raids when the objective is out of range of normal supporting fires.
- Initial phase of an airborne operation until a battalion has completed its assembly and linkup.
- Initial phase of an air assault until the landing zone has been secured and the battalion HQ can coordinate the actions of the companies.

SUPPORT RELATIONSHIPS

3-20. A commander specifies support relationships by assigning one of two standard tactical missions for mortars— either GS or DS. Direct support is a support relationship requiring a unit to support another specific unit and authorizing it to answer directly the supported force's request for assistance. General support is a support relationship requiring a unit to support the supported force as a whole and not to any particular subdivision thereof. For example, the battalion mortar platoon has a DS relationship if it supports one of the maneuver companies directly and a GS relationship when it supports the battalion as a whole.

3-21. The two standard tactical missions of GS and DS carry inherent responsibilities that everyone who is involved in fire support must know. They describe in detail the fire support responsibilities of a mortar platoon or section (Table 3-3). When a commander's intent cannot be adequately supported by a standard tactical mission, a nonstandard one may be assigned. This is done either by issuing a separate mortar platoon or section mission statement along with explicit instructions on each of the inherent responsibilities, or by assigning a standard tactical mission and explaining how it has been altered.

ARMY SUPPORT RELATIONSHIPS

3-22. An Army commander assigns one of the following standard tactical missions:
- GS with priority of fires.
- GS with priority targets.
- GS without established priorities.
- DS.

Table 3-3. Inherent responsibilities of standard Army mortar tactical missions

A Mortar unit with a mission of—	General Support with Priority of Fires	General Support with Priority Targets(s)	General Support without Priorities	Direct Support
Answers call for fire in priority from—	1. Unit with priority of fires 2. All others in order of receipt	1. Unit calling for priority target 2. All others in order of receipt	Elements with the Bn/co in order of receipt of call for fire	1. Supported unit 2. Mortar unit leader 3. All others in order of receipt
Has as its zone of fire in priority—	1. AO of priority unit 2. Bn/co AO	1. Priority target 2. Bn/co AO	Bn/co AO	Supported unit AO
Establishes communication, in priority, with—	1. Priority unit 2. Bn/co CP 3. All others	1. Unit with priority target 2. Bn/co CP 3. All others	Bn/co CP	Supported unit HQ and FISTs/FiSTs. With FOs as directed
Is positioned by—	Bn/co commander	Bn/co commander	Bn/co commander	Coordinated among supported unit, mortar leader, and unit leader
Has its fires planned by—	Bn/co FSO/FSC	1.Bn/co FSO/FSC 2. Unit with priority target	Bn/co FSO/FSC	Supported unit

General Support (With Priority of Fires)

3-23. The assignment of priorities of fire allows a commander to retain overall control of the fires of his organic mortars but also makes them available to subordinate commanders. When two or more observers are calling for fire at the same time, a mortar unit leader has clear guidance as to whom his platoon should support first. A unit also fires for nonpriority observers when priority fire missions are complete. A commander can alter priority of fires at any time as the tactical situation changes.

3-24. If given a GS mission with priorities of fire established, a mortar unit leader must position at least one mortar or section of the unit to cover the company or platoon with priority of fires. He should attempt to locate a position that permits coverage for his entire battalion or company.

3-25. If providing priority of fires coverage to one company or platoon means a mortar unit cannot provide coverage for all the other elements of the battalion or company, a mortar leader must inform his commander and FSO/FSC.

3-26. If a commander changes the company or platoon to which he allocates priority of fires, a mortar platoon or section may be forced to displace to provide coverage. If so, a mortar unit leader must immediately notify the commander of his need to displace.

General Support (With Priority Targets)

3-27. This is a standard tactical mission during which the delivery of fires on a specific target takes precedence over all other fires for the mortar section or platoon. The mortar unit prepares for the engagement of such targets as much as possible. It lays its mortars on this target when not engaged in other fire missions. If any observer calls for the priority target to be fired, the mortar unit does so immediately, even if engaged in another fire mission. Only the maneuver commander can direct the mortar unit to cease firing on a priority target to engage in another fire mission. With the exception of the FPF (a special priority target), once a priority target mission is complete, the mortar unit immediately returns to firing other missions unless the order REPEAT is sent by the FO.

3-28. A commander may designate a priority target by type, location, or time sensitivity. A commander must give his FSO/FSC specific guidance as to when targets become priority targets and when they are no longer priority targets. He must also state the desired effects-on-target and any special ammunition to be used.

3-29. A mortar unit is normally assigned only one priority target at a time. A heavy mortar platoon can be assigned one priority target for each section. Under unusual circumstances, such as in a strongpoint defense, a section can be assigned more than one priority target. This may occur during execution of the battalion's close-in suppression of enemy air defenses fires or during illumination missions. Multiple priority targets require close coordination between the mortar unit leader and maneuver unit FSO/FSC. A commander can alter priority targets as the tactical situation changes.

3-30. An FPF is a special type of priority target. Normally, an FPF target is assigned to the company or platoon that is covering the most dangerous avenue of dismounted approach or covering the most vital area. Most often this company or platoon also has priority of fire. This prevents conflict of missions. In some situations, however, one commander may have priority of fires while another has the FPF. This could occur when a security force has priority of fires initially, but the FPF target is assigned to a defending company. This requires close coordination between a maneuver commander, operations staff officer, FSO/FSC, and mortar unit leader. A specific amount of mortar ammunition is always designated, prepared, and set aside for use with the FPF target. This FPF ammunition may not be used on any other mission without specific authorization from the commander.

General Support (Without Established Priorities)

3-31. A mortar platoon or section assigned a standard tactical mission of GS, but without established priorities, provides fires exclusively at the direction of the battalion or company HQ. Assigning the GS mission without priorities of fire may be appropriate during screening missions and closely phased deliberate attacks.

3-32. General support missions provide mortar fires immediately responsive to the needs of a commander. A mortar platoon or section with this GS mission will be less responsive in attacking targets of opportunity since there is no direct communications link with the FISTs at company level. General support missions are most effective against planned targets. General support without priorities is the most centralized of all standard tactical missions.

Direct Support

3-33. A mortar unit assigned the standard tactical mission of DS is immediately responsive to the fire support needs of a particular maneuver company, platoon, or some other element, such as the reconnaissance platoon. A mortar platoon must establish effective communication with the supported commander. It must coordinate its movements with that commander. The difference between DS and GS with priority of fire is that a mortar unit with a DS mission positions itself to conform to the supported commander's plans, even at the expense of other elements in the unit. The essential feature of the DS mission is the one-on-one relationship between a mortar unit and a supported commander or leader. From the standpoint of battalion control, the DS mission is the most decentralized of the tactical missions. It is often used to place a mortar section in support of a rifle company. A commander who has a mortar platoon or section in DS can further assign priorities of fire and priority targets.

MARINE CORPS SUPPORT RELATIONSHIPS

3-34. A Marine Corps commander specifies support relationships by assigning standard tactical missions of either GS or DS. (See Table 3-4 for the inherent responsibilities of each mortar standard tactical mission.)

Table 3-4. Inherent responsibilities of mortar standard Marine Corps tactical missions

A Marine Corps mortar unit with a mission of—	General Support	Direct Support
Answers call for fire in priority from—	1. Unit w/ priority of fires, if assigned 2. Elements in order of receipt of call for fire	1. Supported unit 2. Mortar unit leader 3. All others in order of receipt
Has as its zone of fire in priority—	1. AO of priority unit 2. Bn/co AO	Supported unit AO
Establishes communication, in priority, with—	1. Priority unit 2. Bn/co CP 3. All others	Supported unit HQ and FiST
Is positioned by—	Bn/co CDR	Coordinated among supported unit, mortar leader, and unit leader
Has its fires planned by—	Bn/co FSO/FSC	Supported unit

General Support

3-35. Marine Corps mortar platoons or sections, assigned a standard tactical mission of GS, support the maneuver force as a whole and remains under the immediate control of the mortar unit's HQ. This ensures mortars are immediately responsive to the needs of a maneuver force commander, and provides fires at the direction of the battalion (or company) HQ. It is the most centralized of the standard tactical missions.

3-36. Marine Corps commanders usually assign priorities of fire to subordinate units when mortars are assigned the GS mission. If priorities of fire are not assigned, a mortar unit responds to calls for fire in the order received.

3-37. The assignment of priorities of fire allows a commander to retain overall control of the fires of his organic mortars but also makes them available to his subordinate commanders. When two or more observers are calling for fire at the same time, a mortar platoon leader has clear guidance as to whom the platoon should support first. A platoon also fires for nonpriority observers when priority fire missions are complete. A commander can alter the priority of fires at any time as the tactical situation changes.

3-38. If given a GS mission with priorities of fire established, a Marine Corps mortar platoon leader must position at least one section of the platoon to cover the company or platoon with priority of fires. He should attempt to locate a position that permits coverage for the entire battalion.

3-39. If providing priority of fires coverage to one company or platoon means a Marine Corps mortar platoon cannot provide coverage for all the other elements of the battalion, a platoon leader must inform the battalion commander and FSC.

3-40. If a commander changes the company or platoon to which he allocates priority of fires, a mortar platoon or section may be forced to displace to provide coverage. If so, the mortar platoon leader must immediately notify the commander of his need to displace.

Direct Support

3-41. A Marine Corps mortar platoon assigned the standard tactical mission of DS is immediately responsive to the fire support needs of a particular maneuver company or some other element such as the reconnaissance platoon. A mortar platoon must establish effective communication with the supported commander. It must coordinate fire and movement with the battle plans of that commander. The difference between DS and GS with priority of fire is that a mortar platoon with a DS mission positions itself to conform to the supported commander's plans, even at the expense of the other commanders in the battalion. The essential feature of the DS mission is the one-on-one relationship between a mortar platoon and a supported commander. From the standpoint of battalion control, the DS mission is the most decentralized of the tactical missions. It is often used to place a mortar section in support of a rifle company. A commander who has a mortar platoon or section in DS can further assign priorities of fire and priority targets.

SECTION V – GRAPHICAL CONTROL MEASURES

3-42. Graphic control measures are graphic directives given by a commander to subordinate commanders to assign responsibilities, coordinate fire and maneuver, and control combat operations (FM 1-02). These measures are shown on maps, charts, overlays, and digital displays. Figure 3-1 displays examples of maneuver control measures and FSCMs discussed in this section. Commanders use graphical control measures to assign responsibilities, coordinate fires and maneuver, and control the use of airspace. Mortar units are primarily concerned with three types of graphical control measures: maneuver control measures, FSCMs, and airspace coordinating measures. The measures reduce the requirements for coordination or restrict firing into certain areas. (See FM 1-02/MCRP 5-12A for more details on graphical control measures.)

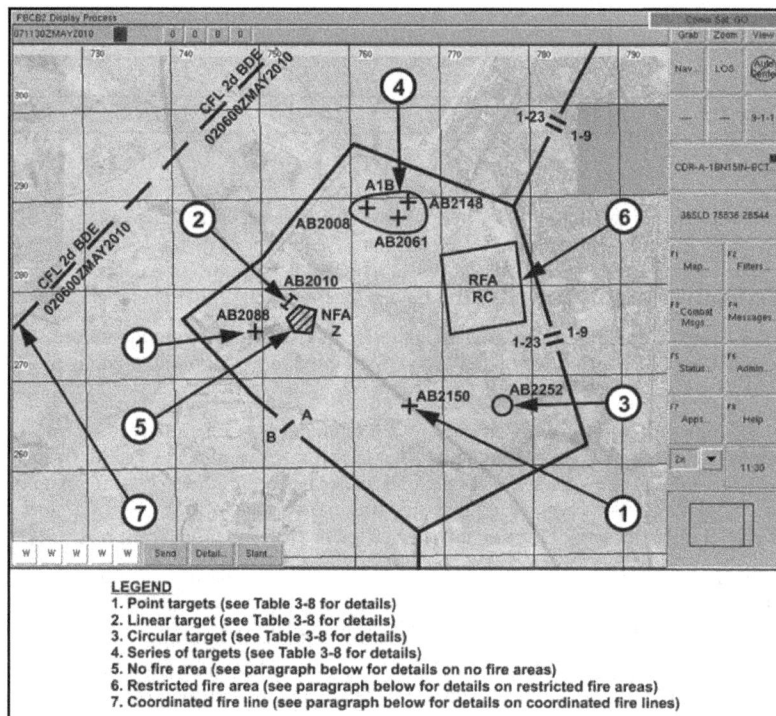

Figure 3-1. Examples of maneuver control and fire support coordinating measures

MANEUVER CONTROL MEASURES

3-43. The most important control measure is the boundary. Boundaries define the AO assigned to a commander. Commanders have full freedom to conduct operations within their AO unless the order establishing the AO includes constraints. Boundaries themselves also act as constraints; they limit commanders by preventing them from creating uncoordinated effects outside the boundaries. They are normally designated along terrain features easily recognizable on the ground. They affect fire support in the following two ways:

- They are restrictive in that no indirect fire support means can deliver fires or effects across the boundary unless those fires are coordinated with the force having responsibility for the area within that boundary.

- They are permissive in that the maneuver commander has complete freedom of fire and maneuver within his boundaries, unless otherwise restricted by a higher HQ. Many times boundaries will reduce the need for other FSCMs.

FIRE SUPPORT COORDINATING

3-44. Fire support coordinating measures are designed to make the rapid engagement of targets easy and, at the same time, provide safeguards for friendly forces (FM 6-20). They ensure that fire support will not jeopardize troop safety, will interface with other fire support means, and will not disrupt adjacent unit operations.

3-45. Fire support coordinating terms, symbols, and colors are standardized and mean the same for both artillery and mortar personnel. Examples of FSCMs and their symbols are discussed below. Black is the only color used to display FSCMs, targets, and other items on the fire support overlay. Standard colors for units include blue for friendly, red for enemy, and green for neutral or unknown.

3-46. The two general classes of FSCMs are permissive and restrictive.

PERMISSIVE FIRE SUPPORT COORDINATING MEASURES

3-47. Permissive FSCMs facilitate the attack of targets.

Coordinated Fire Line

3-48. A coordinated fire line (CFL) is a line beyond which conventional and indirect surface fire support means may fire at any time within the boundaries of the establishing HQ without additional coordination. The purpose of a CFL is to expedite the surface-to-surface attack of targets beyond the CFL without coordination with the ground commander in whose area the targets are located (JP 3-09). A CFL is usually established by a BCT/RCT or division commander, but it can also be established, especially in amphibious operations, by a maneuver battalion. The CFL is located as close to establishing unit as possible without interfering with the maneuver forces. (See FM 6-20-20/MCWP 3-16 more details.)

Fire Support Coordination Line

3-49. An FSCL is an FSCM that is established and adjusted by appropriate land or amphibious force commanders within their boundaries in consultation with superior, subordinate, supporting, and affected commanders. Force support coordination lines facilitate the expeditious attack of surface targets of opportunity beyond the coordinating measure. Forces attacking targets beyond an FSCL must inform all affected commanders in sufficient time to allow necessary reaction to avoid fratricide. Supporting elements attacking targets beyond an FSCL must ensure that an attack will not produce adverse effects on, or to the rear of, the line. Mortar units, except perhaps those in reconnaissance squadrons and light armored reconnaissance units, are unlikely to be involved with FSCLs. (See FM 6-20-20/MCWP 3-16 for details.)

Free-Fire Area

3-50. A free-fire area is a permissive fire control measure that defines an area into which mortars can fire without additional coordination. A free-fire area is a specific area into which any weapon system may fire without additional coordination with the establishing HQ. It is used to expedite joint fires and to facilitate jettison of aircraft munitions (JP 3-09). (See FM 6-20-20/MCWP 3-16 for additional information on the free-fire area.)

Kill Box

3-51. A kill box is an area used to facilitate the integration of joint fires (JP 3-09). A kill box is a three-dimensional FSCM used to facilitate the expeditious air-to-surface lethal attack of targets, which may be augmented by or integrated with surface-to-surface indirect fires. While kill boxes are permissive FSCMs with respect to the deliverance of air-to-surface weapons, they are also restrictive in nature; trajectories and effects of surface-to-surface indirect fires are not normally allowed to pass through a kill box. A kill box is a unique FSCM that may contain other measures within its boundaries, such as no-fire areas, restricted operations areas, and airspace coordination areas. Restrictive FSCMs and airspace coordinating measures will always have priority when established in a kill box.

Battlefield Coordination Line

3-52. A battlefield coordination line is an exclusive Marine Corps FSCM, similar to an FSCL, which facilitates expeditious attack of targets with surface indirect fires and aviation fires between this measure and the FSCL. (See MCWP 3-16 for details.)

RESTRICTIVE FIRE SUPPORT COORDINATING MEASURES

3-53. Restrictive FSCMs provide safeguards for friendly forces and noncombatants, facilities, or terrain. They indicate where firing is restricted or even prohibited without prior coordination. A mortar leader must coordinate with the FSO/FSC to ensure that all restrictive FSCMs are known to all concerned personnel.

Restrictive Fire Line

3-54. A restrictive fire line is a restrictive fire control measure often used to coordinate mortar and other fires during linkup operations. It is a line between converging friendly forces, one or both of which may be moving, and that prohibits fires or their effects across the line without coordination with the affected force. It is established on identifiable terrain, where possible, by the common commander of the converging forces.

Restrictive Fire Area

3-55. A restrictive fire area is an area with specific restrictions and in which fires that exceed those restrictions will not be delivered without coordination with the establishing HQ. This is a common coordination measure used with mortars fires during stability operations.

No-Fire Area

3-56. A no-fire area is an area into which no fires or their effects are allowed. The two exceptions are—
- When the establishing HQ approves fires within the no-fire area on a mission-by-mission basis.
- When an enemy force within the no-fire area engages a friendly force and an engaged commander determines there is a requirement for immediate protection and responds with the minimal force needed to defend the force.

3-57. If possible, a no-fire area is established on identifiable terrain. A no-fire area may also be located by a series of grids or by a radius from a center point. It may be established in conjunction with a host nation to preclude damage or destruction to a national asset, population center, natural or cultural resources such as a shrine, or to minimize environmental impact. It may also be established to protect an element of tactical importance.

AIRSPACE COORDINATION MEASURES

3-58. Airspace coordination measures are rules, mechanisms, and directions governed by joint doctrine and defined by the airspace control plan that controls the use of airspace of specified dimensions. They also ensure that artillery and mortar fires do not endanger aircraft conducting CAS, close combat attacks, or air assaults. The three basic techniques to separate aircraft from indirect fires are by time, lateral dispersion, and altitude (Figure 3-2). No one technique is preferred, but the technique used should be the one that allows the most firepower and flexibility for the systems. If possible, air controllers should avoid simply placing mortars or artillery into a check-fire status when employing CAS and close combat attack.

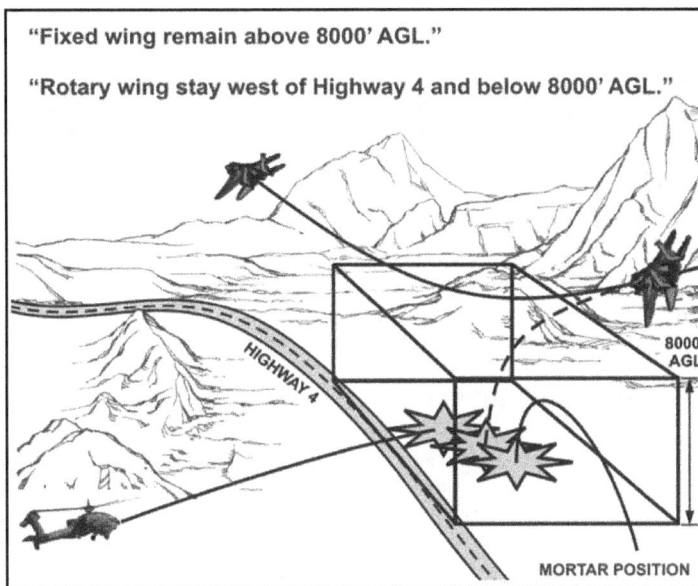

Figure 3-2. Example of lateral and altitude separation

3-59. There are many airspace coordination measures, including coordinating altitude, low-level transit routes, and so on, but the primary one that affects mortar operations is the airspace coordination area. An airspace coordination area is a three-dimensional block of airspace of defined dimensions in which friendly aircraft are reasonably free from friendly surface fires. Artillery, helicopters, and fixed-winged aircraft are given specific lateral or vertical airspace within which to operate. When airspace coordination measures are in place, mortar units should be prepared to identify the maximum ordinate of the rounds being fired and to modify their firing when requested. (See JP 3-09 for details.)

SECTION VI – TARGET IDENTIFICATION

3-60. A target is the most fundamental term used in fire support planning. A target can be personnel, material, or a piece of terrain that is designated and numbered for future reference and firing. Target categories are standard and mean exactly the same to artillery and mortar personnel.

TARGET TYPES

3-61. The two target types are targets of opportunity and planned targets.

TARGETS OF OPPORTUNITY

3-62. Targets of opportunity are targets that appear during combat that were not previously identified. They are targets either identified too late or not selected for action in time to be included in the deliberate targeting process.

PLANNED TARGET

3-63. Planned targets are targets upon which fires are prearranged. The degree of prearrangement varies, but some before-action coordination has been done to facilitate its engagement. Planned targets are subdivided into—

- **Scheduled targets** are planned targets scheduled for firing at a specific time.
- **On-call targets** are planned mortar targets that have not been scheduled for attack at a specific time, but will be attacked when requested.

- **Priority targets** are planned targets that when requested for attack, take priority over all other requests. Priority targets are designated by the maneuver commander, who provides specific guidance as to when the targets will become priority and desired effects.
- FPFs are defensive priority targets and are fired to stop and destroy an enemy force before it can penetrate a defensive position. They are integrated into a maneuver unit's direct fire final protective lines.

PRIORITY TARGETS

3-64.   Priority targets increase fire support responsiveness on specific targets or specific high threat areas. In addition to artillery priority targets allocated to him, a maneuver commander has one or two (one for each section) mortar priority targets he can allocate to his mortar platoon. The importance of a priority target normally justifies the allocation of fires from a mortar section or platoon, especially the fires from a heavy mortar unit. However, because of the size of the AO or the number of targets, leaders may have to allocate a priority target to a squad. If it is a heavy mortar squad, then its lethality may be sufficient to achieve the desired target effects. Light mortar squads may achieve some effects on a priority target, but they can rarely achieve destruction.

3-65.   As a guide, a battalion mortar platoon can be assigned up to two priority targets, one for each section, and the company mortar section can be assigned one. This guideline normally provides adequate target coverage and results. Mortar platoons using medium mortars and light mortar sections usually cover only a single priority target. A commander indicates his priority target in the "remarks" column of his target list. Anticipated changes of the priority target are indicated as "on-order priority targets" on the same target list.

3-66.   Mortar firing units may be assigned priority targets in a sequence identified by the commander. Mortar unit leaders should understand that—

- A single priority target per section is usually best.
- Multiple priority targets are possible where more than one mortar-firing unit of a specified size is available.
- Priority targets may have to be engaged by a single mortar, especially in noncontiguous operations.
- When a mortar-firing unit is not engaged in a fire mission, the mortar should be laid on the firing data for the current priority target.

3-67.   A battalion commander and FSO/FSC must carefully consider priority targets before assigning them. Priority targets should lie in the AO of the company or platoon having priority of fires. This prevents any confusion if a mortar platoon receives several calls at the same time. If a conflict is possible, such as when a reconnaissance platoon has priority of fires, yet a priority target has been allocated to a rifle company, a commander, FSO/FSC, operations officer, and mortar platoon leader must coordinate to avoid confusion.

3-68.   Priority targets are not always fired using HE ammunition. Illumination, smoke, or a mix of HE and white phosphorous (WP) can be used as the designated rounds to be fired.

3-69.   With the exception of FPFs, a predetermined amount of ammunition is set aside to be fired on priority targets. A mortar section fires this ammunition at the maximum rate of fire immediately upon the observer's call for fire. An FDC then modifies the fire command or calls for the section to repeat the mission, shift fires, or cease fire, based on the message from the observer.

3-70.   Final protective fires are the highest type of priority targets and take precedence over all other fire requests. They are planned barriers of both direct and indirect fires designed to protect friendly troops from an enemy dismounted assault.

NUMBERING SYSTEM

3-71.   To designate targets for fire support operations, the Army and Marine Corps adhere to the provisions of STANAG 2934. A target number is comprised of six characters, two letters followed by four number positions, such as AJ1234. Other than the letter Z, there are no permanently assigned first letters. The senior HQ for an operation will establish and publish, in orders, the assigned first letter. A two-letter group may be used to indicate the originator or the target number and the level holding the target data. Target numbers serve as an index to all other information regarding a particular target, such as location, description, and size. Within a major force, normally at corps, a common target numbering system is used. Fire planners and fire support resources at all echelons, including mortar platoons, are assigned blocks of target numbers for their use.

Because target numbers are assigned in blocks to specific users, a target can be readily traced back to its originating source. Standard blocks of numbers are assigned to each BCT and Marine Infantry regiment as listed in Table 3-5 and Table 3-6. A battalion or squadron sub allocates blocks of numbers as listed in Table 3-7 and Table 3-8.

Note. This paragraph complies with STANAG 2934.

3-72. Target numbers are usually established in the division or regimental TACSOP. The numbers sub allocated to BCTs/regiments should be incorporated into the BCT, battalion/squadron, company/troop, and platoon TACSOPs.

Table 3-5. Example standard blocks of numbers assigned to each Army brigade

Numbers	Assigned To
0001 through 1999	Brigade fires cell and combat observation and lasing teams
2000 through 2999	Fires cell, lowest numbered maneuver battalion or squadron
3000 through 3999	Fires cell, second lowest numbered maneuver battalion or squadron
4000 through 4999	Fires cell, third lowest numbered maneuver battalion or squadron
5000 through 6999	Additional fires cell or fire support assets
7000 through 7999	FDC of the BCT fires battalion
8000 through 8999	Counterfire/counterbattery targets
9000 through 9999	Spare

Table 3-6. Example standard blocks of numbers assigned to Marine Corps Infantry Regiments

Numbers	Assigned To
0001 through 1999	Infantry Regiment FSCC
2000 through 2999	Lowest numbered Infantry battalion
3000 through 3999	Second lowest numbered Infantry battalion
4000 through 4999	Third lowest numbered Infantry battalion
6000 through 6999	Attached battalion
7000 through 7999	Attached battalion
8000 through 8999	Unassigned
9000 through 9999	Spare

Table 3-7. Example of Army battalion or squadron sub allocations of target numbers

Numbers	Assigned To
000 through 199	Battalion/squadron fires cell
0200 through 299	A company/troop
300 through 399	B company/troop
400 through 499	C company/troop
500 through 599	D company/troop
600 through 699	Additional companies/ troops or fire support assets
700 through 799	Battalion squadron mortar platoon (or section)
800 through 999	Spare

EXAMPLE

Assume that the Army battalion to which a mortar platoon is assigned is allocated target numbers 3000 to 3999. A mortar platoon's block of numbers would be 3700 to 3799. If a division is assigned a first letter of A, and a division then assigns the BCT a second letter of B, a mortar platoon's block of target numbers could be AB3700 to AB3799.

Table 3-8. Example of Marine Corps sub allocations of target numbers

Numbers	Assigned To
0000 through 0199	Marine Corps Infantry battalion FSCC
0200 through 0299	Lowest lettered Infantry company
0300 through 0399	Second lowest lettered Infantry company
0400 through 0499	Third lowest lettered Infantry company
0500 through 0599	Weapons company
0600 through 0699	Scout sniper platoon
0700 through 0799	81-mm mortar platoon
0800 through 0899	Attachment

SYMBOLS

3-73. The following standard symbols are used in the preparation of maps, charts, and overlays to identify targets by type (Table 3-9). (See FM 3-22.91 or FM 1-02/MCRP 5-12A for details.)

- **Point target** is a target that is less than 200 meters wide.
- **Linear target** is more than 200 meters, but less than 600 meters long. Targets longer than 600 meters require fire support assets other than mortars or must be further subdivided into multiple targets for attack. A linear target is designated on the target list by two grids or a center grid, length, and attitude.
- **Rectangular target** is wider and longer than 200 meters. It is designated on the target list by four grids or a center grid, length, width, and attitude.
- **Circular target** is circular in nature or is vague as to its exact shape. It is designated by a center grid and a radius on the target list.
- **Final protective fires** are types of priority fires that are similar to linear targets. They are a prearranged barrier of indirect fire that prevent or stop the enemy from advancing.
- **A series of targets** is a number of targets or groups of targets planned to support the operation. The fact that a series has been formed does not preclude the attack of individual targets or groups of targets within the series. However, once the series has been initiated, all of the targets must be fired on in the predetermined sequence as provided by the target list or schedule for the series.

Table 3-9. Target symbols

Type of Target	Symbol
Point	⊢ AB4050
Linear	⊢ AB4050 ⊣
Rectangular	AB4050
Circular	AB4050
Final protective fire	AB4050 FPF 1-26 INF MORTAR
Series of targets	DOG A3B AC3459 AC3431 AC4163

<!-- Target symbols illustrations -->

SECTION VII – TARGET SELECTION

3-74. During bottom-up refinement of the top-down planning process, an FO in each Infantry platoon identifies any additional targets as directed by a platoon leader. He forwards his additional targets to the company FSO/FSC who further refines the fire plan to support the company commander's scheme of maneuver and his intent for fire support. The company commander reviews, approves, and forwards the list of additional targets to the battalion fires cell.

3-75. A battalion FSO/FSC analyzes each company's additional target list, resolves duplication by deleting redundant targets, adds any new targets provided by the battalion staff or external agencies, and produces a consolidated battalion target list and overlay.

3-76. Based on the battalion commander's guidance, an FSO/FSC establishes a precedence of targets for engagement. He determines specific weapons and shell/fuze combinations to attack each planned target.

SECTION VIII – FIRE SUPPORT PLANNING AND PRODUCTS

3-77. A battalion commander is responsible for the fire support plan. The fire support plan is based on the commander's intent for fire support, developed by the battalion FSO/FSC, and reviewed by the battalion operations staff officer. It includes targets selected for engagement by mortar platoons.

3-78. A company commander is responsible for his company's fire support plan. The company fire support plan is developed by the company FSO/FSC to support the company commander's plan for maneuver. The commander should give his mortar platoon a specific mission during each phase of an operation. A platoon's mission must be realistic and clearly understood by both the platoon and observers who will be calling for fire.

PLANNING

3-79. Battalion mortar platoons and company mortar sections execute their portion of the fire support plan by engaging planned targets in accordance with schedules of fire provided by the battalion FSO/FSC or company FIST/FiST. They respond to calls for fire on planned targets and targets of opportunity originated by the company FIST/FiST, battalion FSO/FSC, or others. If no designated formal command or support relationships exist, battalion mortar platoon leaders and company section leaders cooperate, responding to targets of opportunity. Mortar platoon and company mortar sections normally have limited fire planning responsibility, other than technical computation of firing data for planned mortar targets and ensuring that a commander's guidance is met. However, mortar platoon and section leaders must be knowledgeable about fire support planning coordination. (See Figure 3-3 and Figure 3-4 for details.)

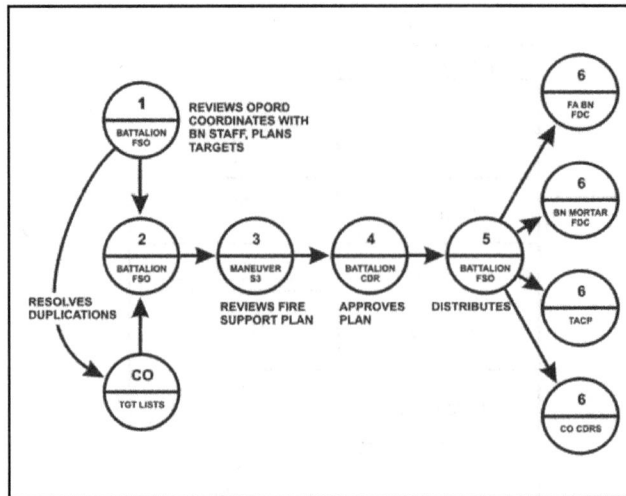

Figure 3-3. Battalion or squadron fire support planning process

Note. Figure 3-3 shows the top-down planning and the bottom-up refinement process.

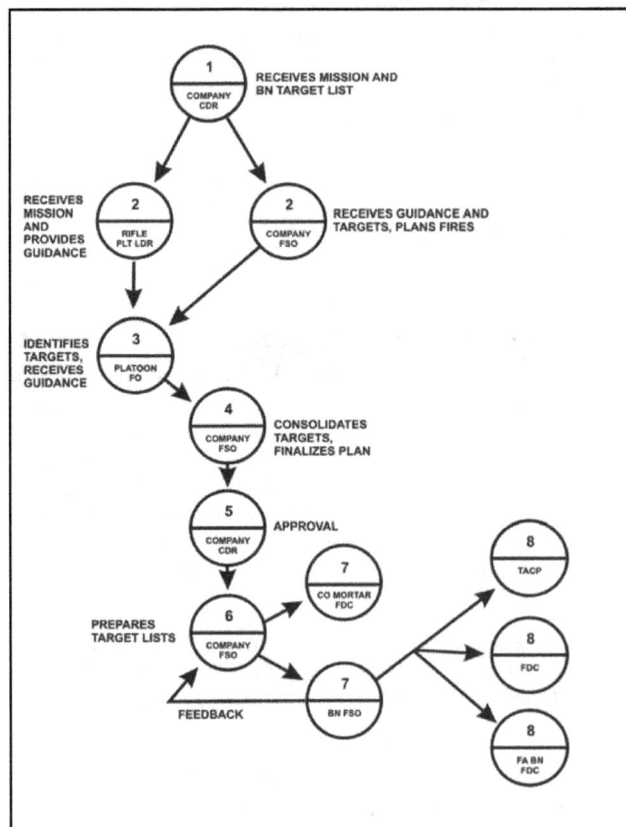

Figure 3-4. Company team fire support planning process

3-80. To ensure timely and accurate execution of a mortar unit portion of the fire support plan, a mortar unit leader must—

- Consider support requirements, terrain and positioning of firing sections commensurate with a battalion's/company's scheme of maneuver.
- Consider the means by which he will control his unit's movement and fires.
- Analyze mortar targets given in the fire support plan to ensure that sufficient quantities of ammunition (by type) are available for firing against planned targets and targets of opportunity to include checking on a commander's intent to use smoke or illumination extensively.
- Identify, reconnoiter, and select firing positions that enable mission accomplishment, provide the ability to mass fires, and are favorable to mortar employment.
- Coordinate the displacement plan, the use of terrain, and resupply routes with a battalion operations staff officer and support platoon leader, or a company commander and executive officer (XO), as applicable.
- Coordinate required field artillery support, such as survey and meteorological data, with a battalion FSO/FSC or battalion FIST/FiST to enhance first-round accuracy and the ability to mass fires from separate firing section locations.

BATTALION FIRE SUPPORT PLAN

3-81. A consolidated target overlay, consolidated target list, and implementing instructions constitute the battalion fire support plan. A copy is provided to a mortar platoon for technical data processing. This enables each mortar platoon to precompute firing data for each planned target, thereby reducing response time. If multiple firing positions are planned, sections can compute firing data from each firing position for each target.

CONSOLIDATED TARGET OVERLAY

3-82. A target overlay in the fire support plan shows targets planned to support the battalion's mission. The overlay also includes any established or planned FSCMs and occupied or planned firing positions. Used in conjunction with the operations overlay, a target overlay is a quick reference for coordinating fires. Coordinating measures shown on the overlay should be transcribed onto firing charts in the FDCs to ensure compliance with any restrictions. An overlay, when transcribed on the operations map, keys the platoon to the status of individual targets in relation to friendly maneuver. Target information and FSCMs are also plotted on the FBCB2 and distributed within the battalion and company. A target overlay that is part of the battalion OPORD, however, is the definitive overlay. A target overlay must be checked continuously against the maneuver graphics to ensure it supports a commander's plan.

3-83. Superimposed over the operations overlay, a battalion target overlay displays planned fires in relation to the scheme of maneuver. This overlay provides a ready means for resolving duplications, ensuring adequate coverage of the AO, and identifying targets that require special coordination. The target overlay contains all planned targets to support the battalion operation. It also contains marginal information that identifies the overlay, references the applicable map sheet(s), and provides orienting data in the form of grid register marks.

CONSOLIDATED TARGET LIST

3-84. A consolidated target list in the fire support plan is the basic document used to communicate planned target data. It is the product of the top-down and bottom-up refinement process, all levels of command from platoon and up providing input and recommending revisions. A target list provided to mortar units contains all of the targets planned to support the operation, regardless of whether mortars or artillery are preferred to attack the target. (See FM 3-22.91 for details.)

IMPLEMENTING INSTRUCTIONS

3-85. In addition to the target overlay and target list, a battalion fire support plan includes implementing instructions. If not written in the fire support plan, implementing instructions can be provided orally.

3-86. A commander routinely makes decisions that affect the way a mortar unit operates. Through his analysis of the METT-TC/METT-T variables, a commander determines how he can best use the mortar unit's firepower to accomplish the mission. He communicates his decisions by providing his intent for fire support to his operations staff officer, FSO/FSC, and mortar platoon leader. He also provides any other guidance that he feels is necessary. While not intended to be an all-inclusive list, the following are representative of the commander's guidance that affect mortar employment:

- Priority of fire to designated subordinate companies or platoons.
- Allocation of mortar fire to attack on-call priority targets.
- Attack guidance or the degree of damage required for particular targets, such as suppress, neutralize, or destroy.
- Establishment of FSCMs.
- Anticipated changes in mortar employment (command relationship, DS, or GS) to support future operations.
- Communication constraints and special requirements.
- Precedence of targets by type for engagement by various firing resources.
- General location of positions to provide for attack of targets and survivability.
- Instructions regarding moves.
- Coordination requirements.
- Special considerations for smoke or illumination use, especially in urban operations.
- An enemy's capacity to fire countermortar fire.
- Ammunition constraints by type and quantity.

3-87. Implementing instructions for a mortar platoon come from several sources. Although a written OPORD is rarely distributed below battalion level, an OPORD can be given via the FBCB2 or orally in the OPORD format. A mortar unit leader pays particular attention to the execution paragraph with emphasis on his commander's intent, scheme of maneuver, and plan for fires. Implementing instructions for targets can appear in the remarks column of the target list.

3-88. Implementing instructions are also provided in the form of schedules for firing. Schedules are prepared for firing a series, program, preparation, or counter preparation. Schedules direct the firing of the mortar unit onto designated targets at a specific time, regardless of the type provided. The schedule designates the time on target and the amount of rounds to be fired, or it gives the time on target and the duration of fire (for example, time on target H-5, duration four minutes). A mortar unit leader studies the schedule of fires closely to determine the ammunition required and the target shifts involved. An FSO/FSC plans a one-minute shift time for mortars. The platoon leader synchronizes his time with the FSO/FSC and keeps the platoon on the schedule. If rounds scheduled for a certain period are not all fired by the shift time, a mortar squads check fire, shift, and stay with the schedule. Any targets not fired are reported to an FSO/FSC immediately.

3-89. A fire support execution matrix is a graphical, easy-to-use way of assigning target responsibilities and allocating fire support resources to a battalion/squadron or company. A matrix shows which targets are most critical to the battalion's success and who is responsible for firing them. The matrix shows the allocation of priority targets and FPFs. It also shows a mortar platoon's firing positions and expected displacements by phase (Figure 3-5).

3-90. A company fire support execution matrix is a tool used to aid in executing a battalion plan. A company FSO/FSC and mortar platoon or section leader develop the matrix. It aids key leaders in the company in understanding and executing the fire support plan without the FSO/FSC (Figure 3-6).

UNIT	PHASE I FPOL	PHASE II ATTACK	PHASE III DEFENSE	PHASE IV TBD		
TF CONTROL		1X PLT ATK AVN ⟶				
TM A/1-35 AR	FA POF AB 1005 (P) ⟶	1X FA PRI TGT	AB 2010 (P)			
TM B/1-35 AR	MTR POF 1X CFZ AB 2005 (A) ⟶	AB 1110(P)	AB 2010 (A) ⟶			
TM C/1-6 IN	AB 1005 (A)		1X FA PRI TGT AB 1115 (A)			
TM D/1-6 IN	O/O FA POF AB 2005 (P)	AB 1110 (A) 1 X MTR TGT	AB 1115 (P) ⟶ FA POF			
TF MTR (4x120 mm)	MFP 1 ⟶ AB 2005 (PLT 6 round of HE)		MFP 2 ⟶ AB 2010 (1 X 5 min 300 m SMK Screen)			
Mortar Priority of Fires	TM B/1-35 AR	TM B/1-35 AR	TF Control	TF Control		
FA Priority of Fires	TM A/1-35 AR	TM A/1-35 AR	TM D/ 1-6 IN	TF Control		

FA Organization for Combat 4-27 FA(2x8 155SP) 2ND BCT 2-3 FA (2x8 155SP) R 4-27 FA	**Mortars** MFP 1 NV 123456 (AOF 1600) O/O move to MPF 2 NV 345321 (AOF 1700)	**Coordinating Instructions** All CO TGTs need to be submitted to the TF FSO/FSC NLT H-6 Hours. Mortars will utilize RTE Softail and RTE Road King for movement w/in the AO. Voice and Digital COMMs checks will be conducted w/ the FSC NLT H-2 hours.	**FSO LOC** w/ TF CDR @ TAC vic GV 123456 **SUCCESSION OF COMD** A-CO FSO, B-CO FSO, C-CO FSO, D-CO FSO
FSCMs CFL: PL HARLEY O/O PL HONDA NFA 1: GV 435678 (250m Radius) RFA 1: GV 465127 (500m Radius) NO DPICM	**HPT/Attack Guidance** 1. Man (Suppress) 2. FS Assets (Neutralize) 3. ADA (Suppress)		**Refinement Cut-Off** NLT H-6 hours **FS Rehearsal** H-4 hours at the TF CP vic GV 765432
Restrictions FASCAM release authority is retained at the DIV level	**Target Blocks** TF 1-35 AR: AB 2000-2199 A/1-35 AR: AB 2200-2299 B/1-35 AR: AB 2300-2399 C/1-6 IN: AB 2400-2499 D/1-6 IN: AB 2500-2599		**CAS** CAS will be on station at H+30min to H+ 1 hour (30 min). All missions need to be formulated and transmitted by assigned JTACs. Type 1 CAS missions only.

Figure 3-5. Example of a battalion fire support execution matrix

COMMANDER'S INTENT FOR FIRE SUPPORT: COMPANY OFFENSE SMOKE ON BB 1001 TO COVER OUR INITIAL MOVEMENT ACROSS THE LD. FIRE GROUP B1B ON OBJ FOX AS 2^D AND 3^D PLATOONS CROSS PL BLUE. USE BB 3109 TO HELP BLOCK A COUNTERATTACK FROM HILL 333

TGT #	GRID	DESCRIPTION	DECISION POINT	EXECUTION	
				PRIMARY	BACKUP
BB 1001	123456	SMOKE OP	WHEN 1ST PLT IS READY TO CROSS LD	1ST PLT	FSO
BB 1002	123567	SUSPECTED INF SQUAD	2^D AND 3^D PLTs CROSS PL BLUE	CO CDR	2^D PLT
BB 3108 (GRP B1B)	125467	AT POSITION	2^D AND 3^D PLTS CROSS PL BLUE	CO CDR	2^D PLT
BB 3109	143335	ROAD JCT	IF CNTRATTCK BRIDGE AT 146578	2^D PLT	3^D PLT
BB 2102	136324	SUSPECTED AT POSITION	IF RECEIVE FIRE FROM POSITION	FSO	XO

HIGH PAYOFF TARGETS: ALL ATGM POSITIONS

ACTIONS UPON: XO MONITORS HVY MORTAR PLT NET FOR FIRE SUPPORT COORDINATION
LOSS OF FSO: PLs SWITCH TO CF2 OR THE MORTAR NET TO FIRE MISSIONS

PRIORITY OF FIRE				AMMUNITION AVAILABLE TO TF	SOI		
	CROSS LD		CROSS PL BLUE			DAY 05	DAY 06
	FA	MTR	FA	MTR		FA NET	31:10	42.00
CO	1ST PLT	1ST PLT	2NF PLT	2^D PLT	FA DPICM/HE 16 BN 3 RDS	MTR NET	56:00	23.65
BN	A CO	B CO	A CO	B CO	FA SMK 23 MIN MTR HE 24 PLT 6	MTR FDC	38:45	26.30
BDE	1-26		1-26		MTR SMOKE: 20 MIN	FA FDC	36:00	47.45
						BN FSO	42:25	31.15

COORDINATING INSTRUCTIONS
1. SHOOT 120-mm MORTAR SMOKE ON BB 1001
2. GP B1B TGTS ARE FA PRIORITY TGTS
3. SHOOT IMMEDIATELY ANY ADA TARGETS

Figure 3-6. Example of a company fire support execution matrix

SECTION IX – PROCESSING AND COORDINATING CALLS FOR MORTAR FIRE

3-91.   This section gives mortar leaders at company and battalion levels a description of the nets available for fire support planning and coordination with FISTs/FiSTs and FSOs/FSCs, and for receiving calls for fire.

3-92.   Radios in a battalion mortar platoon allow it to operate on multiple nets and to pass information to any FM radio station in the battalion. By designating mortar squads within a platoon to monitor the lesser used nets, a mortar platoon remains informed while keeping enough radios free to conduct fire coordination and execution. A company mortar section has fewer radios and its radios nets are simpler than those at battalion level.

3-93.   Wire communications are the most secure and reliable means of coordinating and calling for mortar fires. They are especially effective for communication within a platoon and section. They should be used when units expect to be stationary for a period of time. Stability operations and the colocation of units in operating bases make wire communication more feasible.

RADIO NETS

3-94. Frequency modulation voice and digital are usually the most practical means to communicate. Several radio nets are important to a mortar platoon leader. He does not routinely operate in all of them, but he can enter any of them to accomplish his mission. However, tactical and local conditions, such as restricting call for fires to one net during stability operations, may change the number of available radio nets. Some stations in the artillery-controlled nets may operate in the digital mode only.

> *Note.* The Marine Corps uses different terminology to name their radio nets. Instead of the Army's artillery battalion fire net, the Marine Corps uses the term conduct of fire net.

FIRES BATTALION COMMAND FIRE NET

3-95. An artillery commander uses the fires battalion command fire net to control his batteries and pass tactical information. A battalion FSO/FSC operates in this net to conduct the fire planning. This net is used to pass target lists to a battalion FSO/FSC. A fires battalion FDC is the net control station. A mortar platoon leader may be directed to enter this net when fire plans are tightly controlled by a BCT.

ARTILLERY BATTALION FIRE NET

3-96. The FIST/FiST HQ and FO use a fires battalion fire net to call for field artillery fire. No other information passes over this net. There is a fire direction net authorized for each firing battery in a fires battalion and command fires net. A fires field artillery battalion FDC is the net control station. A mortar platoon leader monitors this net to know when it is being operated in voice mode.

MANEUVER COMPANY COMMAND NET

3-97. A maneuver company command net allows direct coordination between platoon leaders, including mortar unit leaders, a company commander, and a company FSO/FSC. Although this net can be used to request mortar fire, it is the least desirable net to use. Calls for fire and observer's adjustments can quickly clog this important net. A company commander is the net control station. A battalion mortar platoon leader may enter a company command net, especially if one of his mortar sections is attached or under OPCON of his company.

MANEUVER COMPANY FIRE CONTROL NET

3-98. A company FSO/FSC uses a maneuver company fire control net to control actions of FO parties. A company mortar section uses this net. Platoon leaders, platoon sergeants, and other non-field artillery observers also use this net to request artillery and mortar fire through the FIST/FiST. The FIST/FiST HQ is normally the net control station. When firing support planning and coordination must be over an FM radio (rather than face-to-face), this net is used. It is also used for processing fire missions from either platoon FOs or non-field artillery observers. Stations operating this net are FOs, FIST/FiST HQ, and company mortars. Occasionally, a battalion FSO/FSC can enter this net to coordinate with the FIST/FiST chief.

BATTALION MORTAR FIRE DIRECTION NET

3-99. The primary net for processing and controlling fires of battalion mortars is the battalion mortar fire direction net. Normally, battalion mortar platoon leaders, FDC(s), FSO/FSC, and FOs operate on this net when requesting fires from battalion mortars.

BATTALION COMMAND AND ADMINISTRATION/LOGISTIC NETS

3-100. A battalion mortar platoon always operates on a battalion command net. It operates in the administration/logistic net when necessary.

METHODS

3-101. Three methods are available to a commander for controlling FO calls for fire. A commander and FSO determine, based on the experience of the FOs and the tactical situation, if FOs are to send fire requests to the FIST/FiST HQ (centralized control), directly to a mortar FDC (decentralized control), or if fire requests are predesignated. An FSO/FSC monitors all voice calls for fire regardless of the method used.

3-102. Forward observers do not have to be under the same control options at the same time. The three methods for control of FOs must be tailored to the tactical situation. Normally, a combination of methods is used. In tailoring the three options for controlling the fire support assets and FOs, a commander considers the following:

- Decentralized control requires well-trained FOs.
- The platoon requiring the most responsive support should have priority for mortar fires.
- The platoon with the most difficult mission gets the assets that are effective against targets they are expected to locate.
- The FO who can see the farthest should be able to shoot the farthest.
- Each FO must have access to a fire asset.
- Personnel other than FOs can be designated to call for mortar fire.

CENTRALIZED

3-103. A centralized method is the most restrictive. It requires an FO to operate in a company fire control net. When a rifle platoon leader needs indirect fire, his FO calls the FIST/FiST HQ and submits a target description and target location. A company FSO/FSC determines if this request should be fired by company mortars (if available), or sent to battalion mortars or supporting artillery. If a request is to be fired by company mortars, a company FSO/FSC may elect to give verbal authorization for mortars to fire the mission or may establish that silence is consent to fire. Company mortars operate within a company fire control net, monitoring and processing calls for fire pending authorization from a company FSO/FSC. If an FSO/FSC determines that a mission needs to be fired by battalion mortars or supporting artillery, he directs an FO to switch to the applicable fire direction net and to send his request. Once the FO completes his mission, he returns his radio from the fire net back to the company fire control. This method allows the company FSO/FSC the most positive control over the FOs and prevents net overload. It is the slowest and least responsive method (Figure 3-7). However, centralized control is used frequently, particularly in stability operations, where there may be very restrictive ROE.

DECENTRALIZED

3-104. In a decentralized method, platoon FOs are allowed to call for fire from either artillery or mortars, based on their own judgment. An FO sends a request directly to a designated FDC on its fire control/direction net. An FO does not have to contact FIST/FiST HQ before sending his call for fire, but the FIST/FiST HQ monitors all voice transmissions to ensure coordination of fires on target is accomplished. A FIST/FiST HQ can override any decision made by an FO and direct him to use another fire support means or method of engagement, or to cancel a mission. Anytime an FO is not engaged in a fire mission, he operates in the company fire control net. A company FSO/FSC monitors each voice request and, in this situation, silence is consent. A battalion FSO/FSC monitors requests directed to battalion mortars in the same way. When a section or squad is attached or placed under OPCON to a company, the section/squad operates in the company fire control net or as directed by the company commander. The advantage of this method is that it is highly responsive to each rifle platoon; however, to use this method requires highly trained FOs and is difficult for a company FSO/FSC to control. Another consideration is the range of a platoon FO's radio that may not be sufficient and multiple FOs that may overload a net (Figure 3-8).

PREDESIGNATED

3-105. In the predesignated method, a company FSO/FSC assigns any or all FOs a fire net in which to operate. This option includes provisions to assign two FOs to one net. Net assignment is dependent upon tactical considerations. A platoon FO requests as many missions as he desires and FIST/FiST HQ monitors all nets. If an FO requests the use of an asset other than his predesignated asset, he must coordinate with FIST/FiST HQ. If an FO is given a different asset for a particular mission, he will return to the original predesignated asset upon completion of the mission. This method is highly responsive, provides positive control by a FIST/FiST HQ, and prevents net overload. However, predesignation is not as flexible as other methods and may result in a less than optimal utilization of fires assets (Figure 3-9).

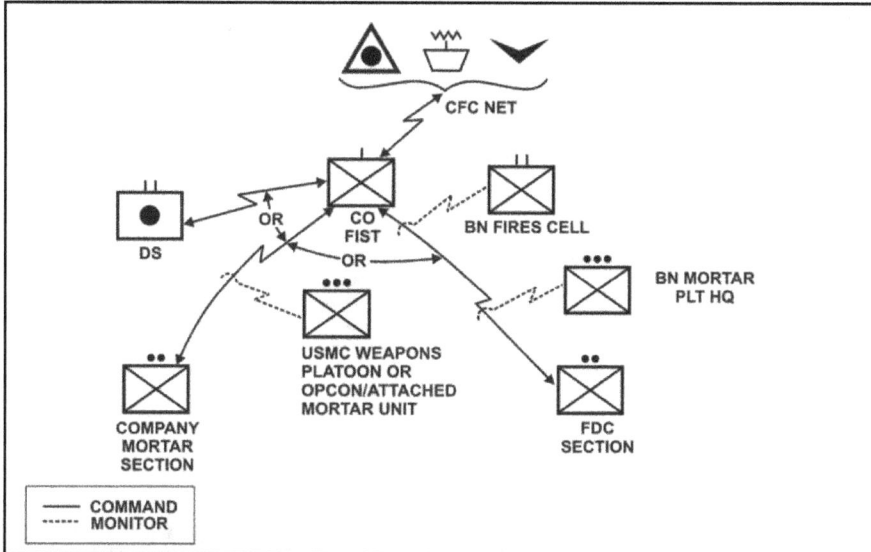

Figure 3-7. FM radio fire request to fire support team headquarters (centralized control)

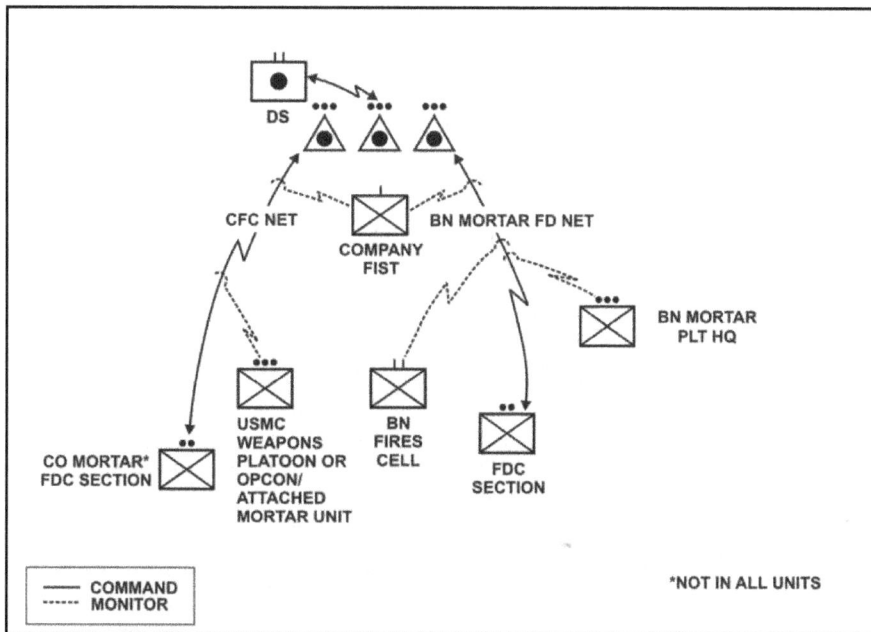

Figure 3-8. FM radio fire request to any fire direction center (decentralized control)

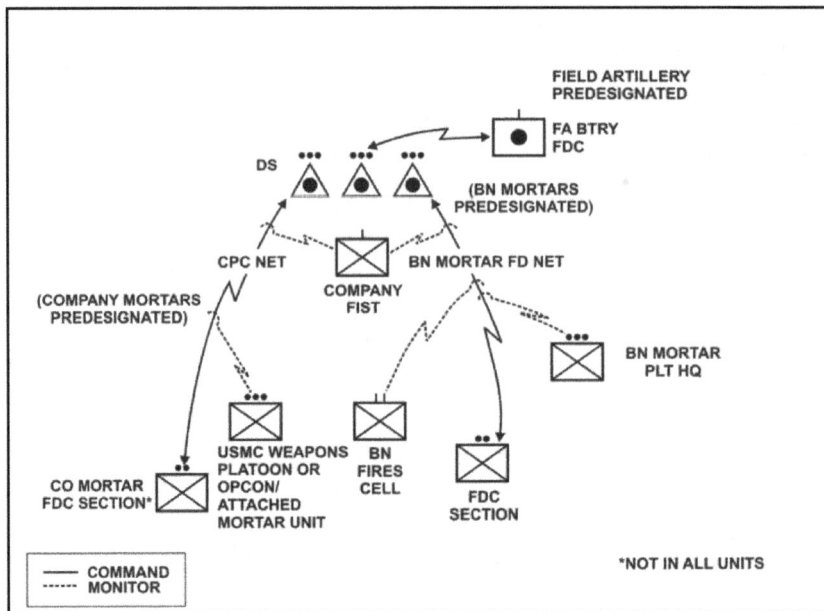

Figure 3-9. Predesignated method

SECTION X – AMMUNITION SUPPLY RATES

3-106. The expenditure of mortar ammunition must be controlled based on tactical priorities and ammunition availability. Tactical commanders provide this control by using ammunition allocations.

REQUIRED SUPPLY RATE

3-107. A battalion or squadron operations officer computes or estimates the type and amount of mortar ammunition needed for a particular combat operation or phase. He then submits these RSRs to the BCT or Marine Infantry regiment HQ. A mortar platoon leader assists an operations officer in determining the RSRs. He uses historical records, rate-of-fire computations, or a combination of both. Once an RSR is determined, it is used to plan transportation requirements for moving a mortar platoon's ammunition to a firing location.

CONTROLLED SUPPLY RATE

3-108. Due to rapidly changing combat situations and problems that may arise in the logistical system, the actual availability of mortar ammunition can be less than an RSR. If so, action must be taken to control expenditures. Each tactical commander announces a CSR of mortar ammunition, expressed in rounds (by type) per mortar per day. A mortar platoon or section leader considers the CSR during his planning and execution of fires. A CSR cannot be exceeded except in emergencies, and then only by the permission of the next higher commander. It is more combat-effective to limit the number of mortar-missions fired, firing enough rounds for each mission, than to ration rounds. Some guidelines are—

- When a CSR is small (10 to 20 rounds), mortar missions should be limited to those that can be observed and can immediately affect friendly troops and operations.
- When a CSR is larger (20 to 100 rounds), mortar fire missions can include those that affect planned operations as well as some that involve planned fires without adjustment.
- Intense operations against a strong enemy force can generate an RSR of 100 to 300 rounds. If a CSR is imposed, a mortar platoon leader should periodically report his ammunition status to the operations officer and FSO/FSC.

Chapter 4

Target Effects

Not only must fire support planners determine what targets to hit and when, but they must also decide how to attack each target. They must consider the complex relationship between a weapon, a round and a fuze combination, type of target, terrain and weather, and the desired effects. Because it is such a complex relationship, there are no definite rules for the number and types of rounds required for a desired effect. An FO's observation and evaluation are critical in determining the effect of fires on a target. FSOs/FSCs, mortar platoon and section leaders, and FDC chiefs should consider all the aspects of target effects when planning fires.

This chapter discusses the purpose and effects of mortar HE, smoke, and illumination fire on targets. More detailed and classified information is found in the U.S. Air Force published Joint Munitions Effectiveness Manual (JMEM).

SECTION I – TEXT REFERENCES

4-1. Within this manual, selected topics are only briefly discussed and readers are referred to another publication for more detail. Mortar and other combat units use these tactics, techniques, and procedures in the same or very similar manner and a detailed discussion in this manual would be redundant. However, they are as important as the subjects discussed in detail. Table 4-1 consolidates the references to additional information.

Table 4-1. Guide for subjects referenced in text

Subject	References
Obscuration	FM 3-22.91
Weather effects	FM 3-22.91
Illumination	FM 3-22.90
	FM 3-22.91

SECTION II – METHODS OF FIRE

4-2. The ability of the fire support system to place effective fires on a target depends, in part, on the method of fire and type of ammunition selected to attack the target. Maximum effect can be achieved through accurate initial and massed fires that surprise and shock the enemy.

ACCURATE INITIAL FIRES

4-3. Mortar units strive for first-round fire for effect. Although not always possible, first-round fire for effect should be the goal of fire support planning. First-round fire for effect requires accurate—

- Location of mortars.
- Location of the target.
- Laying of mortars.
- Direction, elevation, and charge.

MASSED FIRE AND TIME-ON-TARGET FIRE

4-4. Massed fire is fire from a number of weapons directed at a single point or small area. Massing all available fires enables the mortar unit to inflict maximum effect on a target with a minimum expenditure of ammunition.

4-5. Time-on-target fires are a form of massed fires. Time-on-target identifies the actual time at which munitions impact the target (JP 3-09.3). Time-on-target fire reduces a unit's vulnerability to enemy target acquisition devices by providing multiple firing signatures that overload the enemy target acquisition system. It gives an enemy little time to react and seek protection. Time-on-target fire ensures maximum effect in attacking targets that can easily change their protective posture. For example, dismounted enemy in the open can easily become a more difficult target by lying prone, seeking overhead cover, or moving out of the impact area.

4-6. Massed and time-on-target fire is now much more feasible because of the automation of the fire direction process. Automated firing systems and digital communications quickly and accurately provide firing solutions and transmit firing commands and hang times directly to the mortars.

4-7. Artillery units, mortar units, or a combination of the two execute massed fires. It is important that control of all the firing units involved are assigned to a single FDC.

SECTION III – JOINT MUNITIONS EFFECTIVENESS MANUALS

4-8. The U.S. Air Force publishes the JMEMs for all surface-to-surface weapons, to include mortars. These manuals provide detailed data concerning the expected fraction of casualties to personnel targets or, given the number and type of rounds fired, damage to materiel targets. The data in JMEMs are taken from test firings, actual combat performance, and mathematical modeling.

4-9. The JMEMs are normally classified as "confidential." A battalion personnel staff officer can establish the classified document's account with the Air Force to receive these manuals and an intelligence staff officer can store them when they are not being used.

4-10. It takes time to extract usable attack data from JMEMs. JMEMs should be used during training to develop TACSOPs and, rather than during calls for fire, during deliberate planning.

4-11. The JMEMs provide effective data for many fuze/shell combinations, target size, personnel posture, fortification, and terrain. They can be used to determine how many rounds to fire during each mission to cause a predetermined amount of enemy casualties. (See Table 4-2 for general guidance.)

Note. Although users can refer to the JMEMs for more exact guidance on the number of rounds to use for a planned effect, an FO calling the fires determines the actual effect of the fires on a target.

Table 4-2. Ammunition expenditure guide to neutralize platoon-sized targets*

Target	Terrain	Target Posture	Rounds of HE		
			60-mm	81-mm	120-mm
Trucks	NA	NA	28	10	6
Armored † ‡	NA	NA	Suppress	45	35
Personnel	Open	Attacking	14	8	4
Personnel	Open	Defending w/o fighting positions	40	10	6
Personnel	Open	Defending w fighting positions	60	20	12
Personnel	Forest/Jungle	Attacking	18	25	10
Personnel	Forest/Jungle	Defending w/o fighting positions	60	27	15
Personnel	Forest/Jungle	Defending fighting positions	40	50	25

*Neutralization fire does not totally defeat, be prepared to repeat.
† Light armored vehicles, such as BMPs/BTRs, can be suppressed using a combination of HE and WP.
‡ It is difficult for mortar fire to destroy tanks, but it forces crews to close hatches and damages the exterior.

SECTION IV – FUZE SETTINGS

4-12. The position of an enemy determines the fuze setting used. The following are enemy target positions and the fuze setting that is most effective for that position:

- **Standing targets.** Impact or near-surface burst fuze settings effectively engage exposed enemy troops that are standing. The round explodes on, or near, the ground. Shell fragments travel outward perpendicular to the long axis of the standing target (Figure 4-1).
- **Prone targets.** If exposed enemy troops are lying prone, the proximity fuze setting is most effective. The rounds explode above the ground and the fragments coming downward are once again traveling perpendicular to the long axis of the targets (Figure 4-2).
- **Targets in open fighting positions.** The proximity fuze setting is also the most effective if an enemy is in open fighting positions without overhead cover. However, even proximity settings do not always produce effects if the positions are deep (Figure 4-3).
- **Targets with overhead cover.** The delay fuze setting is most effective when an enemy is below heavily wooded terrain or in fighting positions with overhead cover. Light mortars will have little effect against overhead cover; even medium mortars have limited effect. Heavy mortars can destroy a bunker with a hit or a near miss (Figure 4-4).

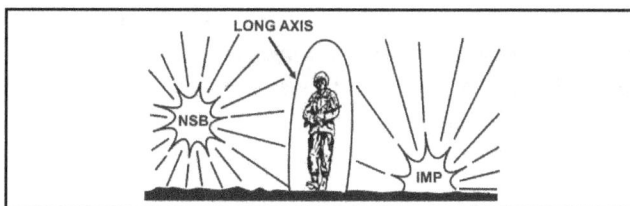

Figure 4-1. Standing targets

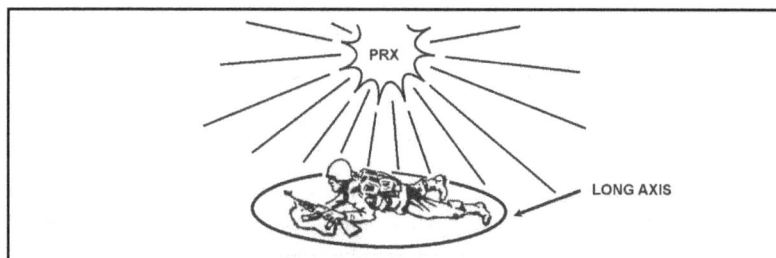

Figure 4-2. Prone targets

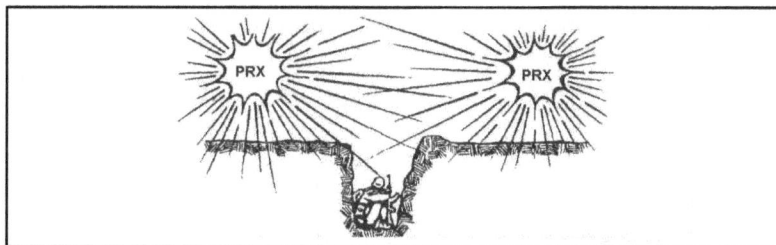

Figure 4-3. Targets in open fighting positions

Figure 4-4. Targets beneath triple canopy jungle

SECTION V – FUZE AND AMMUNITION COMBINATIONS

4-13. Mortar leaders and FDCs should understand what combinations of fuzes and ammunition have the greatest effects on targets.

PLANNING CONSIDERATIONS

4-14. The following guidelines are useful during the planning of mortar fires. As the battle progresses, the actual results should be reviewed and the guidelines should be modified, as needed.

ENEMY

4-15. Considerations for enemy positions are as follows:
- If an enemy is unwarned, standing in the open, fire one impact-fuzed HE round from each mortar. Then fire the following rounds as proximity-fuzed.
- If an enemy is prone or crouching in open fighting positions, fire all rounds as proximity-fuzed.
- If an enemy's status is unknown, fire all proximity-fuzed rounds.

4-16. Considerations for enemy locations are as follows:
- If an enemy is in bunkers, fire half the rounds with point-detonating fuzing and half with delay fuzing.
- Do not depend on light or medium mortar fires to damage heavy bunkers or buildings.
- Expect heavy mortar fire to destroy some heavy bunkers and damage others, but also expect to fire large amounts of ammunition.

TERRAIN

4-17. Considerations for the type of ground are as follows:
- If the ground in the target area is soft, swampy, or covered in deep snow, fire proximity-fuzed or near-surface burst rounds.
- On rocky and hard soil, fire a 50 percent mixture of proximity-fuzed and impact-fuzed rounds.
- If soil type is unknown, fire all proximity-fuzed rounds.

4-18. Considerations for the type of vegetation are as follows:
- If the target is within forest, fire point-detonating fuzes for all rounds.
- In extremely dense forest or jungle, fire point-detonating fuzes mixed with 50 percent delay fuzes.

VEHICLES

4-19. Normally, mortar fires by themselves are not effective against vehicles, especially armored vehicles, but they can be most effective when combined with direct fires of antitank weapons. Mortar fires force the armored vehicle crewmen to button up, reducing their visibility and preventing them from firing the heavy machine guns mounted outside the vehicle. This allows dismounted Infantry to use their antiarmor weapons. Mortar fire also channels enemy vehicles into prepared engagement areas and antiarmor kill zones.

4-20. Field artillery, CAS, and close combat attack are generally more effective against moving, tracked vehicles. The 120-mm heavy mortar has a moderate capability against wheeled and tracked mechanized Infantry vehicles. Mortar fragments from smaller mortars can damage exterior components of lightly armored vehicles, ATGM launchers, or self-propelled antiaircraft guns and can reduce their effectiveness. Firepower or mobility kills are difficult to achieve without expending large amounts of mortar ammunition.

4-21. Against heavily armored moving vehicles, such as tanks or tracked mechanized Infantry fighting vehicles, mortar fires, at best, force the crew to close their hatches. Against stationary tanks or tracked mechanized Infantry fighting vehicles, bursting WP rounds from medium and heavy mortars can be effective. Although the probability of hitting a target the size of a tank is low, a direct hit by a 120-mm HE round can destroy a tank. These rounds must make almost a direct hit on the target to cause any damage. Mortar fire, however, may damage or destroy weapons sighting and communications systems.

4-22. Point-detonating rounds are the most effective against trucks. Their low-angle fragments do the most damage to tires, wheels, and engines. Bursting WP rounds are also effective if mixed with HE rounds.

HIGH EXPLOSIVE FIRES

4-23. When mortar rounds impact, they throw fragments in a pattern that is not truly circular and may even be irregular, based on their angle of fall, slope of the terrain, and type of soil. However, for planning purposes, each mortar HE round is considered to have a circular lethal bursting area. (See Figure 4-5 for a scale representation of the lethal bursting areas of mortar rounds.)

Note. Because newer ammunition has greater lethality, the effects of HE fires discussed below are approximations and for planning purposes only.

4-24. Table 4-3 gives information on the average lethal areas, in square meters, of mortar HE rounds against various targets. Images shown in Figure 4-5 can be used to develop the mortar ammunition RSR. Planners also determine the size of the target or objective area and then divide the lethal areas of the mortar round into this image to determine the number of rounds needed to cover the target with lethal fragments. This gives an idea of the least number of rounds needed to cover the target area once. JMEM data can be used to refine this number and to estimate the total number of rounds required.

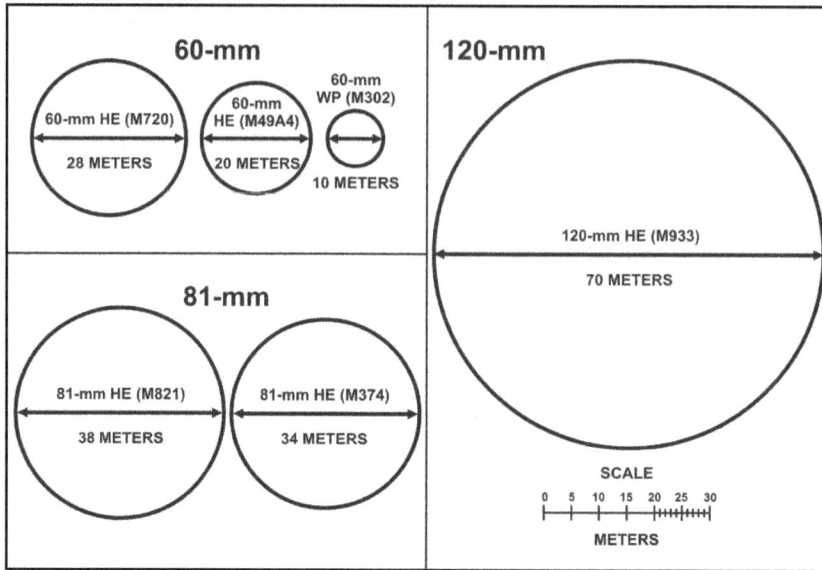

Figure 4-5. Comparison of lethal bursting areas for U.S. mortar rounds

Table 4-3. Approximate lethal areas (square meters) for U.S. mortar ammunition

Mortar and Ammunition	Enemy Posture	Fuze	
		Impact	Proximity
60-mm M720 HE (1 mortar, 1 round)	Standing prone, open terrain crouching, open position	250 100 1	600 200 25
60-mm M720 HE (2 mortars, 1 round)	Standing prone, open terrain crouching, open position	450 200 5	1,000 350 30
81-mm M821 HE (1 mortar, 1 round)	Standing prone, open terrain crouching, open position	700 300 2	900 600 30
81-mm M821 HE (3 mortars, 1 round)	Standing prone, open terrain crouching, open position	1,800 1,000 10	2,400 1,500 85
120-mm M934 HE (1 mortar, 1 round)	Standing prone, open terrain	1,350 520	1,650 900
120-mm M934 HE (3 mortars, 1 round)	Standing prone, open terrain	3,900 1,650	4,500 2,700

4-25. Impact-fuzed rounds are normally the best for adjusting fire. If dense foliage prevents observation of the impact-fuzed round, near-surface burst or proximity settings will cause the round to explode near the top of the trees where the burst can be better observed. If there is a combination of snow cover and fog in the target area, making adjusting rounds difficult to see, the delay setting can be used for adjustments. This causes a plume of dirt or exposes the earth at the point of impact. The dark soil contrasts with the fog and snow, making adjustment easier.

EFFECTS OF TERRAIN ON HIGH EXPLOSIVE ROUNDS

4-26. High explosive fires are the most common for destruction, neutralization, and suppression. Most mortar HE rounds can be fired with the M734 series multioption fuze. This fuze enables HE rounds to be detonated above the target surface, on the target surface, or after a short delay. Older ammunition that cannot use the multioption fuze uses single- or dual-option fuzes to achieve almost the same effects. These effects vary depending on the ground, target, and mortar size.

4-27. Soft ground limits the effectiveness of surface-burst HE rounds for light, medium, and heavy mortars (light mortars being limited the most). One foot of soft ground, mud, or sand, or 3 feet of snow can reduce the effectiveness of surface-burst HE rounds by up to 80 percent. Light mortar rounds can land close (within a few yards) to a target on this type ground and still have no effect.

4-28. Hard, rocky soil and gravel increase the effectiveness of surface-burst HE rounds. Rock fragments are picked up and thrown by the blast, adding to an enemy's casualties (heavy mortars throw the most rock fragments).

4-29. Dense woods cause impact-fuzed HE rounds to detonate in trees, producing airbursts. These airbursts can be dangerous to exposed troops since large wood splinters are added to the round's metal fragments. Wounds caused by large wooden splinters are often severe. Extremely dense woods, such as triple canopy jungle, cause most impact-fuzed HE rounds to detonate high in trees without much of an effect at ground level.

EFFECTS OF COVER ON HIGH EXPLOSIVE ROUNDS

4-30. Enemy forces are normally standing or prone. They may be in the open or protected by varying degrees of cover. Each of these changes target effects of mortar fire.

4-31. Surprise mortar fire is always more effective than fire against an enemy that is warned and seeks cover. Recent studies have shown that a high casualty rate can be achieved with only two rounds against an enemy platoon standing in the open. The same studies required 10 to 15 rounds to duplicate the casualty rate when a platoon was warned by adjusting rounds and sought cover. If enemy soldiers merely lay prone, they significantly reduce the effects of mortar fire. Mortar fire against standing enemy forces is almost twice as effective as fire against prone targets.

4-32. Proximity burst is usually more effective than surface-burst rounds against targets in the open. The effectiveness of mortar fire against a prone enemy is increased by about 40 percent by firing proximity-fuzed rounds rather than surface-burst rounds. The steeper the angle of the fall of the round, the more effective it is.

4-33. If an enemy is in open fighting positions without overhead cover, proximity-fuzed mortar rounds are about five times as effective as impact-fuzed rounds. When fired against troops in open fighting positions, proximity-fuzed rounds are only 10 percent as effective as they would be against an enemy in the open. For the greatest effectiveness against troops in open fighting positions, the charge with the lowest angle of fall should be chosen. It produces almost two times as much effect as the same round falling with the steepest angle.

4-34. If an enemy has prepared fighting positions with overhead cover, only impact-fuzed and delay-fuzed rounds have much effect. Proximity-fuzed rounds can restrict the enemy's ability to move from position to position, but they cause few, if any, casualties. Impact-fuzed rounds cause some blast and suppressive effects. Delay-fuzed rounds can penetrate and destroy a position but must achieve a direct hit. Only a 120-mm mortar with a delay-fuze setting can damage a heavily constructed bunker.

EFFECTS OF TERRAIN ON PROXIMITY-FUZED HIGH EXPLOSIVE ROUNDS

4-35. A proximity fuze functions best over open, firm soil. Figure 4-6 is an example of a proximity-fuzed HE round detonating over open terrain. Snow or sand can cause it to function low or on impact. Water or frozen ground can cause it to function early. If proximity-set, multioption-fuzed rounds are functioning high, they can still be effective. The height of burst can be reduced by using the near-surface burst setting on the fuze. It cannot be increased except by choosing the steepest angle of fall possible.

Figure 4-6. 120-mm proximity-fuzed high explosive detonating over open terrain

4-36. Proximity-fuzed rounds fired over built-up areas can detonate if they pass close by the side of a large building. They can also function too high to be effective at street level. Impact fuzes are the most effective in heavily built-up areas.

4-37. In dense jungle or forest, proximity fuzes detonate too early and have little effect. Impact fuzes achieve airbursts in dense forests, and delay fuzes allow rounds to penetrate beneath the heavy canopy before exploding.

SUPPRESSIVE EFFECTS OF HIGH EXPLOSIVE MORTAR ROUNDS

4-38. Suppression from mortar fire is not as easy to measure as the target effect. Suppression is an effect produced in the mind of an enemy that prevents them from returning fire or maneuvering. Inexperienced or surprised Soldiers are more easily suppressed than experienced, warned soldiers. Soldiers in the open are much more easily suppressed than those with overhead cover. Suppression is most effective when mortar fires first begin; as they continue, their suppressive effects lessen. High explosive rounds are the most suppressive, but bursting WP mixed with HE has a great psychological effect on the enemy. Figure 4-7 shows suppressive effects derived from live-fire studies and combat observations. For example, if a—

- 60-mm mortar round lands within 20 meters of a target, the target will probably be suppressed, if not hit.
- 60-mm mortar round lands within 35 meters of a target, there is a 50 percent chance it will be suppressed. Beyond 50 meters, little suppression takes place.
- 81-mm mortar round lands within 30 meters of a target, the target will probably be suppressed, if not hit.
- 81-mm mortar round lands within 75 meters of a target, there is a 50 percent chance that the target will be suppressed. Beyond 125 meters, little suppression takes place.
- Heavy mortar round (proximity-fuzed) lands within 65 meters of a target, the target will probably be suppressed, if not hit.
- Heavy mortar round (proximity-fuzed) lands within 125 meters of a target, there is a 50 percent chance the target will be suppressed. Beyond 200 meters, little suppression takes place.

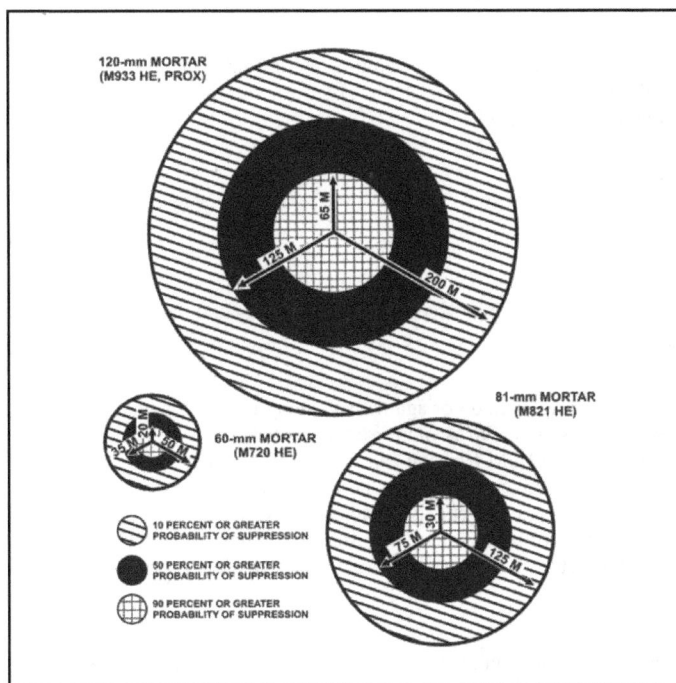

Figure 4-7. Suppressive effects of U.S. mortar rounds

SECTION VI – MORTAR SMOKE OPERATIONS

4-39. Smoke missions are important functions for mortar platoons or sections. Atmospheric stability, wind velocity, and wind direction are the most important factors when planning target effects for smoke mortar rounds. The terrain in a target area also affects smoke rounds.

EMPLOYMENT OF SMOKE

4-40. Smoke can significantly reduce an enemy's effectiveness both in daytime and at night. Smoke reduces the ability of an enemy to deliver effective fires, conduct operations, and observe friendly units. Smoke reduces the effectiveness of laser beams and inhibits electro-optical systems.

TYPES OF MISSIONS

4-41. Smoke missions that mortar units conduct are—

Immediate

4-42. The primary requirement for an immediate smoke mission is speed. When engaging a planned target or a target of opportunity that has taken friendly forces under fire, units can call for immediate smoke. Response is more important than accuracy and the delivery of fires is performed as quickly as possible. Immediate smoke missions are not intended as screening missions. The purpose of immediate smoke is to obscure an enemy's vision for short periods so that maneuver elements can break contact or evade enemy direct fire.

Quick

4-43. A quick smoke mission is planned and requires a substantial amount of ammunition. The objective of quick smoke is to obscure an enemy's vision or to screen maneuver elements. A quick smoke mission is normally conducted in three phases:

- Adjustment.
- Establishment.
- Maintenance.

APPLICATIONS

4-44. Smoke has obscuration, screening, deception, and signaling and marking applications on the battlefield.

Obscuration

4-45. Obscuration smoke is employed on or against an enemy to degrade his vision both within and beyond his location. Red phosphorous (RP) smoke is more effective at degrading enemy weapons using thermal sights. Smoke delivered on an enemy ATGM position can prevent the system from acquiring or subsequently tracking targets, thereby reducing its effectiveness. Employment of obscuration smoke on an attacking armored force can cause it to vary its speed, inadvertently change its axis of advance, deploy prematurely, and force it to rely on less effective non-visual means of control. (See FM 3-22.91 for details on planning the number of smoke rounds required to generate a 500-meter smoke curtain under various weather conditions.)

Screening

4-46. Screening smoke is employed in friendly operational areas or in areas between friendly and enemy forces to degrade enemy ground and aerial observation, and to defeat or degrade enemy vision systems. Screening smoke from mortars is used to conceal friendly ground maneuver, breaching, and recovery operations.

Deception

4-47. Deception smoke is employed to create the illusion that a tactically significant event is occurring to confuse or mislead the enemy. Deceptive smoke from mortars can be used in river crossings, withdrawals, and air assault operations.

Signaling and Marking

4-48. Signaling and marking smoke missions are used to relay prearranged communications on the battlefield and to mark unit locations. Occasionally, phosphorous mortar rounds can be used to signal the end of a preparation on a target and the beginning of an assault. Marking smoke is used to identify targets, evacuation points, landmarks, and so on.

PLANNING CONSIDERATIONS

4-49. All U.S. mortar smoke rounds are filled with either WP or RP. The bursting WP or RP round provides a screening, incendiary, marking, and casualty-producing effect. They both produce localized, instantaneous smoke clouds by scattering burning phosphorous particles. Red phosphorous reduces the effectiveness of thermal sights. Smoke is used to—

- Deny an enemy information by screening or obscuration.
- Reduce effectiveness of enemy target acquisition systems.
- Restrict nap-of-the-earth and contour approaches for enemy aircraft.
- Disrupt an enemy's movement, operations, and ability to control his forces.
- Deceive an enemy as to the intent of friendly forces.

4-50. Technical information regarding ammunition and the employment of smoke is contained in applicable mortar technical manuals and FMs.

4-51. A bursting smoke round can be used to produce casualties among exposed enemy troops and to start fires. The casualty-producing radius of the smoke round is much less than that of the HE round. Generally, more casualties can be produced by firing HE ammunition than by firing WP or RP. However, the burst of a smoke round causes a significant psychological effect, especially when used against exposed troops. A few smoke rounds mixed into a fire mission of HE rounds may increase the suppressive effect of the fire.

4-52. Although there has been confusion among leaders, it is not a violation of the Law of Land Warfare to use WP ammunition against an enemy as long as all normal considerations for using lethal military force are met. White phosphorous rounds, or any mortar round, should not be used in such a manner as to cause unnecessary pain and suffering against inappropriate targets or under inappropriate circumstances.

4-53. White phosphorous rounds can be used to mark targets, especially for attack by aircraft. Base-ejecting smoke rounds, such as the 81-mm M819 RP smoke round, produce a dispersed smoke cloud that is too indistinct for marking targets.

TACTICAL CONSIDERATIONS

4-54. Normally, a commander makes the decision of when to fire smoke missions. The following tactical factors should be considered when employing smoke:

- Effects of smoke on adjacent friendly units.
- Effects of smoke on friendly supporting fires.
- Time required to fire the mission.
- Observation required to conduct the smoke mission.
- Size of the area to be obscured.
- Characteristics of ammunition fuzes.
- Availability of ammunition.
- Time length of desired obscuration.
- Capability of resupply.
- Desirability of dual effect of obscuring and producing casualties.
- Closure rates of moving vehicles (Table 4-4).

Table 4-4. Rates of closure in minutes

Distance Travelled (Meters)	Vehicle Speed (KMH)					
	5	10	15	20	25	30
3,000	36	18	12	9	7.2	6
2,500	30	15	10	7.5	6	5
2,000	24	12	8	6	4.8	4
1,500	18	9	6	4.5	3.6	3
1,000	12	6	4	3	2.4	2

4-55. Obtaining the best combination of smoke effects at the right time requires knowledge of a given type of round. Once the type of smoke to use is decided, the number of rounds required to build and maintain the smoke can be calculated.

4-56. If HE and smoke are to be mixed, it may be desirable to use two separate sources to deliver the rounds. For example, one section of battalion mortars provides obscuration, and the company mortars provide HE. This can increase the effect of the mission and can reduce the problems of FOs who are adjusting both types of rounds on one radio net. Detailed coordination is required for this type mission.

4-57. Normally, a mortar unit carries only a limited number of smoke rounds. This number and the capability of the load must be made known to commanders. Special requests for smoke or changes in smoke round allowances can be made, but they must be prepared in advance and submitted before the required mission.

WEATHER AND GROUND CONSIDERATIONS

4-58. Weather and ground are major considerations for the employment of smoke. Weather determines the effectiveness of smoke missions, the placement of rounds, and storage requirements. (See FM 3-22-91 for details regarding the effects of weather). Ground conditions are also critical for mission effectiveness. Wind, temperature, atmospheric stability, The effects of weather and ground conditions on smoke missions are as follows:

- **Wind**. Wind speed and direction are critical factors for smoke missions. The higher the wind velocity, the more effective bursting phosphorous rounds are, and the less effective burning smoke rounds from field artillery become. Ideal wind conditions are when the direction is across the target and wind speed is between 5 and 15 knots.

- **Temperature.** All bulk-filled WP or RP ammunition needs special care when temperatures are high. A phosphorous filler liquefies at temperatures of 100 degrees Fahrenheit. Since phosphorous does not fill all the space in the cartridge, the result is a hollow space in the upper part of the cartridge filler cavity. This causes the round to be unbalanced and, therefore, unstable in flight. White phosphorous ammunition should be protected from direct sunlight, if possible. When stored at high temperatures, it should be stacked with the fuze up. Keeping the phosphorous ammunition under cover, digging ammunition bunkers, opening only as many rounds as needed, maintaining proper storage, and monitoring the ambient temperature reduces the chances of firing unstable ammunition. In extremely high temperatures, phosphorous ammunition should be fired only if taken directly from vertical storage. This does not apply to the M252 mortar's base-ejecting RP smoke rounds. They do not require special storage.

- **Atmospheric Stability.** The effects of atmospheric stability can determine whether mortar smoke is effective or, if effective, how much ammunition will be needed. These determinations are as follows:

  - During unstable conditions, mortar smoke rounds are almost ineffective. The smoke does not spread but often climbs straight up and quickly dissipates.

  - Under moderately unstable atmospheric conditions, base-ejecting smoke rounds are more effective than bursting WP rounds. A M819 RP smoke round is the only base-ejecting smoke round currently in inventory and has a screening effect of over 2½ minutes.

  - Under stable conditions, both RP and WP rounds are effective. The higher the humidity, the better the screening effects of mortar rounds.

  - An M819 RP smoke round loses up to 35 percent of its screening ability if the ground in the target area is covered with water or deep snow. During extremely cold and dry conditions over snow, up to four times the number of smoke rounds may be needed than expected to create an adequate screen. The higher the wind velocity, the more effective bursting WP rounds are and the less effective burning smoke rounds become.

Ground Conditions

4-59. If the terrain in a target area is swampy, rain-soaked, or snow-covered, then burning smoke rounds may not be effective. These rounds produce smoke by ejecting felt wedges soaked in RP. These wedges then burn on the ground, producing a dense, long-lasting cloud. If the wedges fall into mud, water, or snow, they can be extinguished. Shallow water can reduce the smoke produced by these rounds by as much as 50 percent. The terrain in the target area affects bursting phosphorous rounds very little, except that deep snow and cold temperatures can reduce the smoke cloud by about 25 percent. Although bursting phosphorous rounds are not designed to cause casualties, the fragments of the shell casing and bits of burning phosphorous can cause injuries. Burning smoke rounds do not cause casualties and have little suppressive effect.

Ammunition

4-60. Smoke missions require many of rounds to build up and maintain the effect. For a planned mission, leaders should calculate the number of rounds required and request them well in advance. They may be loaded on vehicles, if available, or prepositioned at the firing point.

SMOKE IN SUPPORT OF OFFENSIVE OPERATIONS

4-61. Specific ways that mortar smoke can be used in offensive operations are as follows:

- **Blind enemy observers/gunners.** This technique is effective when conducting a movement to contact or when enemy contact is likely. Mortars can fire smoke directly on all suspected or known enemy observer/gunner positions. They can also fire smoke between known or suspected enemy observer/gunner positions and the supported unit. The smoke cloud must be maintained until the attacking unit reaches its objective or passes the danger area.
- **Screen an attack.** This technique covers a unit while moving forward in an attack. A smoke screen to the attacking unit's front conceals maneuver. Ideally, the screen is maintained continuously along the axis of advance. It should be terminated for mounted forces about 500 to 800 meters short of the objective to allow for maximum visibility during the final assault. For dismounted forces, this distance is about 100 to 200 meters. By using this technique, a unit can move behind smoke without being effectively engaged. If necessary, the flanks or rear of the supported unit can also be screened.
- **Conceal a bypass.** The two ways to conceal a bypass are—
    - Screen the bypassing unit while it is moving around the enemy. A smoke cloud is fired in front, to the left or to the right of the enemy position. When the smoke is in position, the bypassing unit moves around the screened flank towards its objective.
    - Make an enemy believe they are the object of an attack by firing smoke and HE directly on their position. With the smoke cloud in place, the bypassing unit moves around the enemy to its objective.
- **Cover a breaching operation.** This technique is employed by mortars (or mortars and artillery) generating two smoke clouds at the same time. One cloud is fired directly on an enemy. The other is fired between an enemy position and a breaching force. Continuous smoke is maintained in both areas because obstacles are normally covered by direct and indirect fires.
- **Obscure vehicles from enemy direct fire gunners.** This technique is used to degrade the capability of enemy ATGM gunners. Once a vehicle commander realizes that his vehicle is being engaged by enemy missiles, he employs vehicle smoke or smoke hand grenades and directs his driver to take evasive action. To further degrade every gunner's vision, mortar smoke should also be requested. It can be fired on enemy gunners or between them and friendly vehicles. This prevents enemy gunners from tracking vehicles and guiding missiles to the vehicles.

SMOKE IN SUPPORT OF DEFENSIVE OPERATIONS

4-62. Specific ways that mortar smoke can be used in support of defensive and retrograde operations are—

- **Force enemy infantry to dismount from vehicles.** Ideally, this technique employs mortar and artillery smoke, HE ammunition, and the family of scatterable mines or chemicals together. Smoke is fired to the front of an attacker and may force an enemy to dismount. The smoke is fired beyond the range of direct-fire weapons to give friendly forces more time to engage targets. The family of scatterable mines (if available) and HE are then fired into the smoke.
- **Slow the advance of attacking forces.** This technique causes an attacker to reduce his speed, thus slowing the momentum of his attack. It is employed by firing smoke across the front of an advancing enemy. High explosive rounds are also fired with smoke to make an enemy close the hatches of his tanks and personnel carriers. Vehicles are also silhouetted as they emerge from the smoke, making them easier to track and destroy.
- **Separate and isolate attacking echelons.** This technique is employed by firing smoke between two echelons of an attacking enemy force. The smoke visually separates the two echelons and prevents the second echelon from seeing and supporting the first when it is engaged. The second echelon is also slowed by the smoke. This gives a defender more time to fire at targets in the first echelon without being engaged by enemy in the second. It also provides a defender with silhouetted targets as the second echelon emerges from the smoke.
- **Cover displacement.** This technique fires smoke in front of a defensive position for a supported unit to move without being observed. When the initial smoke screen begins to dissipate, more smoke is fired between an enemy and a displacing unit. Smoke is also fired on suspected enemy locations and routes.

● **Expose enemy helicopters.** This technique makes enemy helicopters vulnerable to air defense systems because smoke forces them to fly at higher altitudes. It may occur as a result of mortar smoke that has already been employed in fighting enemy ground forces. In addition, smoke can be employed in a specific location, such as a flank, to prevent enemy helicopters from attacking undetected by flying nap-of-the-earth. When helicopters fly above the smoke to engage their targets, they are engaged by air defense weapons.

SECTION VII – ILLUMINATION

4-63. Illumination rounds disclose enemy formations, signal, or mark targets. All U.S. mortars have both visible and IR illumination rounds. Infrared light illumination is used in conjunction with personnel equipped with night vision devices.

MORTAR ILLUMINATION ROUND CHARACTERISTICS

4-64. U.S. mortar illumination rounds provide excellent illumination during limited visibility operations. The period of visible and IR illumination lasts from 30-40 seconds for the light mortar to about one minute for the medium and heavy mortars. The light mortar illumination round provides 250,000 candlepower and the heavy mortar illumination round provides about 1 million candlepower. (See FM 3-22.90 and FM 3-22.91 for details.)

4-65. The 60-mm illumination round does not provide the same degree of illumination as the rounds of the heavier mortars and field artillery. However, it is sufficient for local, point illumination. The small size of the round can be an advantage when illumination is desired in an area, but adjacent friendly forces do not want to be seen. The 60-mm illumination round can be used without degrading the night vision devices of adjacent units.

4-66. The M721 and M767 IR 60-mm illumination rounds are ballistically matched with the M720 HE round. They are effective out to the full range of the mortar and produce improved illumination over the M83A3 round.

4-67. To prevent friendly or noncombatant casualties, the point of impact of the illumination round canister is also considered. This is especially important during stability operations and operations in populated areas.

SPECIAL TECHNIQUES

4-68. The following are special illumination techniques that mortars have used effectively:

● An illumination round fired to burn on the ground prevents observation beyond the flare into the shadow. This is one method of countering enemy use of image intensification devices. A friendly force could move behind the flare with greater security.

● During day or night, an illumination round fired to burn on the ground is effective in marking targets for CAS and close combat attack. Illumination rounds have an advantage over phosphorous as target markers during high winds. The smoke cloud from a phosphorous round is quickly blown downwind. Smoke from the burning illumination round continues to originate from the same point, regardless of the wind.

● When IR illumination is limited, visible illumination rounds can be used to simulate the effects of IR illumination. Mechanical time fuzes on visible illumination rounds are set at the highest possible height of burst for the given range. The resulting diffused illumination increases the effectiveness of night vision devices and other optics.

Chapter 5

Mortar Units in Full Spectrum Operations

Full spectrum operations is the Army's operational concept. It combines offensive, defensive, and stability or civil support operations simultaneously to seize, retain, and exploit an initiative to create opportunities to achieve decisive results. Operations conducted outside the U.S. and its territories simultaneously combine elements of offense, defense, and stability operations. Within the U.S. and its territories, operations combine elements of civil support, defense, and offense in support of civil authority. During offensive and defensive operations, the primary mission of mortar units is to provide lethal and nonlethal fires to support a commander's scheme of maneuver.

SECTION I – TEXT REFERENCES

5-1. Within this manual, selected topics are only briefly discussed, and readers are referred to another publication for more detail. Mortar and other combat units use these tactics, techniques, and procedures in the same or very similar manner and a detailed discussion in this manual would be redundant. However, they are as important as the subjects discussed in detail. Table 5-1 consolidates the references to additional information.

Table 5-1. Guide for subjects referenced in text

Subject	References
Risk-estimate distance	FM 3-09.31/MCRP 3-16C

Note. Army and Marine Corps doctrinal definitions are the same. For example, the definition of a hasty attack is the same for both services. The way in which doctrine is presented and organized may be slightly different. In this chapter, discussions of operations are brief and only intended to establish the conditions in which the mortar unit operates. Readers should refer to their service's doctrinal references if they have questions about operations.

SECTION II – OFFENSIVE OPERATIONS

5-2. Offensive operations carry the fight to an enemy to destroy or defeat them. Fires from mortars are integrated with all available direct and indirect fires to support a commander's scheme of maneuver. Mortar units participate in offensive operations as part of a larger force.

TYPES OF OFFENSIVE OPERATIONS

5-3. The types of offensive operations are movement to contact, attack, exploitation and pursuit, raids and ambushes, reconnaissance force, and linkup.

MOVEMENT TO CONTACT

5-4. Movement to contact gains or reestablishes contact with an enemy to further develop a tactical situation. The exact location of an enemy is usually not known. Search and attack is a decentralized movement to contact requiring multiple, coordinated patrols to locate an enemy.

5-5. Mortars provide a maneuver commander the most responsive means of indirect fire support during a movement to contact. Displacement techniques used by a mortar platoon during this operation depend on the distance to be traveled, the likelihood of enemy contact, and the maneuver commander's guidance. For example, if the objective in a movement to contact is beyond the support range of mortars, an entire mortar platoon can be ordered to displace, moving close behind a maneuver element, depending on where enemy contact is expected. While a mortar platoon, section, or squad is displacing, it must be prepared to immediately engage targets using standard indirect fire procedures, direct-lay, direct-alignment, or hip-shoot techniques of engagement. Mortar unit leaders must aggressively seek out information and make recommendations for using mortar fires. Considerations for employment of mortars during a movement to contact are—

- Giving priority of fires to a leading elements/elements in contact.
- Having an FO for the lead element operate under decentralized control.
- Anticipating frequent moves and hip shoots.
- Expecting numerous requests for immediate smoke to occur when contact is established. (Mortar leaders may consider carrying a larger number of smoke rounds and modifying the ammunition resupply mix to include more smoke.)
- Planning fires along the route and on the flanks, especially on high-speed avenues of approach into the lead element's flanks.
- Preparing to fire on enemy forces that directly threaten the mortar unit.
- Maintaining SA and considering methods to increase security, such as moving with a maneuver element.

5-6.   Fire planning on key terrain and likely enemy positions increases mortar responsiveness upon enemy contact. It includes possible targets en route to the march objective, on the march objective, and beyond. Once enemy contact is made, a mortar platoon leader quickly issues a FRAGO to support a maneuver element's hasty attack or bypass.

5-7.   Not only must a commander plan mortar fires, but he must also plan mortar movement. A mortar platoon can be attached, for movement, to a company near the front of the battalion march column or tactical formation. This ensures that mortars are close enough to an enemy to contribute responsive, immediate fires.

5-8.   In a search and attack, mortar units are often in previously prepared positions that can fire within the AO. If a mortar unit is moving with the maneuver units and it receives a call for fire, it immediately moves to the best position available and fires the mission. The mortar unit leader must observe any ROE during a search and attack.

ATTACK

5-9.   Attacks are offensive operations that destroy or defeat enemy forces, seize and secure terrain, or both. Attacks combine maneuver, indirect fires, and close combat to defeat the enemy. The primary difference between a hasty and a deliberate attack is the time available to plan and prepare. The types of attacks are—

Hasty

5-10. Hasty attacks are the most common form of attack, using maximum firepower and rapid movement to maintain momentum. There is usually little or no time for planning additional fire support. Most targets engaged by mortars are targets of opportunity. Considerations for the employment of mortars during a hasty attack are the following—

- Short and intense missions, target series, or target groups may be used to mass fires on critical areas or targets sets.
- Immediate suppression and quick smoke fire missions should be anticipated.
- Rapid shift of massed fires to exploit identified enemy weak points should be expected.
- Ammunition types, especially low-density ammunition such as smoke, may be in short supply as a hasty attack begins.
- SA should be maintained, and fire support requirements anticipated.
- Mortar unit leaders must aggressively seek information and make recommendations for the use of mortar fires.

5-11. Once contact has occurred and a commander decides to attack, the mortar platoon leader issues FRAGOs. He quickly positions any moving elements in defilade and provides maximum indirect fires. Properly positioned and employed, mortars aid a maneuver commander in maintaining the momentum of the attack.

5-12. After a successful hasty attack, mortars must be resupplied quickly. This enables them to support a continuation of the attack, to protect against a counterattack, or to transition to the defense. Any movement during this phase of the operation quickly minimizes a maneuver element's vulnerability to a counterattack.

Deliberate

5-13. Deliberate attacks require more planning time, detailed intelligence, and a more detailed scheme of maneuver, including the plan for fire support. Mortars support consolidation of an objective the same as in a hasty attack.

5-14. A mortar platoon delivers fires on targets. Company mortars may be included in these fires or may be used against targets of opportunity. Mortar unit leaders must consider preparation of ammunition, registration, and resupply. Use of prestocked ammunition, where possible, allows a mortar platoon to save its basic/combat load for the continuing attack. Considerations for the employment of mortars during a deliberate attack are—

- Long preparations increase a unit's vulnerability to counterfire. Mortar units should consider using—
  - Dug-in and well-camouflaged positions.
  - Firing missions at the lowest charge and elevation.
- Frequent displacements, to include firing missions from unprepared positions and then displacing to the prepared ones.
- Split sections.
- Massed fires from multiple sections.

5-15. One common form of maneuver during a deliberate attack is penetration. A battalion must mass combat power against an isolated, narrow portion of an enemy defense. Concentrated direct and indirect fires are used as an assaulting force closes on an enemy's forward defensive positions. A mortar platoon's massed indirect fires keep an enemy suppressed while rifle platoons move forward to destroy them.

5-16. Once assault elements have reached the requisite phase line, a commander of the assaulting force shifts mortar fire onto the rear or onto enemy supporting positions, likely routes of withdrawal, support by fire positions, and likely counterattack routes.

5-17. A final assault is conducted with all available direct fire weapons from support by fire positions and from the assault element. A mortar platoon leader must be prepared to fire large volumes of ammunition near friendly forces. This requires detailed planning and close supervision by mortar leaders at all levels.

EXPLOITATION AND PURSUIT

5-18. **Exploitations** follow successful attacks. They destroy an enemy's defenses and keep them disorganized so they cannot resupply or regroup their forces. Exploitations require rapid advance and violent action. Pursuit normally follows successful exploitation. The primary difference is that it is oriented on the final destruction of retreating enemy units. Other considerations for the employment of mortars during an exploitation or pursuit are—

- More missions from any direction.
- Increased requirement for unit local security.
- Frequent displacements and moving relatively close behind forward units.
- Mortar unit leaders must maintain good SA and anticipate maneuver elements needs for fire support.

5-19. In the exploitation, FRAGOs are common. An operation may require changes in the direction of attack to ensure destruction of an enemy. There may be small groups of enemy throughout the AO, which may be a threat to the security of mortar platoon. A mortar platoon provides its own security and may even be involved in taking and guarding prisoners of war.

5-20. Due to the speed with which an exploitation is conducted, mortars can be directed to move by platoon or section with, or just behind, a maneuver element. Many fire missions are conducted using direct-lay, direct-alignment, or hip-shoot techniques. Since exploitations occur deep behind enemy lines, a mortar platoon leader ensures that ammunition is conserved since resupply may be difficult.

RAIDS AND AMBUSHES

5-21. A raid or ambush is normally conducted by a small unit to secure information, to confuse an enemy, or to destroy their installations. An ambush is a form of attack by fire or other destructive means from concealed positions on a moving or temporarily halted enemy. Company or battalion mortars can be attached or placed under OPCON to the raid or ambush force. Using a different route, mortar units can also displace and establish positions in range of a raid or ambush site. During raids and ambushes, mortar units can support the maneuver force by—

- Isolating an objective or kill zone.
- Destroying or suppressing nearby enemy forces and enemy forces reacting to a raid or ambush.
- Destroying an enemy within an objective area or kill zone. In a vehicular ambush, mortars can also be used to force an enemy to button up.
- Providing illumination.
- Covering the movement of friendly forces after an attack.

RECONNAISSANCE IN FORCE

5-22. A reconnaissance in force is a limited objective attack by a strong force, typically a battalion or larger, to obtain information; to discover or test an enemy's dispositions, strengths, and weaknesses; and to force a reaction by their reserves or fire support assets. A commander ordering a mission must be prepared to extricate his force or to exploit its success. (See FM 3-0/MCDP 1-0 for details.)

5-23. To a mortar platoon leader, a reconnaissance in force is conducted the same as a deliberate attack. Fire planning is detailed to increase responsiveness. A mortar platoon leader can adjust rapidly to changing situations that may include supporting the withdrawal of the force, conduct a hasty defense, or execute an exploitation.

5-24. Depending on the distance to be covered, mortars can be a maneuver commander's only means of indirect fire support. As such, platoon leaders position mortars to provide continuous fire support throughout the operation.

5-25. Sections or squads cover greater distances between displacements and should be prepared to engage targets using emergency techniques.

LINKUP

5-26. A linkup is a meeting of friendly ground forces. Examples of a linkup include—

- Advancing force reaches an objective previously seized by an airborne or air assault force.
- Encircled unit breaks out to rejoin friendly forces.
- Converging maneuver forces meet.

5-27. A linkup requires detailed restricted fire line, close coordination and detailed planning of movement, fires, control measures, and recognition signals. Ideally, an exchange of liaison officers takes place before an operation. Depending on the mission after a linkup, either force can be attached to the other or both can remain under control of the directing HQ. (See FM 3-0/MCDP 1-0 for details.)

5-28. To a mortar platoon leader, a linkup is conducted as a movement to contact if supporting a converging force or as a defense if supporting a stationary force. In either case, he ensures that all restrictive fire control measures are followed as the two forces converge.

MORTAR SUPPORT

5-29. Movement, maneuver, and rapidly changing situations characterize offensive operations. Flexibility in fire support is required to provide effective fires. Commanders integrate all available fires to ensure all known or suspected enemy positions are targeted.

5-30. A mortar platoon plans to conduct fires en route to, on, and beyond the objective. Mortars accomplish this by positioning near the line of departure, using a one-half to two-thirds maximum range rule as a guide, and then moving forward as necessary. However, it is often better to use a firing position with good defilade than to strictly apply the maximum range rule.

5-31. Mortars provide support during an attack to neutralize, suppress, or destroy an enemy while the assault element moves to the final coordination line, screens friendly movement by obscuring the enemy's observation, neutralizes resistance during the final assault, and isolates the objective.

5-32. Mortars neutralize and suppress enemy defenses during the final phase of an attack by short, violent preparations targeted against forward defenses and OPs. Mortar fires are lifted or shifted at the last possible moment before assault elements close on the enemy's position.

5-33. Once an objective is seized, friendly forces consolidate and prepare to repulse enemy counterattacks or to reorganize with minimum loss of momentum to continue the attack. Mortars protect friendly troops during consolidation or reorganization by preventing enemy reinforcements from entering the objective area or by breaking up enemy counterattacks.

FIRES

5-34. Commanders plan mortar fires on the terrain to be traversed and on the flanks to protect the force. If friendly forces make unexpected contact, immediate suppression missions may be fired. Mortar sections establish firing positions within forward assembly areas to protect against enemy attacks. Mortar fires are always planned from these assembly areas, though they may not be registered or prefired.

Fires En Route to an Objective

5-35. Fires en route to an objective can be divided into the following phases:
- Short of the line of departure/line of contact.
    - Because both maneuver and mortar units can identify them, plan fires in the vicinity of checkpoints, passage points, release points, and attack positions to support movement to the line of departure/line of contact.
    - Plan targets to support in the event the enemy conducts a spoiling attack.
- From the line of departure/line of contact to the final coordination line.
    - Fire smoke to screen the obstacle breaching operations and HE to suppress enemy fires.
    - Plan mortar fires in the vicinity of known locations such as friendly rally points, objective rally points, and assault positions.
- From the final coordination line to the limit of advance.
    - Fires on and around the objective to destroy and isolate it. Besides fires on the objective, this includes fires on enemy mutually supporting positions.
    - Plan interdiction fires on the rear of enemy locations and along likely avenues of withdrawal.
    - Plan smoke and HE fires on likely enemy reserve positions and assembly areas.
    - Plan fires on likely enemy counterattack routes and support positions.

Preparation Fire

5-36. Preparation fire is fire delivered on a target preparatory to an assault (JP 1-02). It is an intense volume of fire delivered in accordance with a time schedule. Fires may start at a prescribed time or be held on call until needed. Fires normally begin before H-hour and may extend beyond it. Duration is influenced by factors such as fire support needs of the entire force, number of targets, and firing assets and ammunition. Mortars may not always have adequate ammunition supplies or the range to fire on all planned targets. Commanders plan fires based on sustained rate of fire for each weapons system.

5-37. An example sequence of preparatory fires includes—

- **Phase I** provides for the early attack of enemy indirect fire support assets and observation capabilities. These targets are the slowest to recover. This degrades an enemy's ability to react with indirect fires and to gain intelligence about the friendly force. A battalion mortar platoon may play a major role in this phase of preparatory fires. A commander may mass fires against identified enemy mortar units or reconnaissance elements. Mortars may contribute to the counterfire program to free artillery and to aid in joint suppression of enemy air defense systems.
- **Phase II** concentrates on identified CPs, communications positions, assembly areas, and reserves. The goal is degradation of an enemy's ability to reinforce their defense and to shift forces to counter the main attack. Mortar targets are based on weapons capabilities.
- **Phase III** concentrates on the forward portions of an enemy defensive area and targets that pose an immediate threat to attacking troops. The purpose of this phase is to suppress and obscure enemy direct fire systems until the assault force has closed with them. Mortar fires are most likely used during this phase, especially against enemy reverse-slope positions, which can only be reached by high-angle fire.

On-Call Fires

5-38. On-call fires are planned targets fired on request not influenced by time schedules. On-call targets isolate all or part of the objective, provide illumination during night attack if needed, and disrupt an enemy counterattack.

Fires in Support of Consolidation and Reorganization

5-39. Fires in support of consolidation and reorganization protect friendly units against enemy counterattack or reinforcement. Mortar fires on likely enemy withdrawal routes disrupt his organized retrograde operations.

EXECUTION CONSIDERATIONS

5-40. When lead elements of an attacking force approach a designated phase line or control measure en route to an objective, an FSO/FSC normally begins the preparation. Lead element observers or company team FSO/FSCs track movement rates and confirm them for a battalion FSO/FSC. A battalion FSO/FSC may need to adjust the plan during execution based on unforeseen changes to anticipated movement rates.

5-41. As a unit continues movement toward an objective, the first delivery system engages its targets. It maintains fires on targets until a unit reaches the line that corresponds to the risk-estimate distance (RED) of the weapon.

SECTION III – DEFENSIVE OPERATIONS

5-42. During defense or retrograde operations, mortar units provide a commander with the ability to destroy an enemy, regain the initiative, and counterattack by fire. They participate as part of a larger force.

PLANNING FACTORS

5-43. A mortar unit's primary task during defensive operations is to provide immediate, close, and continuous fires to the defending force. A mortar leader must understand his commander's scheme of maneuver and his unit's role. Factors that determine how battalion and company mortar units are employed include—

- Whether a unit's AO is contiguous or noncontiguous, especially—
  - Sectors of fire.
  - Security.
  - Limits imposed by ROE.
- Size of an AO.
- Enemy capabilities, especially—

- Effectiveness of artillery.
- Countermortar and artillery capability, such as radar.
- UASs.
- Air power.
- Ability to conduct raids or other actions behind friendly front lines.

FINAL PROTECTIVE FIRES

5-44. Final protective fires are an immediately available prearranged barrier of fire designed to impede enemy movement across defensive lines or areas (FM 1-02). They are the highest type of priority targets and take precedence over all other fire requests. Final protective fires differ from standard priority targets in that they are fired at the maximum rate of fire until mortars are ordered to stop or until all ammunition is expended. The RED for a given delivery system is a factor in how close the FPF can be placed in front of friendly front lines. Closer FPFs are easier to integrate into direct-fire final protective lines. The high rate of fire achievable by mortars creates effective barriers of fire. The normal allocation of FPFs is identical to the allocation of priority targets (one for each battery/platoon and one for each mortar platoon). While firing FPFs, mortar sections are not normally allowed to cease fire and displace due to countermortar fire. They must take precautions to avoid or withstand countermortar fire.

5-45. Mortar units normally have a single FPF. A battalion heavy mortar platoon normally has a single four-mortar FPF, but a battalion commander may direct the heavy mortar platoon to prepare two two-mortar FPFs. This should be done only if terrain dictates the need for more FPFs than he has been allocated and only after seeking additional artillery allocations. (See Table 5-2 for the approximate width and depth of FPFs, which are based on the bursting diameters of mortar rounds.)

5-46. A company commander assigned an FPF is responsible for the precise location of the mortar FPF and FPF integration into the direct fire final protective lines. An FDC plots, precomputes, and saves all firing data for the FPF as early as possible.

Table 5-2. Final protective fire dimensions

Size	Number of Mortars	Width (M)*	Depth (M)*
120-mm	4	280	70
120-mm	2	140	70
81-mm	8	300	40
81-mm	4	150	40
81-mm	2	80	40
60-mm	3	90	30
60-mm	2	60	30
*Measurements are approximate.			

5-47. Mortar FPF widths and depths listed in Table 5-1 are neither precise nor restrictive. A mortar sheaf can be opened or closed to cover the specific terrain on which an FPF is located. The bursting radius is the standard method to compare the effectiveness of HE shells and is defined as the radius from the center of impact in which 50 percent of casualties can be expected. It is based on a surface burst against a standing target. The bursting diameter is therefore twice the bursting radius. The following mortar-bursting diameters are estimations since the type of round, fuze, range, and target surface all affect the mortar's bursting diameter:

- M120 (120-mm) mortar: 70 meters.
- M252 (81-mm) mortar: 38 meters.
- M224 (60-mm) mortar: 28 meters (M720 round).

5-48. Artillery FPFs are allocated to companies in the most critical defensive positions. Mortar FPFs may be allocated to cover less critical avenues of approach that are in the same or a different AO. Once allocated to a company, that commander designates the precise FPF location where they can best augment the direct-fire weapons. Figure 5-1 shows how mortar FPFs are positioned to integrate them into the direct-fire final protective lines of the defender.

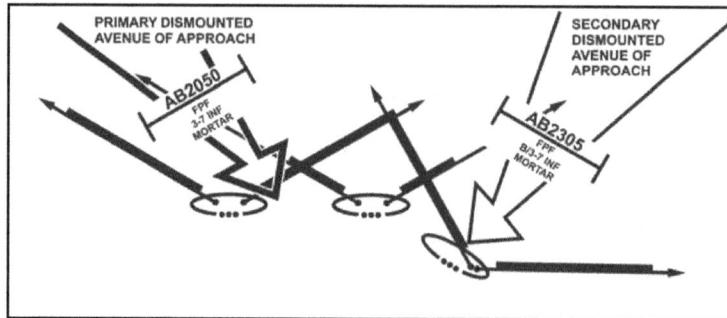

Figure 5-1. Mortar final protective fires integrated with direct fire final protective line

5-49. Mortar FPFs are always targeted on an avenue of likely dismounted attack. They can be any distance from the friendly position that fits into a ground commander's tactical situation but are always within the range of organic direct-fire weapons, normally within 100 to 400 meters of friendly troops. The importance of accurate defensive fires and the proximity of friendly troops means that each mortar firing an FPF should be individually adjusted into place, normally using delay fuze settings and the creeping method of adjustment.

5-50. A company commander may retain the authority to call for the mortar FPF to be fired or he may delegate it to a subordinate. If the decision is delegated to a forward platoon leader, he directs his FO to transmit the request to fire the FPF directly to the FDC or through the company FSO. When the request is transmitted directly to the FDC, the rifle platoon leader must inform the company commander that he has initiated the FPF. The mortar section or platoon leader always informs his commander when he initiates the firing of the FPF.

5-51. A commander and mortar unit leader must have alternate means of communication to call for the FPF. No one means of communication, such as radio, wire, or voice is sufficient; an alternate means must be established. In addition to standard voice messages, the commander and mortar unit leader should establish a simple visual pyrotechnic signal.

5-52. Mortar FPFs are fired only when needed. Once begun, FPFs are fired until ordered to terminate or until all mortar ammunition is gone. High explosive ammunition with point detonating fuzes is normally used in firing the FPF. When planning FPFs, a mortar platoon leader decides how many rounds to prepare, based on ammunition available and the CSR, and sets them aside for immediate use. This allows mortars to quickly begin the FPF and maintain it without pausing to prepare rounds when the call for fire is received. Additional rounds can be prepared during the firing of FPFs if the ammunition requirement exceeds the quantity prepared.

MORTAR DEFENSIVE FIRE SUPPORT TASKS

5-53. In defense, a mortar platoon leader must understand the intent of defensive techniques a commander employs. These techniques affect how a mortar platoon provides support, since specific actions and techniques vary depending on the characteristics of the defense. Mortar fires are used in defense against both mounted and dismounted enemy forces.

5-54. Against a mounted attack, they are used to suppress—
- Armored forces by using proximity-fuzed HE rounds to cause the crews of tanks and fighting vehicles to close the hatches, reducing their field of view and their ability to detect friendly forces.
- Antiarmor guided missile systems while friendly maneuver units are displacing.
- Enemy direct-fire overwatch positions.
- Enemy air defense weapons and vehicles.
- Enemy mortars, automatic grenade launchers, and rocket launchers.

5-55. Against a dismounted attack, they are used to—

- Engage dismounted enemy infantry beyond direct-fire weapon ranges.
- Suppress enemy mortar fires supporting the attack.
- Break up enemy troop concentrations.
- Cover dead space in front of friendly positions.
- Reduce an enemy's mobility and canalize their assault forces into engagement areas.
- Neutralize and destroy enemy forces attempting to breach friendly obstacles.
- Suppress and obscure enemy direct-fire support weapons.
- Provide close-in FPFs against an enemy's dismounted assault.
- Deny an enemy the use of a specified piece of terrain.
- Conceal friendly obstacles from the attacking force.

5-56. Against both mounted and dismounted attacks, mortar fire is used to—

- Screen movement of friendly forces between firing positions.
- Isolate attacking enemy units, especially to separate dismounted Infantry from Armor.
- Illuminate areas where enemy forces are known or suspected to be, so they can be engaged with other weapons.
- Mark targets for attack by direct-fire weapons or aircraft.
- Mark targets for precision guided munitions.

5-57. Mortar fires are often used to support security forces. Security forces can be given priority of mortar fires, OPCON of the mortar platoon (or section), or attachment. Mortar fires are used to engage an advancing enemy at long ranges, inflict casualties, delay and disorganize their movements, and assist the security force in breaking contact. If a mortar platoon or section moves forward of main defensive positions to accomplish these tasks, a leader coordinates the subsequent rearward displacement. He confirms the timing of the displacement, changes in OPCON or fire priority, routes of displacement, passage point through friendly barriers, recognition signals, and plan for occupying the subsequent position.

5-58. Closely coordinated mortar fire can significantly increase the effectiveness and survivability of antitank weapons. Infantry battalion weapons and an SBCT BCT ATGM company commander can be given priority of mortar fires or even OPCON of a mortar platoon or section. They are rarely given OPCON of mortar squads. An antitank company does not have a company FSO/FSC. An FSO/FSC or FO team can be task-organized. However, a mortar platoon leader and antitank company commander must be prepared to coordinate and execute fires in support of antiarmor companies without a FIST/FiST. Because both organizations are organic to the same battalion, this is easily accomplished.

5-59. While HE fires force tank crews to close the hatches, mortar rounds should be set to achieve airbursts to reduce dust and dirt thrown into the air. This interferes less with friendly direct fires.

5-60. Mortar smoke rounds can be fired to isolate the lead element of an advancing enemy force from the main body. The antitank company can then attack this isolated element, free from enemy overwatching fires. Mortar smoke can be placed between an antitank company and an enemy to aid in the movement out of initial firing positions to subsequent ones. Commanders must coordinate the use of mortar smoke rounds. In addition, a mortar platoon leader must be prepared to cease firing smoke rounds immediately if shifting winds move the smoke to an unfavorable area.

5-61. Smoke and HE rounds can be used to complement the effects of antiarmor ambushes and to cover the withdrawal of an ambushing force.

Fires Before Enemy Attack

5-62. Fires delivered before enemy attacks break up an attack before it starts or disorganizes, delays, and weakens the attack. These fires are categorized as follows:

Harassment and Interdiction Fires

5-63. Ammunition resupply constraints severely restrict the amount of harassment and interdiction fires mortar platoons or sections provide. In a high-threat environment, harassment and interdiction fires can expose the mortar firing location to enemy targeting and counterfire. Against a dismounted enemy on close terrain, mortar platoons may fire harassment and interdiction fires to slow and disorganize the enemy as they concentrate forces and supplies to continue their offensive. Mortar harassing fire limits the enemy in preparing OPs. If an enemy must move men and supplies through a defile or across a ford, interdiction fire severely hampers reinforcement and carrying parties. Mortar harassment and interdiction fires are usually unobserved and they require coordination to ensure accuracy and safety. Some may be fired based on recurring patrol reports, sniper/observation teams, stay-behind forces, aerial sightings, or sensor alerts. Close coordination with field artillery survey teams and target locating radars can greatly increase the effectiveness of mortar interdiction fires.

Planned Defensive Targets and Targets of Opportunity

5-64. Defensive fires are planned on all known, likely, and suspected enemy locations. This does not mean that an unmanageable number of targets are planned. Known enemy locations are the first priority, followed by suspected, and then likely enemy locations. As enemy forces appear near planned targets, mortar fire is delivered on them. Targets of opportunity are engaged by shifting fires from planned targets.

Counterpreparation Fires

5-65. Counterpreparation fires are prearranged fires delivered when an enemy attack is imminent. Since the mortar's range is limited compared to artillery, artillery fires most of the counterpreparation fires. Mortar platoons and sections fire against enemy forces that are massing near friendly forward positions. Mortar smoke obscures the view from suspected enemy OPs. Mortar illumination confirms or denies the presence of enemy forces near defensive positions, while not revealing individual weapon locations. Because U.S. mortars outrange most threat mortars of similar caliber and can hit targets in defilade, mortar units may provide countermortar fires.

Fires During Enemy Attack

5-66. Once an enemy attack begins, mortar fires break up their formations to suppress and neutralize supporting weapons and to destroy as much of their force as possible. Targets in relation to friendly defensive positions are planned as follows:

- **In front of the position** on all confirmed and suspected enemy locations, on likely avenues of approach, and on prominent terrain features that can be used by enemy overwatch elements.
- **In front of friendly barriers and obstacles**, these fires are often critical to the defense. Any obstacle not covered by both direct and indirect fires can be obscured and breached. High explosive with proximity settings can effectively prevent enemy dismounted forces from breaching an obstacle. Mortar fire is preferred for this task since it is always available to the commander. Its use permits a field artillery to concentrate destructive fires against enemy formations backed up behind the obstacle.
- **On the position**, so that if an enemy penetrates friendly defenses, effective fire can be delivered on them immediately. If friendly forces are fighting from properly constructed fighting positions with sufficient overhead cover, the mortar fire from rounds with a proximity fuze can be placed directly on them to destroy the exposed enemy. This is a combat emergency technique, since some friendly casualties could still result. Mortar fires planned on friendly positions also aid immediate counterattacks.
- **Behind friendly positions** to provide flexibility to the defense if an enemy surprises the defender by attacking from an unexpected direction. They also aid the defender in blunting enemy penetration, making the counterattack decisive.
- **Avenues of approach** into the flanks of a unit's position.

Counterattack Fires

5-67. Fire support for a counterattack is similar to that for the offense, except fire support priorities are divided between the forces still defending and the forces counterattacking. Mortar platoons may have to provide all or most of the fire support to the defending forces while the artillery supports the counterattack.

COUNTERING THE ENEMY'S STAND-OFF ATTACK

5-68. Mortar units face the possibility of many different types of attack on today's battlefield. Enemy attacks include, but are not limited to, the traditional ground assault, intense preparatory fires, and heavy direct-fire weapons. The stand-off attack is an increasingly common type in which an enemy attempts to inflict casualties and to damage U.S. forces without actually engaging in a close assault. Mortar units must counter stand-off attacks while remaining prepared to conduct a fully integrated defense against a ground assault by delivering counter-preparation fires, close-in fires, and FPFs.

DEFINING THE STAND-OFF ATTACK

5-69. A stand-off attack is a surprise attack by fire and is a common enemy tactic, one used extensively by insurgent and guerrilla forces. In U.S. doctrine, this type of attack is called an attack by fire. The stand-off attack is an asymmetric tactic often intended not only to inflict casualties, but also to have a strategic psychological impact.

5-70. A stand-off attack is normally delivered from beyond the effective range of U.S. small arms fire and is often over before the U.S. unit can bring counter-fire or air strikes against the attackers. These types of attacks are normally initiated from long range and from within defilade. They deliver sudden and intense fires against the U.S. unit. Stand-off attacks are sometimes conducted from a single location, but often they are complex surprise attacks from multiple firing locations.

5-71. An enemy normally plans when they will cease fire and break contact. They may plan to fire a specific number of rounds or may fire as many rounds as possible for a set period of time. Sometimes they will only cease fire and break contact when they start receiving effective counter-fire or are threatened by reaction forces maneuvering against them.

5-72. A stand-off attack is seldom decisive by itself, but it can be used by an enemy to achieve the following:
- Cause damage and inflict casualties.
- Harass and fatigue U.S. forces.
- Create a siege mentality by forcing U.S. units to remain in their fortifications.
- Demonstrate an insurgency's presence and strength, enhancing morale and recruitment.
- Suppress U.S. indirect fires in support of other units.
- Distract U.S. units and conceal enemy intentions.
- Prevent U.S. forces from moving to assist another unit under attack.
- Gauge strength and reaction times for U.S. supporting weapons.
- Entice U.S. reaction forces into planned ambushes or areas seeded with improvised explosive devices.
- Undermine U.S. political will with a steady trickle of casualties.

5-73. A stand-off attack can be conducted using a variety of weapons, often combining both direct and indirect fires. The most common stand-off attacks include fires by mortars, rockets, recoilless rifles, and rifle-propelled grenades, and sometimes fires of machine guns and even rifles. Artillery fires may be part of the attack, but normally the weapons systems used are lighter and more easily displaced than artillery pieces.

5-74. Normally, an indirect fire stand-off attack does not achieve significant precision. Fires are often spread over a wide area and not concentrated on any one target. However, enemy forces have access to modern maps and electronic navigation devices. Coupled with simple math and rudimentary fire control systems, such as a gunner's quadrant and a compass, these allow a fair degree of accuracy with mortars and rockets.

5-75. Precise direct-fire, stand-off attacks are possible by insurgents from long range if they are equipped with modern sniper rifles or guided antitank weapons. The advantage to an insurgent force conducting a stand-off attack is that it minimizes the chance it will suffer significant casualties, while at the same time allowing it to potentially inflict such casualties and damage on a U.S. unit.

5-76. In the traditional ground assault, an enemy force is fully committed. The assault forces have few options once the attack begins. They must continue to assault, possibly enduring heavy losses, or attempt to break contact and withdraw under fire, something that is tactically difficult and often costly. On the other hand, an enemy force conducting a stand-off attack is not fully committed and can cease fire and break contact almost at will.

5-77. A stand-off attack can be conducted without large numbers of troops needed for an assault and is therefore easier to conceal during the movement-to-the-objective phase. After a stand-off attack is complete, a small enemy force can more easily disperse and withdraw out of the area using multiple small covered and concealed routes.

RESPONSIBILITIES AT ALL LEVELS

5-78. Commanders at all levels are responsible for predicting and countering stand-off attacks. Information gathered by all sources should be analyzed for indications of an impending attack. Indicators vary depending on the local situation. Patrol sightings, reports of the enemy stockpiling ammunition, local populations being pressed into service as porters, increases in local radio and phone traffic, and tips from locals should all be monitored and considered. Unexplained movement out of an area by the populace is a possible indicator of an impending attack.

5-79. Historical reports should be reviewed for information on previous attack times and firing locations. Patrols should be directed to search for and report the locations of suspected repeat firing positions. Baseplate and bipod marks in the dirt, discarded arming pins or ammunition packing material, rocket and back blast burn marks, or rocks piled up to brace rockets are all indications that a position has been used before and might be used again.

5-80. Fortifications and protective positions should be built wherever possible. As in any defense, these should be constructed to allow U.S. forces not only to survive a sudden onslaught of fire, but also to continue to return fire without being suppressed.

5-81. Unit leaders should make a determination of the type and caliber of weapons likely to be used in a stand-off attack and construct fortifications adequate to protect the unit. Mortar unit leaders should ensure that their mortars are protected and that they can be brought into action against any likely enemy firing positions within range.

5-82. It is important to maintain observation of possible infiltration routes, assembly areas, and firing positions by patrols, OPs, UASs, and aerial observers.

5-83. Reaction forces, both ground and aerial, should be on alert for immediate employment. The HQ that is controlling the AO must integrate supporting fires from other unit locations.

ROLE OF MORTAR UNIT LEADER

5-84. A mortar unit leader is not the only person responsible for preparing for and countering a stand-off attack, but he is uniquely qualified to play a key role at the company and platoon level as an indirect fire planner.

5-85. Through training and experience, he understands the limitations and capabilities of indirect fire weapons. He has experience planning fires based on terrain analysis. He also has good SA gained through the communications that link him to the firing units, FDC, supporting indirect fire units, and unit commander. He controls the fires of the unit's most lethal, most responsive, and longest ranged weapons, the ones most suitable to countering a violent stand-off attack.

5-86. The key to his success in this role is the ability to plan, prepare, and execute counter-fires that are delivered quickly enough to hit the attacking force while it is still in the firing position or as it is withdrawing.

STEPS TO COUNTER THE STAND-OFF ATTACK

5-87. A mortar unit leader should be proactive and advise his unit commander on the potential for a stand-off attack, possible types and numbers of weapons that might be employed, possible firing locations, and, most importantly, how immediately responsive fires of the mortar unit can be used to counter the enemy attack quickly. These actions fall under the concept of—

Plan

5-88. The planning phase starts with the mortar unit leader conducting extensive terrain analysis of the area around the unit's location to identify and template likely enemy firing positions. He gathers data on the range and capabilities of the type of weapons the enemy uses in the AO. By drawing range circles for various enemy weapons, he can look at the terrain those circles encompass and template where an enemy is most likely to locate his firing positions.

5-89. The effective range of sniper weapons is highly dependent on the skill and training of the sniper. As a rough guide, Table 5-3 shows the maximum ranges of some common threat weapons.

Table 5-3. Example of maximum ranges of threat weapons

Weapon	Approximate Range (in meters)
GP-25 series 40-mm grenade	400
7.62x54-mm sniper rifle	600
Rocket propelled grenade	1,000
7.62x54-mm medium machine gun	1,500
AGS-17 automatic grenade launcher	1,700
73-mm SPG-9, 82-mm series recoilless rifle	1,800
12.7-mm machine gun, 14.5-mm and 20-mm heavy sniper rifles	2,000
60-mm mortar	2,500 or 5,500 (long-range version)
Guided AT missiles Milan, Arrow 8, AT-4, AT-5, AT-7	3,000
82-mm mortar	4,000
120-mm mortar	7,000
107-mm artillery rocket	9,000
122-mm artillery rocket	18,000

5-90. There are many other possible sources for information on the threat of a stand-off attack to any specific unit location. A mortar unit leader should discuss enemy capabilities with the unit intelligence staff officer, the reconnaissance platoon leader, and the supporting field artillery unit representative. The company FSO/FSC is also a potential source of information.

Prepare

5-91. The preparation phase begins with a unit commander directing local security patrols to report the precise grid location of any positions identified as previously used by an enemy for either firing or observing fires against the unit location. Additionally, identifiable infiltration and exfiltration routes should be identified.

5-92. If identified likely enemy firing positions are not easily recognizable from the mortar firing position, a marking may be required. This can be as simple as improvised aiming posts around the rim of the firing position. More elaborate steps can be taken by a unit to either overtly or covertly mark the actual area around the likely stand-off attack position. Painted rocks or tree stumps can be used as target reference points.

5-93. When conducting this terrain analysis to identify and locate likely enemy positions, a mortar unit leader should not limit himself to identifying only distinct single points. An enemy may move their weapons around among several good defilade positions along the reverse slope of a hill or ridge. The ability of mortar crews to fire searching or traversing missions should be considered as a technique for covering these likely firing positions.

5-94. The result of a mortar unit leader's analysis will be a number of potential enemy firing positions. These should then be converted to targets. This is followed by determining the most appropriate weapons to engage each individual target, group, or series.

5-95. For those targets assigned to a mortar unit, further analysis is required to determine the most appropriate type and amount of ammunition to plan and prestock for their engagements. Normally, a mix of bursting WP and HE rounds set for proximity burst is the most effective against enemy gun/mortar crews firing from defilade but without overhead cover.

5-96. A mortar unit leader must determine the optimum amount and type of ammunition to have prepared for countering a stand-off attack. He rarely will have as much ammunition as he thinks he might need and too much ammunition broken out at one time is a risk when exposed to heavy enemy fire. Crew members should be identified ahead of time to move to the ammunition storage area and begin the replenishment of ammunition.

5-97. An important part of preparing to counter a stand-off attack is for a unit to conduct detailed and realistic rehearsals of actions to be taken by leaders, FDC personnel, and mortar crews. The fleeting nature of a stand-off attack demands that counter-actions be rapid and consistent. Everyone in the unit should be aware of what actions to take if an enemy initiates a stand-off attack.

Execute

5-98. The execution phase of countering a stand-off attack begins once a unit is able to identify known or suspected enemy firing positions. As soon as a unit can initiate fires, it should engage these identified positions. There are many ways to identify known or suspected enemy firing positions. Direct observation from the mortar firing position during an attack is only one way. Others include reports or data collected before or during an attack from—

- UAS operators.
- OPs and local patrols.
- Countermortar radar operators.
- Adjacent units.
- Aerial observers and forward air controllers.
- Artillery FOs.
- Crater analysis matched to the terrain template.
- Unattended ground sensors.
- Attached or supporting sniper teams.
- Radio and telephone intercepts.
- Tactical questioning of local personnel.
- Interrogation of prisoners of war or detainees.

5-99. A tactically proficient enemy may make it difficult to precisely locate their position even while they are firing from it. Sometimes the best a unit can do is identify possible enemy locations. These should be checked quickly against a pre-attack analysis list (template) of likely firing positions.

ENGAGING AND COUNTERING THE STAND-OFF ATTACK

5-100. Countering the stand-off attack (execution) is a series of key actions that integrate all planning and preparation efforts by the mortar unit leader.

5-101. A mortar unit is capable of delivering large volumes of exceptionally lethal counterfire that can search out and destroy enemy forces even when they are firing from long range and within defilade.

5-102. Keys to executing those fires in a timely manner are the planning and preparation done before the attack. Planning and coordination must include a detailed analysis of possible collateral damage as well as considering no-fire or restricted-fire areas. The location of patrols and other friendly elements must be tracked continuously.

5-103. A unit that has planned and prepared for a stand-off attack can initiate counter-fires on planned targets almost immediately, firing series and groups of planned targets. A well-rehearsed mortar unit can engage multiple planned targets in a matter of minutes, without lengthy coordination or detailed orders from the commander.

5-104. Stand-off attacks are normally conducted from hasty positions that are particularly vulnerable to air bursting munitions. Direct-fire, stand-off attacks are often visually targeted by enemy gunners. This makes mixing smoke in with the air-bursting HE particularly effective. High explosive fires can disrupt the firing devices of an enemy remotely or time-delay fired weapons. If any firing devices can be recovered, they can provide valuable intelligence.

5-105. While targets are being engaged, a commander has the opportunity to further refine his understanding of where enemy is firing from and how attackers can best be defeated. At an appropriate time, a commander may order a mortar unit to shift fires from known, suspected, and likely enemy firing positions to other targets, such as withdrawal routes or enemy OPs.

5-106. As supporting units, such as attack helicopters or fixed-wing aircraft, are brought to bear against an enemy, a mortar unit may be ordered to shift or temporarily cease fire. If a ground reaction force is committed, a mortar unit may be ordered to fire in support of that unit, using either planned or immediate fires.

RETROGRADE OPERATIONS

5-107. Mortars participate in the retrograde by providing responsive indirect fire support to harass, delay, destroy, suppress, obscure, or illuminate the enemy. In addition, a mortar platoon can screen the displacement of a rifle companies and provide deceptive fires to confuse an enemy as to a commander's intent to withdraw or delay.

5-108. A mortar platoon supporting the delay or withdrawal provides a commander with a quick and effective means to support his maneuver. Mortar fire can be used to screen movement of friendly units between positions and delay lines, or to suppress enemy weapons so the maneuver platoons can move to break contact without heavy enemy fire. Positioning of ammunition must be planned to allow for an increased use of smoke. Mortar fires may be used to deceive an enemy by maintaining a heavy volume of fire while friendly elements withdraw.

5-109. In a delay or withdrawal, a mortar platoon plans its displacement so that it is in position to fire when needed. When and how to displace relies on how far mortars are behind the forward units, how far to the rear those units will move, and the intensity of enemy contact. The platoon usually displaces by section.

5-110. In withdrawal, a mortar platoon can be effective when employed in support of the security force. Employing mortars in split sections allows mortars to be used in the deception plan and to support withdrawing maneuver elements. An effort must be made to keep mortar fire at the same level during withdrawal to increase effectiveness of the deception plan.

5-111. A section or squad can be attached or placed under OPCON of the security force or detachment in contact. If enemy pressure is great, the entire mortar platoon can be employed to support the disengagement.

5-112. In a delay not under pressure, a mortar leader can expect to have half of his unit assigned to the detachment left in contact. These mortars are expected to fire the same number and types of missions as the complete unit.

5-113. While retrograde operations are conducted similarly for both the Army and the Marine Corps, a retrograde is part of defensive operations for the Army. The Marine Corps considers a retrograde as part of other tactical operations that enable a Marine air-ground task force to execute offensive and defensive operations. (See FM 3-0/MCDP 1-0 for details.)

SECTION IV – STABILITY OPERATIONS

5-114. Mortar units conduct stability operations as part of a larger force. The AOs, ROE, and system for clearance of fires are key factors in the employment of mortars during stability operations. The mortar units conduct offensive and defensive tasks as part of stability operations as described previously in this chapter. In stability operations, mortar units may also be required to conduct missions that are not related to the delivery of indirect fires. These missions are diverse and a mortar leader and his unit must plan, train, rehearse, and execute them in the same manner as they do their primary mission.

DECENTRALIZED OPERATIONS

5-115. Stability operations are normally planned centrally and conducted in the form of decentralized, small-scale, noncontiguous actions conducted over extended distances. Responsibility for making decisions on the ground falls to battalion and company level leaders. However, procedures to conduct operations, ROE, clearance of fires, and many other policies that directly affect small unit operation are issued and controlled by higher HQ.

5-116. Mortar units provide a commander with a flexible and adaptive force that has mobility, communications, and full spectrum capabilities. Because mortar units can cause large amounts of collateral damage, they are usually tightly controlled. In stability operations, excessive collateral damage adds to the number of active enemy and increases their covert support.

ENEMY CAPABILITIES

5-117. Stability operations cover a wide range of situations, primarily based on a threat. At one end of the spectrum, an enemy may be active and have the support of a large portion of the population, control large areas, and attack friendly forces with sophisticated tactics and weapons. Operations against such an enemy resemble traditional offensive and defensive operations with large units attacking, fixing, and destroying the enemy. At the other end of conflict, an enemy may be covert, use the local population to protect themselves and hide their identity, and conduct limited operations against friendly forces, such as emplacing improvised explosive devices. Operations against this type of enemy primarily entails separating them from the rest of the population and is characterized by extensive patrolling, intelligence gathering, raiding, executing population control measures, and conducting joint operations with local military forces.

COMPONENTS

5-118. Stability operations have an offensive and defensive component. They may require working closely with non-U.S. military personnel and accomplishing tasks for which the unit is not routinely trained. Because of their lethal nature, mortars units are usually involved in the offensive and defensive components of stability operations.

Offensive Related Tasks

5-119. A key element in the employment of mortars in stability operations is mobility. Combined arms, SBCT, and Infantry battalions employ their heavy mortar units if the mission requires them to do so, and the ground can support their maneuver. Helicopter support can provide the means to move heavy and medium mortars to establish a base of fire to support the maneuver elements. Infantry and SBCT Army battalions and Marine light armored reconnaissance battalions may employ their medium mortars when conducting dismounted operations. However, the amount of ammunition that can be carried may affect their ability to support a commander.

5-120. Stability operations often consist of company- and platoon-level offensive missions. In these situations, light mortar provides effective and mobile fire support. It is often used in the hand-held mode firing direct lay or alignment missions.

Defensive Related Tasks

5-121. During stability operations, U.S. forces conduct defensive operations primarily to protect a force or to secure key facilities. U.S. mortar units may be constantly switching between offensive and defensive operations. Mortar units may be called upon to—

- Protect the local population.
- Guard local bases.
- Protect and facilitate sustainment/logistics operations.
- Escort and protect resupply efforts.
- Monitor and control personnel and vehicle movement.

5-122. Stability operations often require Infantry units to be responsible for large AOs that require constant actions to control. However, some AOs may be too large for the assigned unit to physically control. To provide mortar coverage to as much of the AO as possible, commanders often split platoons and sections. Individual mortar squads are often located separately and under control of their own FDC. Units with multiple mortars, such as SBCT units, may be required to man both primary and secondary mortar systems. Units may also receive additional mortars and mortar equipment once they arrive in-country. Operating more mortars requires minimum crew manning, thorough training, and cross training, along with training of non-mortar personnel to augment crews. In stability operations, mortar units may—

- Operate over wide areas with 360-degree fire coverage responsibility.
- Be called upon to operate semi-independently as sections or squads.
- Be subject to detailed and restrictive ROE.
- Have stringent procedures for clearing fires.
- Be in static positions for long periods of time.
- Move often to support operations.
- Establish firing positions within perimeters defended by U.S. or other forces.
- Be called upon to perform nonstandard, nonfiring missions.
- Conduct fire missions to—
  - Defend their own position against direct ground attack or attacks by fire.
  - Support units in the field.
  - Provide illumination fires as a show of force.

PREPARATION FOR STABILITY OPERATIONS

5-123. Deployment to an area to conduct stability operations normally includes a period of time to prepare for operations. Units may also have the ability to contact and gain extremely valuable information from the unit they are replacing. However, once in-country the unit may immediately conduct the mission hand-over and begin conducting missions. If possible, mortar units must prepare at home and at training centers to immediately conduct effective missions.

5-124. Mortar leaders should consider the following when preparing for deployment:

- Preparing subordinates physically and mentally for expected conditions.
- Cross training mortar crews and FDC personnel.
- Training on all mortar systems.
- Training for continuous operations.
- Conducting operations with minimum mortar crews and FDC.
- Developing close relationships with the FSO/FSC and FOs.
- Acquiring any needed equipment and supplies.
- Conducting operations with the same number of mortar systems as currently operating in the AO.
- Planning the shipment of equipment and supplies down to the individual firing position.

NONSTANDARD MISSIONS

5-125. Because of the mission and ROE, mortar men may not be able to conduct fire missions or otherwise perform the duties they were trained to do. Mortar men and their equipment may be used for other duties. However, mortar leaders must maintain proficiency in individual skills and collective tasks.

5-126. Nonstandard missions are missions that a unit is not designed to conduct, but is capable of performing. Examples include conducting mounted or dismounted patrols or carrying supplies during civil support operations. The types of nonmortar-related missions are many, but the following duties are mortar-related:

- Designate as another mounted or dismounted maneuver element (may require additional equipment and weapons).
- Man the battalion or company CP.

- Provide security.
- Use mortar carriers for Infantry related missions.

SECTION V – CIVIL SUPPORT OPERATIONS

5-127. Civil support operations are operations conducted within the U.S. and its territories to support U.S. civil authorities during domestic emergencies, and for designated law enforcement and other activities. It includes support in response to natural or man-made disasters, accidents, terrorist attacks, and incidents. Army forces conduct civil support operations when the size and scope of events exceed the capabilities or capacities of domestic civilian agencies. Mortar units conduct civil support operations as part of a larger force. Army forces execute civil support tasks for the following general purposes:

- Save lives.
- Restore essential services.
- Maintain or restore law and order.
- Protect infrastructure and property.
- Maintain or restore local government.

5-128. Army forces perform civil support tasks under U.S. law. However, U.S. law carefully limits actions that military forces, particularly Regular Army units, can conduct in the U.S. and its territories. The following are some general tasks that a mortar unit may conduct during civil support operations:

- Provide support in response to disaster or terrorist attack.
- Support civil law enforcement.

5-129. Mortar units in support of civil support operations conduct nonstandard missions and requirements are unique. Because the types of missions assigned to a mortar unit cannot be predicted, this discussion of civil support missions is only descriptive and provides minimal guidance to mortar units and their leaders because—

- Each civil support mission is different. Tasks may include supporting rescue efforts of citizens, conducting reconnaissance to determine the extent of damage during a natural disaster, or providing support to local police forces.
- Missions may be assigned to a unit based primarily on their capability to command, control, move, and conduct operations with disciplined forces. Mortar units do not conduct fire missions.
- Units are under the control of civil authorities.

SECTION VI – TACTICAL ENABLING OPERATIONS

5-130. A commander conducts tactical enabling operations to assist the planning, preparation, and execution of any of the four types of military operations: offense, defense, stability, and support. Tactical enabling operations are never decisive operations in the context of offensive and defensive operations; they are either shaping or sustaining operations. The following are tactical enabling operations that are often used in offensive operations in which mortar units may have a substantial role:

RECONNAISSANCE AND SECURITY OPERATIONS

5-131. Mortar units support reconnaissance and security operations in the same manner as they support offensive and defensive operations. Although reconnaissance troops have their own mortars, a commander may decide to provide them with additional combat power by assigning them additional mortar units. Considerations for the employment of organic and attached mortar units include—

- Units conducting these missions often operate within a large AO that cannot be completely covered by a mortar unit in a single location. The commander decides whether to keep direct control of his mortars or allocate mortar squads, sections, or platoons to subordinate units.
- During reconnaissance operations, the movement of mortars is based on the progress of a unit. While the mortar section is on the move, it should be prepared to provide immediate fires using direct lay, direct alignment, or hip shoot techniques. The movement of the unit is planned so that it is in position

to support the maneuver unit at critical times, such as when the unit is crossing danger areas or when it must clear complex terrain.

- Considerations for using mortars in security operations are similar to those for reconnaissance operations. To reduce potential sustainment/logistics problems during security operations, a commander and section leader may consider the stockpiling of ammunition at subsequent firing positions based on METT-TC/METT-T variables.

PASSAGE OF LINES

5-132. Passage of lines occurs when one unit passes through the positions of another, as when elements of a covering force withdraw through main battle areas. A passage can be designated as a forward or rearward passage of lines. It can be conducted in offensive or defensive operations. Army doctrine lists a passage of lines as a tactical enabling operation. The Marine Corps considers a passage of lines as part of other tactical operations that enable the Marine air-ground task force to execute offensive and defensive operations. (See FM 3-0/MCDP 1-0 for details.) Detailed reconnaissance and coordination ensure that a mortar platoon conducts the passage quickly and smoothly. Personnel can be overly concentrated, fires of the stationary unit can be masked temporarily, and a mortar platoon may not be able to react to enemy action. Direct and indirect fires of a stationary unit are normally integrated into the fire support plan of the passing unit. Mortars and FIST/FiST can be collocated to provide coordinated and responsive support. Often mortars from a stationary unit provide fire support to the moving unit out to the limit of range. Particular attention is given to restrictive fire measures used to control these fires. The use of fire direction nets is also coordinated. A mortar platoon usually operates within a stationary platoon's fire direction nets. Call signs are exchanged and FDC personnel are informed that calls for fire can be received from a passing unit.

5-133. A passing unit's mortars conduct a rearward passage of lines using appropriate displacement techniques until the maneuver element is within range of the stationary mortar platoon. Mortars can then move to and through the passage point either as a platoon or in sections.

5-134. A mortar platoon normally conducts a forward passage when the maneuver element is just short of the stationary mortar platoon's maximum range. Passing mortars then begin displacement techniques to support their maneuver element with continuous fire.

RELIEF IN PLACE

5-135. Relief in place is an operation in which a unit replaces a unit in combat. The incoming unit assumes responsibility for the combat mission and the assigned AO of the replaced unit. Army doctrine lists a relief in place as a tactical enabling operation. The Marine Corps considers a relief in place as part of other tactical operations that enable a Marine air-ground task force to execute offensive and defensive operations. (See FM 3-0/MCDP 1-0 for details.) Mortar sections and their FOs are normally relieved after the maneuver companies. The mortar platoon remains in position, ready to fire, until relief is nearly completed. The mortar element being relieved passes on its target lists and overlays to the incoming mortar platoon to ensure effective delivery of fires. Mortar baseplates (if ground mounted), aiming posts, telephones, and wire lines can be left in place and exchanged. Authority to do so would be included in the relief order of the next higher commander. This simplifies the effort and lessens the time required to affect the relief.

5-136. To ease occupation of positions during hours of limited visibility, an incoming platoon leader should conduct both a day and night reconnaissance.

SECTION VII – ECHELON AND CLEARANCE OF FIRES

5-137. Mortar units operate as part of larger units during full spectrum operations. During operations, leaders must ensure that friendly maneuver forces are not endangered by indirect fires and that targets are approved and cleared at the appropriate command level. Echelonment of fires, along with detailed consideration of the RED, allows a commander to maintain constant fires on the objective while accepting a known level of risk of casualties from friendly fire. Clearance of fires prevents inadvertent engagement of friendly elements or noncombatants.

ECHELONMENT OF FIRES AND RISK-ESTIMATE DISTANCE

5-138. The purpose of echeloning fires is to maintain constant fires on a target while using the optimum delivery system up to the point of its RED in combat operations or minimum safe distance in training. (Since it is used in training, minimum safe distance is not discussed further in this manual.) Echeloning fires provides protection for friendly forces as they move to and assault an objective, allowing them to close with minimal casualties. It prevents an enemy from observing and engaging the assault by forcing them to take cover, allowing the friendly force to continue the advance.

ECHELONMENT OF FIRES

5-139. The concept behind echeloning fires is to begin attacking targets on or around the objective using the weapons system with the largest RED. As a maneuver unit closes the distance, crossing the RED line for that specific munition en route to the objective, fires cease, shift, or switch to a different system, such as the 120-mm or 60-mm mortar. This triggers engagement of the targets by the delivery system with the next largest RED-combat. The length of time to engage targets is based on the rate of the friendly force's movement between the RED-combat trigger lines. The process continues until the system with the least RED-combat ceases fires and the maneuver unit is close enough to eliminate the enemy with direct fires or make its final assault and clears the objective.

5-140. Using echelonment of fires within the specified RED-combat for a delivery system requires a unit to assume some risks. A maneuver commander determines, by delivery system, how close he will allow fires to fall in proximity to his forces. He makes the decision for this risk level, but relies heavily on the FSO/FSC's expertise. The commander considers the effects of terrain and weather, experience of the observers, and communication systems involved. While this planning is normally accomplished at the battalion level, the company FSO/FSC has input and should be familiar with the process.

RISK-ESTIMATE DISTANCE

5-141. Risk-estimate distance takes into account the bursting radius of munitions and characteristics of the delivery system. It associates this combination with a probability of incapacitation for personnel at a given range. Risk-estimate distance is the minimum distance at which friendly troops can approach friendly fires without 0.1 percent or more probability of incapacitation. A commander may maneuver his units into the RED area based on the mission, but he is making a command decision to accept the additional risk to friendly forces. (See FM 3-09.31/MCRP 3-16C for details.)

EXAMPLE

When a battalion makes contact with an enemy during a movement to contact, an example of the use of echelonment of fires and REDs is when an Infantry battalion commander and an FSO/FSC, in close coordination with ground maneuver, directs and executes—

- On-call CAS on the objective.

- The DS fires/DS battalion 155-mm artillery fires on the objective while the CAS shifts to another target.

- When the maneuver element reaches the RED for 155-mm fires, the artillery shifts to another target and the 120-mm mortars commence firing.

- When the maneuvering force reaches the RED for 120-mm mortars, the 120-mm mortars shift to another objective and the company 60-mm mortars commence firing.

- When the maneuver element reaches the RED for 60-mm mortars, the maneuver element begins direct fire on the objective from a support by fire position.

- The maneuver force assaults and seizes the objective.

CLEARANCE OF FIRES

5-142.   Clearance of fires is the process of approving or obtaining approval for attacking targets with indirect fires both within and outside the boundaries of a maneuver unit for which fires are provided. Fires must be cleared to prevent inadvertent engagement of friendly elements and noncombatants. Understanding the current ROE is critical for the clearance of fires process. The ROE may limit the types of systems and ammunition permitted to fire. The ROE may also limit the types of targets and their proximity to specified locations, such as towns and mosques.

5-143.   Commanders clear fires. An FSO/FSC may be designated by a commander to clear fires. In stability operations, clearance of fires may require coordination with civilian organizations and local government. This may increase the time between the call for fire and permission to fire the mission. When clearing fires, commanders should consider all possible factors. This includes the point of impact of illumination round canisters.

This page intentionally left blank.

Chapter 6

Section and Platoon Operations

This chapter presents mortar unit operations. It includes mortar employment, helicopter operations, and operations in urban and mountainous terrain. The chapter also includes employment by unit, position reconnaissance and occupation, displacement, movement, and firing positions. Operations described in this chapter have been successful in the past, but are no guarantee of future success. A successful mortar unit leader must apply his understanding of a commander's intent, knowledge of tactics, and analysis of METT-TC/METT-T variables to develop a course of action.

SECTION I – TEXT REFERENCES

6-1. Within this manual, selected topics are only briefly discussed and readers are referred to another publication for more detail. Mortar and other combat units use these tactics, techniques, and procedures in the same or very similar manner and a detailed discussion in this manual would be redundant. However, they are as important as the subjects discussed in detail. Table 6-1 consolidates the references to additional information.

Table 6-1. Guide for subjects referenced in text

Subject	References
Overhead and mask clearance	FM 3-22.90
Surface conditions	FM 5-103
Fires without an FDC	FM 3-22.91
Terrain mortar positioning	FM 3-22.91
Crater analysis	FM 3-09.12/MCRP 3-16.1A
CBRN factors and crater analysis	FM 3-11.4/MCWP 3-37.2
Helicopter operations	MCWP 3-11.4
Air assault planning	FM 3-21.8/MCWP 3-11.1/MCWP 3-11.2
Sling load operations	FM 4-20.197/MCRP 4-11.3E VOL I
External cargo carrying devices	FM 4-20.197/MCRP 4-11.3E VOL I
	FM 4-20.198/MCRP 4-11.3E VOL II
Mortar units in urban operations	FM 3-06.11/MCWP 3-35.3
Magnetic interference	FM 3-22.90
Effect of mountains on mortar operations	FM 3-97.6/FMFM 7-29

SECTION II – EMPLOYMENT CONSIDERATIONS

6-2. A maneuver commander employs a mortar unit based on his analysis of the METT-TC/METT-T variables. There is no mortar employment option that is routine; each has advantages and disadvantages. Mortar leaders must also consider how to configure their units if vehicles or personnel are not available.

EMPLOYMENT TECHNIQUES

6-3.   When considering how to use the battalion mortar platoon, a battalion commander has three general options: employ the unit by platoon, section, or squad. A company commander with a company mortar section has only two options: employ the unit as a section or by squads. Although individual light mortars can be very effective when employed in the direct lay or alignment mode, company commanders must consider their limited capability for indirect fire control when using this method.

EMPLOYMENT BY PLATOON

6-4.   Using the employment option, a platoon operates from one or two firing positions and usually fires all mortars on each target, under the control of a platoon leader. Firing from one location may be the only option for an under-strength platoon. Even when a mortar platoon is being used as a single firing unit, it can still fire multiple missions simultaneously. It can displace from its firing position either by echelon or as a complete platoon. Platoons may occupy two separate firing positions. If these positions are up to 300 meters apart, it greatly decreases an enemy's chance of neutralizing them with counter mortar fire (Figure 6-1). If a platoon occupies two positions, the distance between mortar sections is limited primarily by their ability to cover the target area, terrain, enemy threat, and limits in communications. Separated firing positions must not be so far apart as to prevent a platoon leader from controlling them both. Separating the sections must not prevent massing the fires of a platoon on a single target.

6-5.   When employed by platoon, the controlling FDC is the mortar fire direction net control station. The controlling FDC issues the fire command designating the platoon, a section, or squad to deliver fire.

6-6.   Massing fires requires FDCs to compute data for each section on the same target. With automated fire direction systems, an FDC designates the type of sheaf desired, such as linear or converged, and sends the commands to the mortar squads. When operating in a degraded mode with an inoperable fire direction automated system, an FDC computes the fires of both sections on a single adjusting point. This produces a smaller, more concentrated sheaf in the target area. The other section FDC plots an imaginary adjusting point at a distance of the bursting diameter, left or right of the fired adjusting point, and computes fire-for-effect data based on the imaginary adjusting point. Registration and meteorological data improve the accuracy for a nonadjusted section.

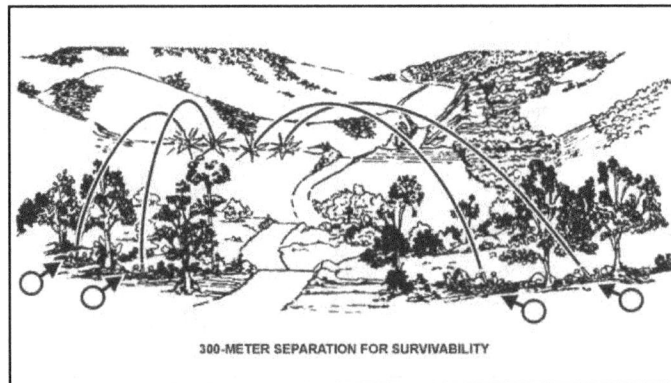

300-METER SEPARATION FOR SURVIVABILITY

Figure 6-1. Firing locations (300-meter separation for survivability)

6-7.   When sections are separated and in degraded mode, each FDC section prepares firing data for its section. However, one FDC remains the controlling FDC. If a fire mission requires the firing of only one or two mortars, such as in a smoke or illumination mission, the controlling FDC designates which mortars are to be fired.

6-8.   Some of the advantages for a mortar platoon firing in one location are—
- Simplifies control of a unit.
- Simplifies sustainment/logistics actions.
- Enables a unit to rest personnel and rotate duties to maintain alertness.

- Allows for the most efficient use of personnel.
- Improves a unit's ability to maintain local security.

6-9. Some of the disadvantages are—

- Unit is massed and, therefore, more vulnerable to counterfire.
- Requires more space and therefore may limit a leader's choice of positions.
- May limit the portion of a unit's AO that can be covered by fires.

EMPLOYMENT BY SECTION

6-10. Employment by section places each section as a separate firing unit. Each section acts semi-independently and covers its own targets or area. The section without an FDC configures one mortar as the mortar/FDC and controls the other.

6-11. A mortar platoon is normally employed by section when it needs to cover wide frontages. Each section is positioned so that it can provide fires within a defined AO. Depending on the range to the target and the separation of sections, more than one section may be able to mass fires on the same target.

6-12. Section employment is more appropriate when rifle companies operate over wide frontages or move along widely separated axis. It is more difficult to control and to support logistically.

6-13. Sections operate on a platoon's mortar fire direction net. Depending on the type of control, an FSO/FSC or FOs must request fire from a designated section using that section's call sign. If separate frequencies are available, each section may operate on its own fire direction net.

6-14. Mortar and section leaders control the displacement of each section. Displacement is coordinated with the movement of the part of the battalion or company that the section is supporting. Since both sections cannot cover the entire area, they may be moving at the same time.

6-15. Some of the advantages for the mortar platoon splitting sections under separate FDC control or the company mortar's establishing a single position are—

- Greater area coverage.
- Less vulnerable to counterfire.
- Easier to find covered and concealed firing positions.

6-16. Some of the disadvantages are—

- Sustainment/logistics more difficult.
- More difficult to provide local security.
- Increased radio traffic.

EMPLOYMENT BY SQUAD

6-17. Employment by squad places one or more mortar squads on the battlefield as separate firing units. This usually supports special requirements, such as—

- Widely dispersed unit positions across a large AO.
- Security force operations.
- One mortar illumination missions.
- Roving mortar adjustment technique.
- Combat patrols.
- Withdrawals not under enemy pressure (as part of a detachment left in contact).

6-18. An entire mortar platoon may be divided and employed by squads. This is the least desirable method of employment and is used only when the situation or terrain prevents adequate support if otherwise employed. The following are examples of when it may be necessary to employ a platoon by squads:

- When a supported maneuver element is required to cover a large front, such as a battalion task force screening a division's flank.

● During decentralized operations where units are assigned very large AOs and must cover them with mortar fire.

6-19. These situations may not occur often. If adequate support can be provided by a section, employment by squads should be avoided. Employment by squads reduces the effects on a given target, increases control problems, and exposes the mortar squads to destruction by small enemy forces. It is also the most difficult option to support logistically. The following are some considerations when mortar units are employed by squads:

● The crew is configured as a mortar/FDC team and the squad leader must be prepared to compute firing data.

● Each squad is normally attached to a maneuver element, such as a rifle platoon. The attached squads normally operate on the supported unit's radio net or as directed by the supported commander. The FO then requests fires using that mortar squad's call sign.

● If a target is within range of more than one squad, fires may be massed to engage that target. The massing of fires requires more effort due to clearance of fires and the increased number of radio nets involved.

6-20. Some of the advantages for the employment of single mortar squads are—

● Greater area coverage.

● Less vulnerable to counterfire.

● Easier to find covered and concealed firing positions.

● More responsive to unit if attached.

6-21. Some of the disadvantages are—

● Sustainment/logistics more difficult.

● Greater stress on mortar unit leaders to maintain standards.

● More difficult to provide local security.

● Radio traffic.

● More reliance on communications.

● Inability to conduct coordinated illumination missions.

● Difficulty in conducting simultaneous fire missions.

AVAILABILITY OF PERSONNEL AND EQUIPMENT

6-22. Mortar unit leaders should be prepared to operate without their full complement of personnel and equipment. Personnel may be not available, vehicles may not be operable or restricted to certain areas, and equipment may be damaged. Leaders should cross-train their personnel so that they are proficient in more than one position. Contingency plans for vehicle cross-loading should be included in the TACSOP and practiced. For example, an FDC should know which vehicle to use if their vehicle is inoperable or cannot go on operations. Likewise, mortar crews should know what equipment to carry and what vehicles to transfer to if their vehicle breaks down.

6-23. Mission accomplishment determines whether a leader, with his commander's concurrence, should reduce the number of mortars carried. As a general rule, a mortar leader's last option is reducing the number of mortars carried. This rule may not always apply. For example, a light mortar leader may determine that he can accomplish the mission with fewer mortars while carrying a greater amount of ammunition.

SECTION III – RECONNAISSANCE, SELECTION, AND OCCUPATION OF MORTAR POSITIONS

6-24. The tempo of the modern battle and the threat of enemy counterfire mean that mortar platoons and sections may have to move often. To reduce the time spent displacing, a mortar platoon must be able to accomplish the reconnaissance, selection, occupation, and movement tasks quickly and efficiently. The key to a successful reconnaissance, selection, and occupation of position is frequent and effective training. Although FBCB2 and automated fire direction systems provide extremely accurate locations and greatly simplify the techniques used to occupy and fire from a new position, mortar leaders must be prepared to conduct operations under degraded conditions.

RECONNAISSANCE

6-25. Mortar units conduct reconnaissance to identify suitable primary and alternate mortar unit firing positions and routes. A continuous and aggressive reconnaissance is essential to timely and accurate fire support. A platoon leader must continually perform this reconnaissance and plan ahead to meet any contingency. He may be given the general location of new positions, or he may have to select them himself and recommend them to his commander.

METHODS OF RECONNAISSANCE

6-26. Platoon leaders may conduct a reconnaissance by using a map and FBCB2, by air, or on the ground.

Reconnaissance with Map and FBCB2

6-27. A mortar leader conducts a map reconnaissance and uses the factors of observation, cover and concealment, obstacles, key terrain, and avenues of approach to systematically analyze the terrain in his AO. Reconnaissance can be conducted using a map or the FBCB2 with the requisite overlays. When using the FBCB2, a mortar leader has available current friendly and enemy locations and can use the line-of-sight, navigation, and steer-to tools. Potential positions and routes to the new position can be chosen. This method is fast and allows unsuitable routes to be eliminated. It also identifies possible ambush sites. In some combat situations, a map reconnaissance may be the only one possible. The major disadvantages of conducting only a map inspection are—

- Terrain and other features may have changed. For example, a bridge shown on a map may no longer exist. Military load classifications of bridges are not listed on maps and must be physically inspected.
- The surface conditions of a route and position cannot be determined. For example, soil texture may not support a mortar carrier or a mortar prime mover.
- Enemy and friendly locations may not be current.

6-28. If available, aerial photographs and UAS feeds should be used to supplement maps because they are more recent, show more detail, and present a clearer picture of the current condition of the terrain to be crossed.

Air Reconnaissance

6-29. If time and resources are available, information gained from an air reconnaissance can be beneficial in selecting routes to be used and areas to be occupied. Although this is a fast method, true surface conditions can be indistinguishable or may appear distorted.

6-30. A commander or platoon leader must be careful that his flight plan does not compromise the route or the new position area. This method may not be available to a platoon leader in all operations or theaters.

Ground Reconnaissance

6-31. The preferred method of reconnaissance is ground reconnaissance, since the suitability of routes can be physically examined. The true condition of the terrain is critical if the surface has been affected by enemy action, such as CBRN attack, or weather conditions. Ground reconnaissance has the disadvantage of being the slowest method of reconnaissance.

PLANNING THE RECONNAISSANCE

6-32. To maximize its tactical benefit, reconnaissance must be thoroughly planned before it is executed. As part of the planning phase for any OPORD or reconnaissance, selection, and occupation of position, the METT-TC/METT-T variables must be considered before any action is taken.

Reconnaissance Party

6-33. A platoon leader or his designated representative performs the reconnaissance. A platoon sergeant and section leaders should be able to perform a detailed ground reconnaissance. The reconnaissance party should be as small as possible while still able to accomplish the mission. The platoon leader, a noncommissioned officer, and a driver normally compose the reconnaissance party.

POSITION SELECTION CONSIDERATIONS

6-34. Mortar firing positions are selected based on mission accomplishment (the most important factor), tactical situation, range criteria, target area coverage, survivability, overhead and mask clearance, surface conditions, communications, and routes.

Mission Accomplishment

6-35. Mission accomplishment is the most important factor. The position must permit a mortar section or platoon to accomplish its primary mission. Mortar unit leaders must ensure that the potential position can support the mission. For example, even though a position may have excellent defilade, it may also limit the range of the mortar and therefore the ability of a unit to support the mission.

Tactical Situation

6-36. A platoon leader must understand the tactical situation, the supported unit's mission, the location of friendly units, and potential enemy threats. By considering the tactical situation, a mortar platoon leader can ensure that the mortar platoon provides effective indirect fire support, while maintaining security for the mortars.

Range Criteria

6-37. Maximum and minimum mortar ranges determine whether mortars can support from selected firing positions. Mortars should be able to fire at least one-half to two-thirds of their range to the front of the forward elements of the supported friendly force. These range criteria are only a guide, not inflexible rules. These may vary due to METT-TC/METT-T variables or due to a commander's guidance. Mortars must be positioned far enough back so that fires can be placed directly in front of and behind the rifle platoon positions. Longer ranges available from the M252 and M120 mortars do not mean platoons equipped with these weapons must be located further to the rear. The added range allows a platoon leader flexibility in choosing firing positions. For example, he can fire out of deeper defilade and still cover the battalion (or company's) sector. Positions that place targets at the extreme edge of mortar range should be avoided, if possible.

Target Area Coverage

6-38. Mortar positions should give maximum coverage of the battalion or company AO. To do this, the mortar platoon leader begins by analyzing the defensive plan, the locations of priority targets, and the enemy avenues of approach. To cover the supported unit, the mortar unit often positions itself near the center of the unit's position. Positioning in the center does not take precedence over priority targets or priority of fires that a commander assigns to a specific mortar element. For example, if mortars must be positioned on a flank to support the company with priority of fire, a priority target, or because of terrain, then positioning in the center of the AO becomes a secondary concern. A mortar platoon leader must choose an area that allows him to cover the company with priority of fires or his priority targets. He then chooses a firing position within that area that maximizes the fires he can provide for the rest of the battalion without reducing support to the priority company. If the priority of fires is planned to change, the mortar platoon leader must choose a position from which he can cover both units, plan a displacement, or operate by section to cover the other unit.

SURVIVABILITY

6-39. Mortar crews face many threats on the battlefield, including CBRN hazards, countermortar fire, ground attacks, and air attacks. These must all be considered when a mortar position is selected. The position should facilitate both active and passive defense measures so it—

- Cannot be hit by direct or low-angle indirect fire (defilade) (Figure 6-2).
- Can be entered without enemy observation.
- Offers good cover and concealment.
- Avoids obvious avenues of approach.
- Has more than one entrance and exit route.
- Takes advantage of existing terrain features and natural obstacles.

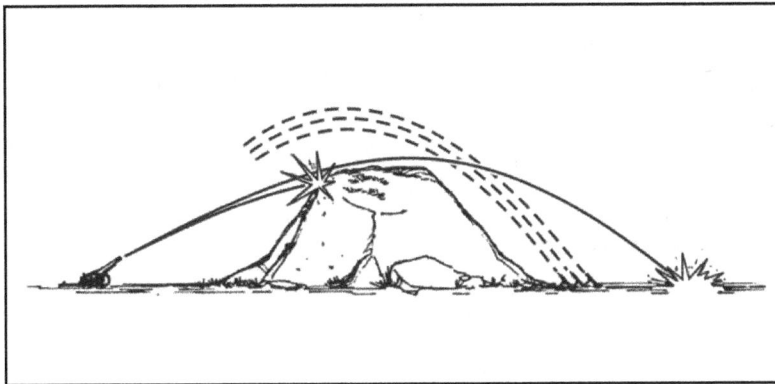

Figure 6-2. Defilade

OVERHEAD AND MASK CLEARANCE

6-40. Concealing and positioning the mortars should not interfere with their operation. Interference is caused by overhead and masking. (See FM 3-22.90 for details about overhead and mask interference.)

SURFACE CONDITIONS

6-41. Soil at each mortar position must be well-drained and firm so that mortar baseplates do not sink into it when the mortars are fired. If mortars are mounted on carriers, the soil must be firm for the carriers to remain stable when mortars are fired. When fired on ground that is not stable, firing pads are constructed. (See FM 5-103 for details.) Sandbags and other material can be used when firing from a hard surface, such as a road or other areas found in urban terrain. When the ground is frozen, slots should be chopped into the earth for the baseplate spades and extra time must be allotted to emplace mortars. When temperatures cycle repeatedly above and below freezing, personnel must ensure baseplates do not become frozen into the earth.

COMMUNICATIONS

6-42. A mortar platoon must be able to communicate with a supported unit, and mortar squads must be able to communicate with an FDC. During reconnaissance, radio checks are made at the position to be occupied.

6-43. Maximum effort must be made to protect a platoon from direction-finding capabilities of the enemy. Direction antennas and maximum use of wire communications reduce the electronic signature of the platoon. Digital messaging devices allow a mortar unit to communicate quickly and accurately.

ROUTES

6-44. Mortar positions should be close to access routes to speed resupply and displacement, but should not prevent concealment. If required, helicopter landing zones should be identified for sustainment/logistics or maneuver purposes.

ADVANCE PARTY OPERATIONS

6-45. After the reconnaissance has been conducted, an advance party is sent to the initial or next position. If time is limited, reconnaissance may be performed in conjunction with advance party operations. An advance party operation includes a minimum of personnel and equipment needed to prepare a position for occupation. It accompanies a mortar platoon leader, or his representative, and begins preparations when he confirms the firing locations. For either a deliberate or a hasty occupation, a prearranged signal or procedure should be used to alert and assemble the advance party. The signal should be in the unit TACSOP, which also lists the personnel, equipment, vehicles, and place of assembly.

6-46. Many improvements in mortar fire control associated with the fielding of the FBCB2, MFCS, and GPS navigation systems have greatly enhanced the process of preparing and occupying positions. In some cases, these systems have also greatly simplified the process.

6-47. A platoon leader determines the personnel and equipment required for the advance party on the basis of the tactical situation and assets available. In some instances, a complete mortar squad may be in an advance party and establish a firing position to support the movement of the rest of the unit. It should become the base mortar at the new firing position. Equipment required to prepare a new position should be identified, maintained, located and loaded on prescribed vehicles.

6-48. An advance party also—

- Verifies and marks the route with engineer tape, signs, lights, aiming posts, or road guides. If tentative routes are determined to be unsuitable, the advance party leader contacts the remainder of the platoon, recommends an alternate route and, sends an overlay showing the alternate route, if required.
- Checks to ensure that tentative routes and positions have the best cover and concealment.
- Locates and marks minefields and obstacles, as time allows. It reports the discovery of minefields to the battalion CP and mortar leaders mark these areas on their maps and digital displays. TACSOPs should prescribe actions taken when minefields are encountered.
- Uses CBRN detection equipment during movement and at the position to detect and identify contaminated areas. It reports the location of all contaminated areas, marks the locations of contaminated areas in FBCB2 and on maps, and reports to the displacing element and alters the route.
- Determines and reports the time required to displace to the next position.
- Verifies tentative emergency occupation positions along the route selected during map reconnaissance. It informs the displacing element of any changes in the suitability of these positions.

6-49. After reconnaissance, an advance party occupies a new mortar position. It prepares the position to the maximum extent possible before the main body arrives. The main body continues to improve the original position.

OCCUPATION

6-50. An advance party starts the occupation of the new firing position and works continuously until the main body arrives. Therefore, occupation by the main body is a continuation of the actions by the advance party.

6-51. An advance party starts the occupation by—

- Verifying position location.
- Checking the position and surrounding areas for mines, CBRN contamination, and enemy forces.
- Establishing local security and OPs.
- Marking mortar positions with stakes or lights.
- Marking entrances to and exits from positions.
- Guiding the displacing element into position upon arrival. The FDC is positioned near the middle of the formation to allow FDC members to announce fire commands to the mortars by voice, if necessary.

- Determining and clearing mask and overhead obstructions.
- Improving security and defensive measures.
- Erecting camouflage or cutting and arranging it.
- Preparing alternate and supplementary positions, as time permits. It continually improves the positions until the mortars displace.
- Identifying a tentative landing zone for resupply and medical evacuation.

6-52. An advance party conducts the following additional duties when operating under degraded conditions:
- Setting up the aiming circle or using an M2 compass to determine the azimuth of fire. The advance party identifies the direction of fire with direction stakes.
- Completing a rough lay of the mortar positions, if time allows, which is useful for night occupations.
- Laying the mortars and wire. Plotting boards should already be prepared.

6-53. Before moving, a mortar platoon leader ensures that the following tasks are accomplished:
- HQ is informed of the move.
- Platoon position is inspected for documents, overlays, or anything that may compromise security.
- Obstacles and claymore mines are retrieved.
- Early warning devices are retrieved, such as trip flares and the platoon early warning system.
- Communication wire is retrieved.
- Personnel at the OPs are returned to the position.
- Carrier-mounted mortars are remounted, if ground-mounted on carriers.
- Ammunition is fired if it cannot be moved (if the tactical situation permits).
- Automated fire direction systems are initialized for the next firing position (if known).
- Mortars are ordered out of action.

MOVEMENT BRIEFING

6-54. Before leaving to reconnoiter the new position, a unit leader briefs key personnel on movement information.

6-55. As a minimum, a movement briefing should cover the following:
- **Situation**, including—
  - Enemy situation, to include activity, major avenues of approach, air activity, and potential ambush sites.
  - Friendly situation, to include changes in tactical missions and locations of friendly maneuver units and supporting artillery.
- **Mission**: changes in the mission of the maneuver unit.
- **Execution**, including—
  - Concept of the operation, to include general location of platoon positions, azimuth of fire, routes, order of march, location of start point and release point, and times.
  - Mission-oriented protective posture status.
  - Areas of known CBRN contamination.
- **Administration and logistics**, including—
  - When and where to feed personnel.
  - Priority for maintenance recovery.
  - Ammunition resupply.
  - Refueling location.
- **Command**, including—
  - Changes in the location of the CP.
  - Location of the commander.
- **Signal**, including—
  - Movement radio frequencies.
  - Net control restrictions.
  - Signals for immediate actions at the halt and during movement.

NIGHT OCCUPATIONS

6-56. Night occupations present special problems of control. Night vision equipment has improved and simplified the process but even with night vision devices limited visibility makes almost every task associated with position occupation harder to accomplish. To conduct efficient night occupations of firing positions, a mortar platoon leader must establish a detailed TACSOP and train his platoon in its use.

6-57. Guides must be thoroughly briefed and should pace the routes to and from a platoon's different elements before and after darkness. They should have filtered flashlights to guide vehicles.

6-58. Although night vision devices do not allow users to distinguish colors, color coding of individual squads or sections may facilitate identification during night operations.

6-59. Light discipline must be maintained. Chemical lights are useful during night occupations, but their use must be standardized and controlled.

TYPES OF OCCUPATION

6-60. The three types of occupation are deliberate, hasty, and emergency.

DELIBERATE

6-61. Deliberate occupations are planned and have an advance party preceding a platoon to conduct extensive preparation of a new position. A deliberate occupation may take place during daylight hours following a daylight operation, at night after a daylight preparation, or at night following a nighttime preparation. Only the minimum number of vehicles and personnel should go forward. Too much activity during preparation risks compromise. When a tactical situation allows, a good procedure for deliberate occupations of a new position is to do the preparation before darkness and to move the sections by night. Deliberate nighttime occupation following a nighttime preparation is often necessary, but it can be time-consuming.

6-62. A guide meets a platoon at a pickup point and leads their vehicle to the entrance of the position area. There the vehicle guides wait to lead the vehicles to selected locations.

6-63. A platoon sergeant implements the security and defense plan as personnel become available.

6-64. Considerations for night occupations are as follows:

- Light discipline must be practiced. Proper preparation for a night occupation minimizes the need for lights.
- Noise discipline is most important, since noise can be heard at much greater distances at night.
- The time for occupation is increased.
- Each vehicle guide should know where his vehicle is in the order of march so the platoon can move smoothly into position without halting the column.
- Vehicles should not move within the position without a guide.

HASTY

6-65. Hasty occupations are also planned. They differ from deliberate occupations mainly in the amount of time available for preparation by the advance party. A hasty occupation may be necessary because of rapid combat operations or unforeseen circumstances. An advance or reconnaissance party may be able to accomplish site preparation such as marking firing positions, manning the release point, and establishing security.

6-66. In a day or night hasty occupation, a platoon may require more time to occupy. This is because some preparatory tasks cannot be completed during the limited time available for the reconnaissance and selection phase. However, an MFCS greatly speeds up the process of occupying a firing position.

EMERGENCY

6-67. Emergency occupations result when a call for fire is received while a platoon is making a tactical movement. They require a mortar platoon or section to occupy the first available location without any prior site preparation.

POSITION IMPROVEMENT

6-68. Position improvements are continuous and performed in the priority determined by a platoon leader. These actions include the following:

- Improve position defense plans.
- Improve camouflage.
- Harden positions.
- Perform maintenance.
- Rehearse.
- Cross train.
- Resupply.
- Complete position area survey.

6-69. Care must be taken in the way ammunition is resupplied and vehicles are refueled, particularly in tracked mortar platoons. These activities can reveal the location of the platoon and should be accomplished at night.

SECTION IV – DISPLACEMENT PLANNING

6-70. After he considers the scheme of maneuver and his commander's guidance, a mortar unit leader develops a displacement plan based on his part of the fire plan. The displacement plan normally includes a map overlay that shows initial positions and subsequent positions. If time permits, a platoon leader selects and includes alternate and supplementary positions. The displacement plan also includes routes to be taken between positions and any pertinent control measures to support a specific operation or for a specific time (Figure 6-3).

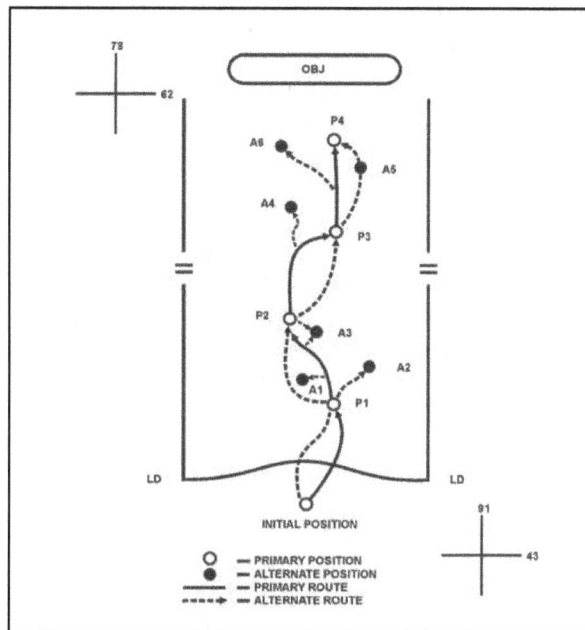

Figure 6-3. Example mortar displacement overlay

DISPLACEMENT TIMING

6-71. A battalion or company commander controls the displacement of the mortar platoon by an on-order or event-oriented displacement.

ON-ORDER DISPLACEMENT

6-72. He can direct the mortar unit to displace only on order, which is the most restrictive way to control displacement. The commander himself orders the unit to displace or directs the operations officer or FSO/FSC to relay the order.

6-73. A mortar unit leader is responsible for keeping the battalion/company CP informed of his status. At a minimum, he reports whenever his fires are falling beyond two-thirds of the maximum range in the offense or less than one-third of the range in the defense. These reports help the commander make timely decisions about mortar displacement. The unit leader maintains SA so he can anticipate the order to displace and be prepared to execute it. If the mortar unit leader feels he must displace, he informs the commander of the situation and requests permission.

6-74. If a mortar unit leader loses total communications with a CP or commander, he uses his best judgment to displace. He tries all possible means to reestablish communications with the CP or its designated alternate.

6-75. If he cannot reestablish contact, a mortar unit leader changes to the command frequency of the company (or platoon) having the priority of mortar fires to reestablish his link to the battle. He must play an active role in keeping the lines of communication open to maintain effective fires.

EVENT-ORIENTED DISPLACEMENT

6-76. A commander directs mortar platoon units to displace whenever certain predetermined events occur. This is less restrictive for a mortar unit leader, but it reduces the flexibility of a battalion or company commander.

6-77. An event-oriented displacement plan is established based on a time schedule, planned phases of an operation, crossing of designated phase lines, or completion of some event. Whatever events are chosen, a mortar unit leader anticipates the one most likely to happen next and is ready to execute the displacement plan immediately. He maintains SA and monitors communications to learn when a specified event occurs. If he loses communications, he actively seeks information as to the course of the battle once communication is restored.

6-78. When the situation changes and a mortar leader feels he must displace out of order with events, he informs the CP and requests permission. If communications are lost, he makes a decision. He always seeks to take whatever action is needed to keep the mortar platoon in range and in communication with the supported maneuver elements.

DISPLACEMENT PLANS

6-79. The rapidly changing conditions of modern ground combat require a mortar leader to always be prepared to displace. Detailed displacement planning aids in providing immediately responsive fires.

6-80. After a tentative displacement plan has been developed, an advance party conducts a reconnaissance to verify routes and positions. It then departs to perform actions that aid displacement and occupation by the displacing element. At the new position, the advance party prepares the position for occupation to the maximum extent possible until a displacing element arrives.

6-81. After a displacement plan is finalized, copies of the overlay are distributed to the commander or operations officer, the FSO/FSC, the platoon and section leader, or the FDC chief. This plan is used to help control the movement of mortars. As the tactical situation and mission change, the displacement plan is updated. Often these changes are the result of the reconnaissance.

OFFENSIVE

6-82. To support offensive operations, a displacement plan must permit rapid displacement of the mortars and immediate fire support when needed. It must be flexible to allow for changes in the scheme of maneuver. The enemy situation, the distance to be covered, and the requirement for continuous fire support determine the number of mortars to be moved at one time and the displacement technique.

DEFENSIVE

6-83. A defensive displacement plan has the same requirements as an offensive plan. A platoon leader also plans for extensive use of alternate and supplementary positions. He anticipates future operations and plan displacements to assume the offense or to conduct a retrograde operation. The same factors affecting the displacement in the offense apply to the defense.

6-84. In retrograde operations, initial employment of mortars may be by platoon or section, depending on the situation and front to be covered. Displacement is planned to provide continuous mortar fire support throughout the operation. Plans should include designated locations for prestocking ammunition, when possible. Close coordination and communication with supported elements ensure that displacement is planned and timed to allow the mortars to move in advance of maneuver elements. Therefore, maneuver element's movements are covered, which prevents mortars from being left behind.

SECTION V – DISPLACEMENT TECHNIQUES

6-85. A maneuver commander's OPORD provides a mortar unit leader the needed information and guidance for deciding which of the three techniques to employ. The integration of FBCB2 and automated fire direction systems has made displacing units much easier and less risky because, even while moving, mortar units can quickly and accurately respond to a call for fire. When displacing part of the mortar unit while the other part provides fire support, platoon or sections use alternating or successive bounds. The displacement technique used for a particular operation depends on the METT-TC/METT-T variables. Specific considerations include—

- Scheme of maneuver of supported unit.
- Enemy activity.
- Trafficability of terrain.
- Number of sections/mortars in a platoon.
- Availability of supporting artillery.
- Time available. (Time is often the limiting variable that determines the displacement technique.)

DISPLACEMENT BY PLATOON AND COMPANY/TROOP SECTION

6-86. Displacement by platoon and company/troop section is used when there is little immediate likelihood of enemy contact or when artillery can provide adequate support during displacement. This technique requires a platoon or company/troop section to displace all of its mortars in one move. This is the fastest way to displace a platoon; however, the platoon cannot provide immediate responsive fire support while moving. If a platoon must fire during movement, it uses hipshoot or emergency techniques to engage. Movements from the assembly area to the initial firing position are usually by platoon and company/troop section. Fielding of the MFCS has greatly increased the ability of mortar units to provide fires even while displacing.

PLATOON DISPLACEMENT BY SECTIONS

6-87. This technique requires one section to remain in position while the other section moves. When a displacing section is in position and ready to fire, the remaining section displaces. The platoon FDC displaces with one of the sections. Displacing by sections is accomplished when continuous fire support from the mortar platoon is required. Since one section must be ready to provide fire support while the other section moves, this technique is slower than displacement by platoon.

DISPLACEMENT BY SQUAD OR SECTION

6-88. This technique is similar to displacement by sections except fewer mortars are involved and is usually employed by platoons or sections. This displacement technique involves displacing one mortar while the other provides continuous support.

6-89. When mortars are in position and ready to fire, the remaining mortar displaces. When required or operating under degraded fire direction condition, part of an FDC is sent with the displacing squad(s), or a squad leader is sent with an M16 plotting board, who serves as the temporary FDC. Units equipped with an MFCS have the ability for individual mortars to perform as a technical FDC.

6-90. When displacing by squads, successive or alternate bounds can be used (Figure 6-4). Alternate bounds are normally used when displacement must be rapid in order to stay up with supported elements. Using alternating bounds is somewhat less secure and a leader has less control. Successive bounds are used when a maneuver element's movements are not so rapid such as in defensive or retrograde operations. Successive bounds are somewhat more secure and give a mortar leader more control.

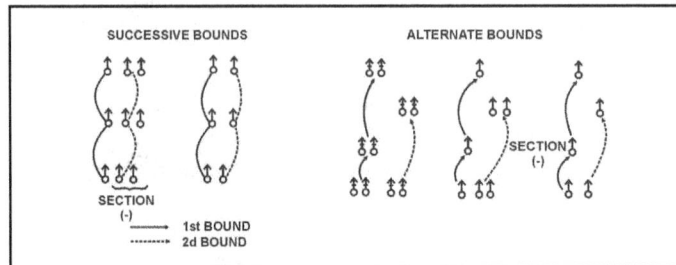

Figure 6-4. Types of bounds

SECTION VI – MOVEMENT

6-91. METT-TC/METT-T variables determine the type of movement used by mortar units. As an enemy threat increases, a mortar leader increases the distance between vehicles or units. Because of their weight, heavy mortars are usually moved by vehicle. Medium mortars are both carried by hand and moved by vehicles. Infantry light mortars are usually hand carried. Mortar platoons or sections move independently or as part of a larger unit.

INDEPENDENT

6-92. A mortar platoon moves as part of a larger group, but it may move independently for short distances.

6-93. When moving dismounted, mortar units employ the same dismounted movement techniques as other Infantry squads: traveling, traveling overwatch, or bounding overwatch. Bounding overwatch is not often used because a mortar platoon or section does not normally seek to make direct contact with the enemy.

6-94. When moving mounted, a mortar platoon leader has several options for moving a platoon in a tactical configuration. Each option has specific advantages and disadvantages. A platoon leader decides which method is best for the existing METT-TC/METT-T conditions.

OPEN COLUMN

6-95. A platoon uses the open column road movement for daylight movements when there is an adequate road network that is not overcrowded, when enemy detection is not likely, when time is an important factor, and when considerable travel distance is involved. Vehicle interval in an open column is about 100 meters.

6-96. Advantages of this method are—
- Speed (the fastest method of march).
- Flexible.
- Reduced driver fatigue.
- Improved vision on dusty roads.
- Fewer accidents.
- Ease in dispersing vehicles as a passive defense measure against an air attack.
- Less chance of the entire platoon being ambushed.

6-97. Disadvantages of this method are—

- Greater column length requires more road space.
- Other traffic often becomes interspersed in the column.
- Communication within the column is complicated.
- Proper vehicle spacing is hard to maintain.

CLOSED COLUMN

6-98. For closed column movement, vehicle interval is less than 100 meters. During limited visibility, each driver can observe the cat's-eyes of the blackout markers on the vehicle in front of him and maintain an interval of 20 to 50 meters. During daylight, the platoon uses closed column when maximum control is needed, such as during limited visibility or when moving through built-up or congested areas.

6-99. Advantages of this method are—

- Simplicity of control.
- Reduced column length.
- Concentration of defensive firepower.
- Full traffic capacity of the road can be used.

6-100. Disadvantages of this method are—

- Column is vulnerable to enemy observation and attack.
- Quick dispersion is difficult.
- Strength and nature of the column are quickly apparent to enemy observers.
- Convoy speed is reduced.
- Driver fatigue increases.
- May cause congestion at point of arrival.

INFILTRATION

6-101. When a platoon moves by infiltration, it dispatches vehicles individually or in small groups without reference to a march table. FBCB2 aids a platoon leader in maintaining SA. This technique is time-consuming, and vehicles are difficult to control. The platoon uses it when an enemy has good target acquisition means and quick reaction capabilities.

6-102. Advantages of this method are—

- Least vulnerable to hostile observation.
- Ideal for covert operations.
- Provides passive defense against air and artillery attack.
- High speeds are possible.
- Deceives an enemy as to the size of the infiltrating force.
- Does not hinder cross traffic.

6-103. Disadvantages of this method are—

- Control is difficult.
- Small elements are more vulnerable to ground attack.
- It is time consuming.

OFF-ROAD MOVEMENT

6-104. A platoon or section using this type of movement should travel close to tree lines, along gullies, and close to hill masses. Off-road movement should be conducted when enemy observation or interdiction by artillery fire or air attack is likely. A platoon may move safely on a road for some distance and then off-road at a point where enemy observation becomes likely or vehicle congestion provides an enemy an inviting target.

6-105.   Advantages of this method are—
- The strength and nature of a column are difficult to determine.
- Traffic is avoided.
- Passive defense against air and artillery attack is provided.

6-106.   Disadvantages of this method are—
- Displacement time may be increased.
- Ground reconnaissance is required.
- Soil conditions may complicate movement.
- Improper movement leaves wheel or track marks to the new position.
- Extensive coordination is required to avoid traveling through other unit areas.

6-107.   A platoon using off-road movement may move in open column, in closed column, or by infiltration. It can also displace either as a unit or by echelon.

SECTION VII – FIRES WITHOUT A FIRE DIRECTION CENTER

6-108.   Fire with an FDC increases the effectiveness of a mortar section. A section sets up and operates an FDC whenever it occupies semi-permanent positions or makes a long halt. An FDC influences the outcome of the battle by massing mortar fires, by furnishing prearranged fires during reduced visibility, by lifting and shifting fires, by effecting time-on-target missions, or by providing fire support to other units within range. However, fire with an FDC is not always possible and the mortar unit may be more responsive without it. The mortar section can be effective without using an FDC if the members are trained to do so. (See FM 3-22.91 for details.)

6-109.   The primary techniques to fire without an FDC are—
- **Direct-lay method**. In the direct-lay method of emplacing a mortar, a gunner sees the target through the mortar sight. No directional or aiming posts, FO, or FDC are used. The firing table should be used to try to obtain a first-round hit. If the first-round hit is not achieved, the firing table should be used to obtain a bracket. Depending on the location of friendly troops to the target, the bracket method, modified ladder method, or creeping method of adjustment apply. This is the primary method for firing the 60-mm mortar in the hand-held mode.
- **Direct-alignment method**. A squad leader positions himself where he can see both the target and the mortar. He computes the firing data for the initial round, spots its fall, and makes corrections.

SECTION VIII – MORTAR SECTION AND PLATOON FIRING FORMATIONS

6-110.   A mortar platoon or section leader must always consider METT-TC/METT-T variables when he decides the firing formation for his mortars. The main emphasis must be on mission accomplishment, but METT-TC/METT-T variables will also affect the choice of the firing formation. A platoon leader always considers the appropriate amount of dispersion, the need for position hardening, overhead and mask clearance, defilade, range, and available camouflage and concealment.

FIRING POSITIONS WITH AUTOMATED FIRE DIRECTION SYSTEMS

6-111.   With the introduction of automated fire direction systems, mortar leaders are no longer limited to positions that produce a parallel sheaf, provide a set pattern of rounds on target, or positions where all the mortars have to have line of sight to an aiming circle. Each mortar can now quickly receive individual fire commands from an FDC without lengthy calculations. A mortar unit leader is now more concerned with—
- The ability to support his commander by positioning his unit to effectively hit assigned targets.
- The effective use of existing cover, concealment, and defilade.
- The ability to establish local security.

6-112.   However, mortar unit leaders have to be prepared to operate under degraded fire direction conditions.

FIRING FORMATIONS UNDER DEGRADED CONDITIONS

6-113.   When automated systems are not available, a mortar leader has to continue to accomplish his assigned mission. He establishes a firing position that enhances the ability control fires with the M16/M19 plotting board.

TERRAIN MORTAR POSITIONING

6-114.   When the threat of enemy counterfire and aerial attack is high, a platoon leader should consider dispersing mortars over a larger area. He should maximize the use of natural cover and concealment offered by the local terrain. This type of dispersal, without regard to any set distance between mortars or effects on a parallel sheaf, is called terrain mortar positioning. This requires the computation of corrections by an FDC to fire a standard sheaf (Figure 6-5). The time required to compute these corrections decreases the responsiveness of the mortars from a given location, unless terrain mortar position corrections can be computed before occupation of the position. Since mortars move often, computing such corrections before occupation may be impossible. A modified version allows a platoon to use a form of terrain mortar positioning that does not decrease mortar responsiveness. (See FM 3-22.91 for details.)

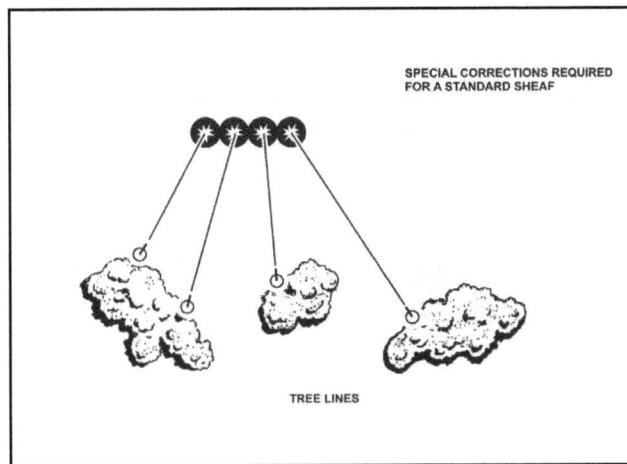

Figure 6-5. Terrain mortar positioning

PARALLEL FORMATION

6-115.   A parallel formation has the mortars on line. The distance between mortar positions is the bursting diameter of HE ammunition for the particular mortar employed. A parallel formation is used to employ two or more mortars where the terrain allows dispersion of the mortars and maximum cover and concealment. A parallel sheaf is formed in the target when all mortars fire the same data. A parallel formation provides maximum coverage of a linear target. However, it does present an easy linear target for enemy aircraft and artillery to engage and makes all-round security difficult to provide. This formation is one of the easiest to move into during a hasty occupation of a firing position since individual mortar placement is by TACSOP.

LAZY W FORMATION

6-116.   The lazy W formation lays mortars on a modified line. It provides better flank security with almost the same target coverage as the parallel formation when all mortars fire the same data. The lazy W is used when the terrain affords little cover and concealment. It adds depth to the sheaf, which is useful when engaging area targets.

DIAMOND FORMATION

6-117.   A diamond formation allows a four-mortar platoon to fire in all directions with equal ease (Figure 6-6). It is used when 6400-mil coverage is required (for example, in support of encircled forces). It creates a tight, defensible position against ground attack and is excellent for use in restricted terrain. Special corrections, similar to those used in attitude missions, are required to fire a standard sheaf. Since distance between mortars is decreased, the formation is more vulnerable to air attack and counterfire. A diamond formation is also useful in built-up area (Figure 6-7). By selecting the mortars to fire, an FDC can create different sheaf patterns in the target area without computing time-consuming deflection and elevation corrections.

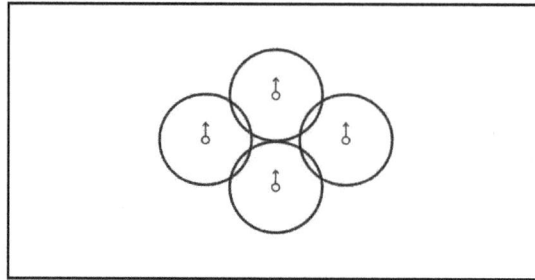

Figure 6-6. Diamond formation

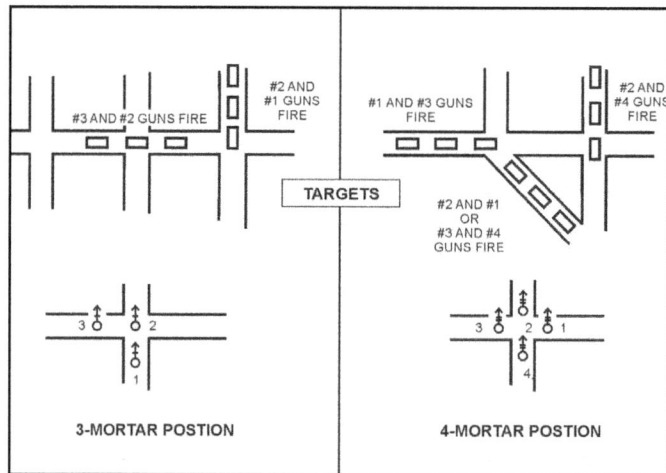

Figure 6-7. Diamond formation used in built-up areas

TRIANGLE FORMATION

6-118.   A triangle formation is a modification of the diamond formation in that only three mortars are used (Figure 6-8). It is used also when the 6400-mil coverage is required. It has the same advantages and disadvantages as the diamond formation.

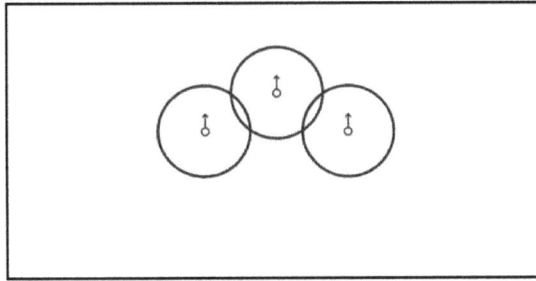

Figure 6-8. Triangle formation

Note. A platoon leader must understand and evaluate the trade-offs required in using the diamond and triangle formations. The ability to provide 6400-mil coverage and increased defensibility is gained by decreasing platoon dispersion and increasing a unit's vulnerability to counterfire.

SECTION IX – CRATER ANALYSIS

6-119.   Crater analysis is an important step toward defeating an enemy's indirect fires. By conducting a simple analysis of the craters produced by enemy fire and by reporting the results, a mortar leader can provide valuable information about the enemy. Crater analysis is the responsibility of all mortar leaders. It can be accomplished during all operations but is most feasible during the defense and stability operations. (See FM 3-09.12/MCRP 3-16.1A for details.)

EQUIPMENT

6-120.   Most of the equipment needed to conduct crater analysis is available in the mortar platoon or section. A key piece, the curvature template, must be constructed. Equipment used to conduct crater analysis include—

* A declinated aiming circle or M2 compass, engineer tape, stakes, and twine or communications wire are used to determine and mark the direction from the crater to the weapon that fired the projectile.
* A curvature template is used to measure the curvature of a fragment to determine the caliber of the shell (Figure 6-9). The template can be constructed of heavy cardboard, acetate, wood, or other appropriate material. Because this figure may be copied and not retain its original dimensions, users should ensure its accuracy by confirming the curves with a protractor.

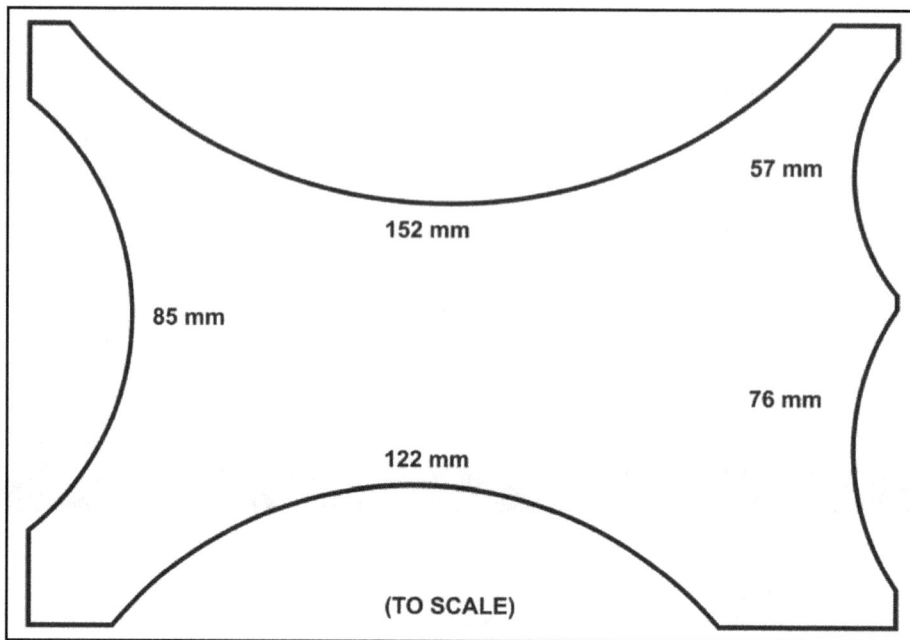

Figure 6-9. Curvature plate

VALUE OF ANALYSIS

6-121.   By studying shelling reports based on crater analysis, artillery experts can—
- Confirm the existence of suspected enemy locations.
- Confirm the type of enemy artillery and obtain an approximate direction to it.
- Detect the presence of new types of enemy weapons, new calibers, or new ammunition manufacturing methods.

INSPECTION OF SHELLED AREAS

6-122.   Shelled areas should be inspected as soon as possible after the shelling. Craters that are exposed to the elements or disturbed by personnel deteriorate quickly and lose their value as a source of information.

CRATER LOCATION

6-123.   Craters must be located accurately for plotting, on charts, maps, or aerial photographs. Deliberate survey is not essential; hasty survey techniques or map spotting usually suffices. Grid locations provided by GPS receivers are sufficiently accurate. Direction can be determined by using an aiming circle or a compass.

DETERMINATION OF DIRECTION

6-124.   A clear pattern produced on the ground by the detonating shell indicates the direction from which the shell came.

6-125.   In determining direction, a mortar leader considers the following:
- The effects of stones, vegetation, stumps, and roots in the path of the projectile.
- Variations in density and type of soil.
- Slope of the terrain at point of impact.

6-126.   From any group, only the most clearly defined and typical craters are used.

6-127.   The direction from which a round was fired is often indicated by the marks made as it passes through trees, snow, or walls. Leaders must not overlook the possible deflection of the shell upon impact with these objects.

6-128.   Often, when an artillery round with a delay fuze is fired at low angle, it bounces or ricochets from the surface of the earth. In doing so, it creates a groove, called a ricochet furrow. Leaders must determine if the shell was deflected before or while making the furrow.

CRATER ANALYSIS PROCEDURES

6-129.   The actual crater created by enemy fire is an excellent source of information to the artillery counterfire planners. A mortar platoon leader should conduct immediate crater analysis and report the results.

6-130.   The first step in crater analysis is to locate a usable crater for determining the direction to the hostile weapon. The crater should be clearly defined on the ground and reasonably fresh. Since the crater is the beginning point for plotting the direction to the enemy weapon, a mortar unit leader determines the grid coordinates of the crater. He determines the direction to the firing weapon by one of the methods described in the following paragraphs. He can collect shell fragments for identifying the type and caliber of the weapon.

6-131.   The projectile direction of flight is determined with reasonable accuracy from its crater or ricochet furrow. By accurately locating the crater and determining the direction of flight, a mortar leader can obtain the azimuth that will pass through or near an enemy position. He can determine the direction to an enemy battery from only one crater or ricochet furrow. However, plotting the intersection of the azimuths from at least three widely separated groups of craters is more accurate (Figure 6-10).

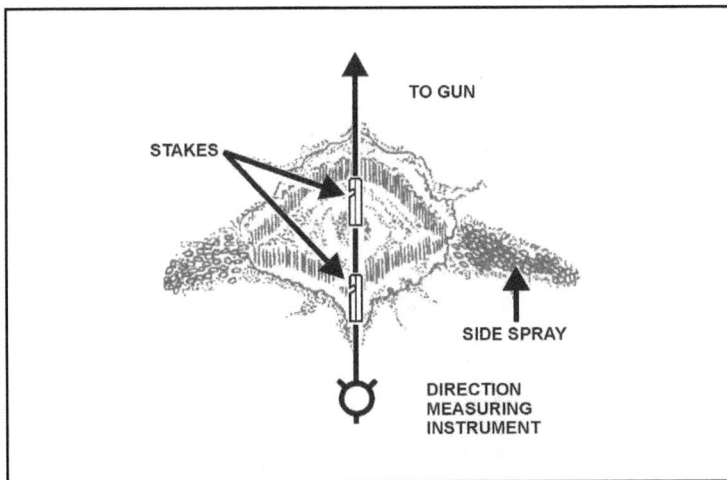

Figure 6-10. Fuze furrow and center of crater method

6-132.   Differences in angle of fall, projectile burst patterns, directions of flight, and time fuze settings can help to distinguish between enemy batteries.

Note. Refer to FM 3-11.4/MCWP 3-37.2 for guidance on friendly troop safety from effects of craters contaminated with CBRN hazards.

LOW-ANGLE FUZE QUICK CRATERS (ARTILLERY)

6-133.   The detonation of a low-angle artillery projectile causes an inner crater. The burst and momentum of the shell carry the effect forward and to the sides, forming an arrow that points to the rear (toward the weapon from which the round was fired). The fuze continues along the line of flight, creating a fuze furrow.

LOW-ANGLE FUZE DELAY CRATERS (ARTILLERY)

6-134.   The two types of fuze delay craters are—

Ricochet Furrow

6-135.   The projectile enters the ground and continues in a straight line for a few feet, causing a ricochet furrow. The projectile normally deflects upward; at the same time, it changes direction, usually to the right as the result of the spin of the projectile. The effect of the airburst can be noted on the ground. Directions obtained from ricochet craters are considered to be the most reliable (Figure 6-11).

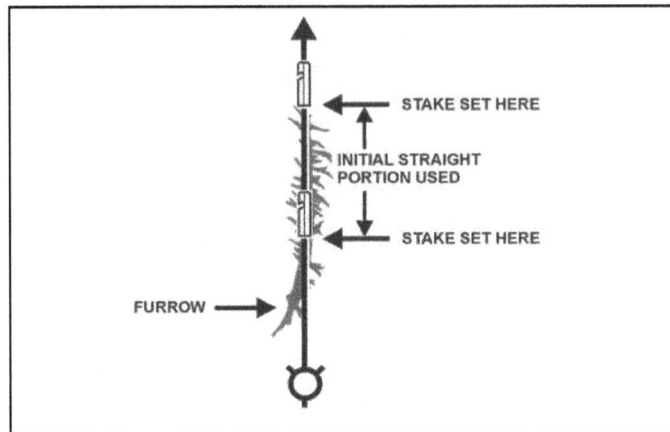

Figure 6-11. Ricochet furrow method

Mine Action

6-136.   A mine action crater occurs when a shell bursts beneath the ground. Occasionally, such a burst leaves a furrow that can be analyzed the same as the ricochet furrow. A mine action crater that does not have a furrow cannot be used to determine the direction to the weapon.

MORTAR SHELL CRATERS (HIGH ANGLE)

6-137.   In typical mortar crater, the turf at the forward edge (the direction away from the hostile mortar) is undercut. The rear edge of the crater is shorn of vegetation and grooved by splinters. When fresh, the crater is covered with loose earth, which must be carefully removed to disclose the firm, burnt inner crater. The ground surrounding the crater is streaked by splinter grooves that radiate from the point of detonation. The ends of the splinter grooves on the rearward side are on an approximate straight line. This line is perpendicular to the line of flight if the crater is on level ground or on a slope with contours perpendicular to the plane of fire. A fuze tunnel is caused by the fuze burying itself at the bottom of the inner crater in front of the point of detonation (Figure 6-12).

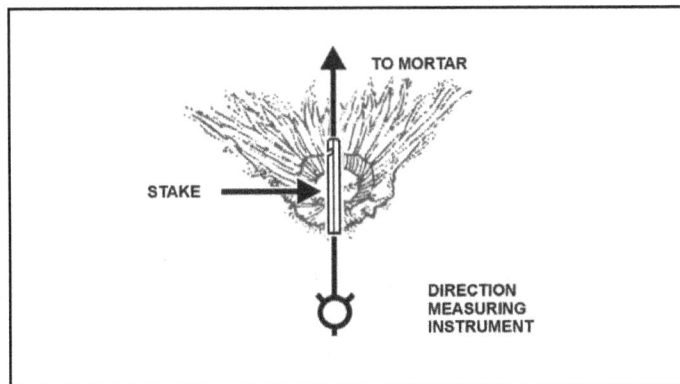

Figure 6-12. Determining direction with mortar crater

ROCKET CRATERS

6-138.   A crater resulting from a rocket impacting with a low or medium angle of fall is analyzed the same as a crater resulting from an artillery projectile armed with fuze quick (Figure 6-13). However, if a rocket impacts with a high angle of fall, the crater is analyzed the same as a crater resulting from a mortar round. The tail fins, rocket motor, body, and other parts of the rocket may be used to determine the caliber and type of rocket fired.

Figure 6-13. Soldier conducting crater analysis of a rocket crater

SHELL FRAGMENT ANALYSIS

6-139.   An expert can identify a shell as to caliber, type, and nation of origin from shell fragments found in the shell crater. (Figure 6-9 is an example of a curvature plate used to determine the caliber of the projectile from its fragments.)

SHELLING REPORTS

6-140.   Bombing, shelling, and mortar bombing reports should be forwarded as soon as possible through fire support channels. Regardless of how little information has been obtained, leaders must not hesitate to forward these reports. Fragmentary or incomplete information (a radio or telephone report) is often valuable in supplementing or confirming existing information. This radio or telephone report may be followed by a written report. Any usable fragments obtained from crater analysis should be tagged (shoe tag) and sent to the battalion intelligence staff officer. As a minimum, the tag must indicate the following:

- The location of the crater.
- The direction to the hostile weapon.
- The date-time group of the shelling.
- The estimated number of rounds fired.

SECTION X – HELICOPTER OPERATIONS

6-141.   Helicopters can rapidly move mortar units and ammunition directly to where they are needed. Mortars usually participate in air assault operations as part of a larger unit. Battalion and company HQ are responsible for the planning, coordination, and control of the air assault operation. (See MCWP 3-11.4 for more details.)

6-142.   Planning and execution of operations involving helicopters require trained, experienced, personnel and proper equipment. This is especially true when using exterior helicopter loads. This chapter provides only a very basic overview for mortar units involved in helicopter operations. Mortar personnel must receive the proper training and certifications before they can execute these operations effectively and safely.

AIR ASSAULT OPERATIONS

6-143.   A mortar unit can use a variety of utility and cargo helicopters. Helicopters allow mortar units to move rapidly to firing positions that may be difficult or impossible to reach. However, helicopter capabilities are greatly affected by weather and altitude and a mortar leader has to consult with his commander, battalion operations section, or aviation liaison officer to get the current lift capacities.

6-144.   Preparation and planning for an air assault is the same for mortar units as it is for other Infantry units. (See FM 3-21.8/MCWP 3-11.1/MCWP 3-11.2 for details.) Forecasting ammunition requirements for the mission is especially important because of the time required to resupply. Depending on the ground tactical plan, mortar units either accompany the Infantry moving toward the objective or maintain their firing position on or near the landing zone. Staying at the landing zone eases ammunition resupply.

6-145.   Mortar units usually participate in air assault operations as part of a larger force. They provide a maneuver force with immediate fire support. A mortar unit's relatively small size and weight makes it a versatile force with the ability to be easily air-lifted. Some employment considerations include—

- Support relationships, priorities, and targets are determined prior to the mission.
- Crew, weapon, and ammunition should be carried together.
- The mortar squad should land on or near the firing position.
- The mortar firing position and firing should not interfere with the aircraft flight patterns.
- The mortar crew should be prepared to fire immediately in any direction.
- Communications should be established immediately.

MORTAR RAIDS

6-146.   A mortar raid is the rapid movement of mortar assets by air or ground into a position to attack a high-priority target with fires. Normally, the raid is for an extremely short duration and should not involve sustained operations. Detailed planning, surprise, and speed in execution are the key factors in the successful conduct of a raid.

MISSION COMMAND/COMMAND AND CONTROL

6-147.   In a mortar raid, three commanders are required: single ground, security force, and firing force.

TIMING AND REHEARSALS

6-148.   Timing is critical. Last minute updates on the enemy are important. These updates may be provided by a unit pre-positioned prior to the raid or a UAS, although units must ensure that the observation of the target landing zone or objective does not alert the enemy. For example, a sniper team may infiltrate to a position to observe the objective, make any fire adjustments necessary during the raid, and provide a battle damage assessment after the raid.

6-149.   Rehearsals are critical to a successful mortar raid. Mortar units should repeatedly practice to quickly and accurately—

- Mount and lay the mortar onto the first target.
- Break out and prepare ammunition.
- Fire the mortar.
- Re-lay to another target.
- Break down the mortar and prepare for extraction.

PLANNING AND PREPARATION

6-150.   Standard air assault procedures apply in the conduct of a mortar raid, with some additional considerations. Because the target is likely to be temporary, the planning phase may be very short. An effective TACSOP is essential. Pilots must understand load composition and configuration. Some planning considerations are as follows:

- An Infantry unit, preferably a platoon or larger, may be designated as the security force. They normally land prior to the mortars, secure the firing position, provide security during the mortar unit extraction, and be the last lift off of the position.
- The number of mortars taken forward on the raid is determined by target analysis, munitions effects tables, aircraft availability, and desired damage effect.
- Additional personnel may be attached to assist in moving ammunition and re-rigging equipment.
- A pathfinder unit may be assigned to control the aircraft and landing zone.
- Mortars, ammunition, and mortar crews may all be carried internally or the mortar system and ammunition may be carried externally.
- The type and amount of ammunition carried and its effect on the target.
- Firing data can be precomputed by the FDC.
- When determining landing zone location, the highest charge possible should be planned to increase stand-off range.

PICKUP ZONE OPERATIONS

6-151.   Pickup zone operations are generally the same as with the air assault mission.

LANDING ZONE OPERATIONS

6-152.   Considerations for the control of the landing zone include—

- Designated personnel control the landing zone. The advance party orients aircraft on the landing points as with any air assault mission.
- When aircraft have delivered their loads to the landing zone, they move to the lager area.
- When the fire mission is complete, mortar crews prepare weapons for sling load extraction. Designated members of the advance party assume the duties as hookup team(s). Security for the area is most difficult at this time, and mortar squad members may have to be designated to provide security.

RESPONSIBILITIES

6-153.   Three different elements are normally involved in a mortar unit helicopter operation: a maneuver unit HQ requests the mission, an aviation unit provides the aircraft, and a mortar unit or designated unit loads and receives the cargo. The responsibilities and functions of each element are discussed below.

6-154. A battalion, squadron, or company requesting the mission is responsible for—
- Selecting, preparing, and controlling the landing site. (Pathfinders can be of great assistance in this area.)
- Requisitioning all equipment needed for sling-load operations, including slings, cargo bags, nets, and containers.
- Storing, inspecting, and maintaining all sling-load equipment.
- Providing enough trained ground crews for rigging and inspecting all the loads, guiding the helicopters, hooking up the loads, and clearing the aircraft for departure.
- Securing and protecting sensitive items of supply and equipment.
- Providing load de-rigging and disposition instructions to the mortar platoon.
- Providing disposition instructions to the mortar platoon and aviation units for the return of slings, bags, cargo nets, and containers.

6-155. The aviation unit is responsible for—
- Coordinating with the battalion and appointing a liaison.
- Advising the unit of the limitations on the size and weight of acceptable loads before they are rigged.
- Advising on the suitability of the selected pickup and landing sites.
- Assisting in the recovery and return of the slings, cargo bags, nets, and containers.
- Establishing safety procedures to ensure uniformity and understanding of duties and responsibilities between the ground crew and flight crew.

6-156. The commander of the operation designates the unit to control and manage the operations at the pickup site. These include marking, loading, rigging, and hooking up cargo. The mortar unit may be tasked for—
- Selecting, preparing, marking, and controlling the landing site.
- Ensuring trained ground crews are available to guide the aircraft in and de-rig the load.
- Coordinating with the battalion logistics staff officer for the control and return of all air items.
- Preparing, coordinating, and inspecting backloads, such as slings and cargo bags, and having them ready for hookup or loading.

SITE SELECTION AND PREPARATION

6-157. Logistics and tactical considerations must be analyzed to ensure the landing site is in the proper location to support the mission, the area is accessible to the aircraft, and the mortar firing does not interfere with aircraft operations. (See MCWP 3-11.4 for details.)

MARKING THE LANDING SITE

6-158. During daylight operations, the landing site can be marked with signal panels. Because the rotor wash from the helicopters, they must be securely staked down. During daylight operations, the landing site can also be marked with colored smoke or by the ground guide. The guide holds both arms straight up over his head or holds a folded VS-17 signal panel chest high. (See MCWP 3-11.4 for details.)

SLING LOAD OPERATIONS

6-159. This section discusses general load hookup and release procedures. (See FM 4-20.197/MCRP 4-11.3E VOL I for details.)

PLANNING

6-160. Prior planning, along with the coordination of plans with an aviation liaison officer, is essential for a smooth, safe operation. During the planning phase, the entire mission is reviewed to include aircraft limitations, landing site selection, and items to be lifted along with their weights. Commanders and staffs should consider the following planning factors:
- Equipment to be moved.
- Alternate means of movement available.

- Number of aircraft and sorties required.
- Landing site and required delivery time.
- Special lifting devices required.
- Primary and alternate radio frequencies and quantity of radios required.
- Ground crew and aircraft emergency procedures.
- Review of maps, landing site description, and local terrain features.
- Safety hazards.

PLACEMENT OF LOADS FOR PICKUP

6-161. Loads for external pickup should be arranged for ease of pickup. Loads should be placed on level ground away from obstacles and should be prearranged for the type of aircraft being used. When triple-hook nets or cargo loads are to be used, loads must fit under the aircraft and rigged to allow some movement and not bind on each other when released separately.

RESPONSIBILITIES

6-162. Since the unit owning the equipment is responsible for properly rigging the equipment and using correct procedures during the sling load operation, the ground crew must be thoroughly trained in the complete operation. Ground crew duties include—

- Clearing the landing site.
- Rigging and de-rigging the loads.
- Directing the aircraft over the load for hookup and over the landing point for load release.
- Hooking up the load.

SAFETY CONSIDERATIONS

6-163. Ground crew personnel must be careful and alert at all times while working near operating aircraft because the hazards found in operating under a hovering helicopter are not always apparent. Only trained crews should be used to rig loads and hook them to the aircraft.

Discharging Static Electricity

6-164. In flight, stored static electric energy of any helicopter increases with helicopter weight, low humidity, and amount of debris blown by the rotor system. When a helicopter touches the ground, this charge is grounded out. However, while a helicopter is in flight, this charge remains stored in the aircraft. A ground crewman provides a path for this charge to follow into the ground when he connects the apex fitting to the cargo hook. This charge may cause severe electrical burn or injury and has to be discharged safely prior to the ground-crew touching the aircraft.

Personal Protective Equipment

6-165. Ground personnel involved in helicopter sling load operations are exposed to hazards that could cause serious injury. These hazards include noise, rotor wash, static electricity, flying debris, and operations around suspended cargo. Certain items of personal protective equipment must be worn to provide for maximum personnel safety. These include—

- **Head and neck protection**.
- **Eye and ear protection**.
- **Hand protection**. All personnel should wear leather gloves to help protect their hands and fingers. If available, all static wand persons should serviceable electrical workers gloves.

- **Clothing**. The ground crew should roll their sleeves down and button their shirts and jackets. Personnel should remove watches, rings, and jewelry to prevent them from being caught in the sling set or load. Personnel must wear their identification tags during a sling load operation.
- **Other equipment**, to include—
  - The static discharge wand is used to protect the hookup man from static electric shock.
  - Smoke grenades are used to mark the location of the landing site and indicate wind direction.
  - Flashlights with wands are used to give hand-and-arm signals at night.

PERSONNEL REQUIREMENTS

6-166. The number of ground crew personnel needed for sling load operations depends primarily on how a commander plans to accomplish his mission. Selected personnel or all unit members can be trained as ground crew members. Consideration for the number of crews needed should include the quantity and type of equipment to be sling loaded and the number of available aircraft.

PERSONNEL BRIEFING

6-167. All personnel involved with the mission should be thoroughly briefed on their duties and responsibilities. The briefing should include, but not be limited to, discussion of the following items:
- Cargo to be carried.
- Operating area description and peculiarities.
- Aircraft approach direction, cargo hookup/release, and aircraft departure.
- Ground/aircrew duties including communications, static grounding, personnel approach/exit procedures, and special safety precautions.
- Procedures to follow in the event of aircraft emergency.

GROUND CREW

6-168. Ground crew teams are classified by their locations. A hookup team is at the supported unit landing site and a receiving team is at the receiving unit landing site. They are organized as follows—
- **Hookup team** consists of a minimum of three persons. The team is made up of the signalman, static wand person, and the hookup man. (See FM 4-20.197/MCRP 4-11.3E VOL I for more detailed instructions for each member.)
- **Receiving team** consists of a signalman to direct the placement of the load and, if required, both a hookup and static wand man. The hookup and static wand individuals are necessary if they have to manually open the cargo hook.

HOOKUP AND RECEIVING TEAM RESPONSIBILITIES

6-169. Each member of the hookup and receiving team has the following specific responsibilities:
- **Signalman**. The signalman directs the movement of the helicopter with standard hand signals. (See FM 4-20.197/MCRP 4-11.3E VOL I for more details.)
- **Static wand person**. The static wand person must be thoroughly familiar with the effects of static electricity. He provides the primary protection against severe electrical shock for the hookup/manual release crew by touching the static discharge wand to the cargo hook and maintaining contact until the hookup/manual release crew clears the load.
- **Hookup man**. The hookup man positions himself on or near the load in a stable position and attaches the sling or net apex fitting to the cargo hook. If required, he performs the manual release of the cargo hook and therefore must be trained in manual release procedures for aircraft used.
- **Additional personnel**. Any extra personnel, such as equipment operators, will be positioned so that they are clear of the maneuver area and away from the landing points. The rendezvous point is a good position for these additional personnel.

RECEIVING TEAM RESPONSIBILITIES

6-170. A receiving team, along with a helicopter support team supervisor, is responsible for—
- Locating, clearing, and marking the receiving landing site.
- Establishing and maintaining required communications.
- Directing and controlling helicopters within the landing site.
- Discharging static electricity if manual release is required.
- Conducting manual release of the sling from the cargo hook, as required.
- De-rigging delivered cargo.

PREPARING FOR THE OPERATION

6-171. A sling load operation requires the following:
- **Establishing security**. A unit commander designates a separate unit for local security. Prior to the operation, a security element clears the landing zone area and establishes positions.
- **Preparing the landing zone**. Once a commander has designated the areas to be used for sling load operations, ground crew personnel clear the zone and set up markings to identify the area from the air.
- **Inspecting the cargo**. Before the operation starts, ground crews must make sure that the cargo to be transported has been correctly prepared, rigged, and inspected for sling load movement. (See FM 4-20.197/MCRP 4-11.3E VOL I for details regarding inspections of all loads.) Inspection includes checking for—
    - Bolts and retention pins in lifting shackles.
    - Unauthorized repairs or improper replacement parts on lifting devices. Equipment could be damaged if not prepared and rigged properly.
    - Breakaway safety ties.
    - Other ties.

GENERAL HOOKUP PROCEDURES

6-172. The following is general guidance for hookup procedures. (See FM 4-20.197/MCRP 4-11.3E VOL I for details.)

PRIOR TO HOOKUP

6-173. Guidelines for procedures prior to hookup are as follows:
- Positions in relation to the aircraft are referred to by a clock system with 12 o'clock being the direction of flight. Avoid approaching or departing under the aircraft from the 4 o'clock position clockwise around to the 8 o'clock position due to hazards presented by landing gear, tail rotor, and the inability of aircrews to monitor ground crews.
- One side of the load is designated as the aircraft emergency landing area and the other side is safety side/rendezvous point.
- A static wand person drives the grounding rod into the ground on the side of the load opposite the rendezvous point/exit path.

POSITIONING OF PERSONNEL

6-174. Personnel are positioned as follows:
- A signalman positions himself upwind of the load, facing the load and aircraft.
- A hookup man and static wand person are on top of the load. The hookup man is the first to depart the load; he should be on the side of the load closest to the rendezvous point exit path. The static wand person is the last person to leave the load, so he should be on the opposite side of the load.
- A hookup team may be stationed on the ground along the side of the load if the load is difficult or unsafe to stand on.

HOOKUP

6-175. Hookup team personnel should kneel down, brace themselves, and hold securely to the load because of the rotor wash. A hookup man will have the apex fitting/web ring in his hands ready for hookup. A static wand person will hold the static discharge wand high enough so that the red line or the red area is above the hookup team's helmets. Hookup is achieved as follows:

- The signalman identifies himself and the load to the aircraft.
- The hookup team must alertly watch the helicopter during the complete operation.
- The pilot maneuvers in position over the load as directed by the signalman and the aircrew member.
- The hookup team stands up and watches for the cargo hook or moves under the aircraft for hookup on signal from the aircrew if not pre-positioned on or by the load.
- Once the helicopter is in a stable hover and correctly positioned, the signalman signals the pilot to maintain his hover and the ground crew begins the hookup.
- The static wand person grounds the cargo hook prior to any contact by the hookup man and maintains that grounding contact until the hookup is complete.
- The hookup man places the apex fitting/web ring on the cargo hook as soon as he can reach it after the hook is grounded.
- After completing the hookup, the hookup man climbs off the load. The static wand person breaks contact with the cargo hook and then drops the static discharge wand to the ground. Both proceed to the rendezvous point or other briefed location.
- The signalman signals to the pilot that the load is hooked up. He then signals the pilot to move upward to take the slack out of the sling legs.
- As the aircraft rises, the signalman and hookup team watch the load for any problems with the rigging or if the load may require correction.
- When the load is 10 to 20 feet higher than the surrounding loads or obstacles, the signalman gives the takeoff signal in the direction he wishes the pilot to depart the landing site.

RECEIVING TEAM AND LOAD RELEASE

6-176. Landing site preparation, safety precautions, protective equipment, and ground crew requirements for load release are similar to those required for hookup. A release team signalman is located in the same position with respect to the helicopter and landing point and directs the pilot to the load release point. When the load is over the release point, he signals the pilot to lower the load to the ground and hover to the side before giving the pilot the "release-load" signal. After the aircrew signals to the ground crew, they approach the cargo hook to manually release the load. The static wand holder uses the static discharge wand to contact the cargo hook. The hookup man either depresses the spring-loaded keeper on the cargo hook or rotates the manual release knob/lever. When the load is released, the signalman gives the "affirmative" signal, followed by the "take-off" signal.

EXTERNAL CARGO CARRYING DEVICES

6-177. The mortar unit must be able to rig and de-rig all of the common helicopter sling-load carrying devices. (See FM 4-20.197/MCRP 4-11.3E VOL I and FM 4-20.198/MCRP 4-11.3E VOL II for more details.)

RIGGING EQUIPMENT

6-178. The following equipment may be available for rigging mortar equipment and ammunition:

- **Sling sets**. The two standard helicopter sling sets are the 10,000-pound and 25,000-pound capacity and come in their own aviator kit bag.
- **Pallet slings**. By using a pallet sling, palletized cargo can be moved directly to the mortar platoon by helicopter without having to reconfigure the load. The pallet sling used by the Army has a 4,000-pound carrying capacity and carries a standard 40- by 48-inch pallet.
- **A-22 cargo bag**. An A-22 cargo bag is used to transport any standard palletized load, ammunition, or loose cargo up to 2,200 pounds.

- **Cargo nets**. Two sizes of cargo nets are currently in the Army system—the 5,000- and 10,000-pound capacity cargo nets. These nets provide a means to externally transport ammunition or general cargo.
- **The 5,000- and 10,000-pound capacity net**. The 5,000- and 10,000-pound capacity octagon-shaped cargo nets are constructed from interwoven nylon cord.

LONGLINE SLING PROCEDURES

6-179.   The longline sling system improves tactical efficiency and integrity of operations by carrying the crew and sling-loading ammunition and equipment on the same aircraft. This system reduces aircraft lift requirements and ensures mortar crew integrity. Using a longline sling, the aircraft lands next to the rigged load. A ground crewman crawls under the helicopter and connects the apex fitting to the aircraft cargo hook. The entire mortar crew boards the aircraft to include the hookup person. As the aircraft lifts off the ground, an air crewmember observes the load and directs the pilot over the top of the load. This system allows all of the equipment, crew, and accompanying ammunition to be transported in one lift. Also, all ground personnel can load onto the aircraft leaving no one on the ground.

SECTION XI – MORTAR UNITS IN URBAN OPERATIONS

6-180.   Mortar is the most-used, indirect-fire weapon in urban combat. Mortars can be used to obscure, neutralize, suppress, or illuminate during urban operations. Mortars have distinct advantages during urban operations. Their high rate of fire, steep angle of fall, and short minimum range give mortar sections the ability to mass fire power on specific enemy positions in the tight confines of city fighting. The use of multioption fuzes and variety of ammunition increases mortar fire versatility. (See FM 3-06.11/MCWP 3-35.3 for details.)

POSITION SELECTION AND PREPARATION

6-181.   Selection of mortar positions depends on the size of buildings, size of the urban area, and mission. Special techniques can be used to position and lay mortars. These include—

- When the depth of the defensive position is shallow, or when suitable firing positions are not available, mortars may have to be positioned directly behind the reserve.
- Displacement is often executed by section or squad.
- Key considerations for selection of positions include the minimum range of the weapon, mask and overhead clearance, terrain suitable for setting baseplates, dispersion, and accessibility.

6-182.   Use of existing structures for hide positions is recommended (for example, garages, office buildings, or highway overpasses) to afford maximum protection and minimize the camouflage effort. With proper use of mask, survivability can be enhanced. If the mortar has to fire in excess of 885 mils to clear a frontal mask, an enemy counter battery threat is reduced. These principles can be used in both offense and defense. (See Chapter 8 for more details on survivability techniques.)

6-183.   Mortars should not be mounted directly on concrete. However, sandbags may be used as a buffer as follows:

- Use two or three layers.
- Butt them against a curb or a wall.
- Extend them at least one sandbag width beyond the baseplate.

6-184.   Rubble may be used to make a parapet for firing positions.

6-185.   Mortars are usually not placed on top of buildings because lack of cover and mask make them vulnerable. They should not be placed inside buildings with damaged roofs unless the structure's ability has been checked. Overpressure can injure personnel, and the shock on the floor can weaken or collapse the structure.

RULES OF ENGAGEMENT AND CLEARANCE OF FIRES

6-186.   When civilians and significant cultural and religious structures are present, ROE will probably affect how mortar units fire. Rules of engagement may restrict ammunition, targets, and conditions under which mortars can fire. Clearance of fires may also reduce responsiveness of fires.

COMMUNICATIONS

6-187. Satellite communications can reduce interference usually encountered when using FM radios in urban areas. Structures reduce radio ranges; however, remoting of antennas to upper floors or roofs may improve communications and enhance operator survivability. Another applicable technique is use of radio retransmissions. Digital systems are affected the same way as FM communications. Other possible techniques to increase communications reliability include using—

- Existing civilian systems to supplement a unit's capability.
- Wire communications, messengers, and visual signals.
- Wire communications between FDC and mortars squads since these elements are usually close to each other.

MAGNETIC INTERFERENCE

6-188. All magnetic instruments are affected by surrounding structural steel, electrical cables, and automobiles. Minimum distance guidelines for M2 aiming circles are difficult to apply. (See FM 3-22.90 for details.) Such features as the direction of a street may be used instead of a distant aiming point.

AIMING POSTS

6-189. Posts can be placed vertically in dirt-filled cans or ammunition boxes if the frontal area is covered by concrete or asphalt. Natural aiming points, such as edges of buildings or lampposts, may also be used.

HIGH-EXPLOSIVE AMMUNITION

6-190. During urban combat operations, mortar HE fires are heavily used. Some of their greatest contributions are interdicting supplies, implementing evacuation efforts, and reinforcing an enemy rear just behind their forward defensive positions. Although mortar fires are often targeted against roads and other open areas, the natural dispersion of indirect fires with unguided projectiles can result in many hits on buildings. Leaders must use care when planning mortar fires during urban operations to minimize collateral damage.

6-191. High-explosive ammunition gives good results when used on lightly built structures within cities, particularly a 120-mm projectile. It does not perform well against reinforced concrete found in larger urban areas.

6-192. When using HE ammunition in urban fighting, point detonating fuzes are normally the most effective. A delay fuze setting allows the projectile to penetrate floors before detonating. The nature of built-up areas can cause proximity fuzes to function prematurely. However, proximity fuzes are useful in attacking targets, such as OPs on tops of buildings.

ILLUMINATION

6-193. In the offense, visible illuminating rounds are planned to burst above the objective to put enemy troops in the light. If illumination is behind the objective, enemy troops would be in shadows rather than light. In the defense, illumination can be planned to burst behind friendly troops to put them in shadows and place enemy troops in light. Buildings reduce the effectiveness of illumination but continuous illumination requires close coordination between the FO and FDC to produce the proper effect by bringing illumination over defensive positions as enemy troops approach buildings. (See Figure 6-14.)

6-194. Infrared illuminating rounds should be used in the same manner as visible-light illuminating rounds. When employing IR illumination, leaders and FOs should consider whether an enemy has night vision devices.

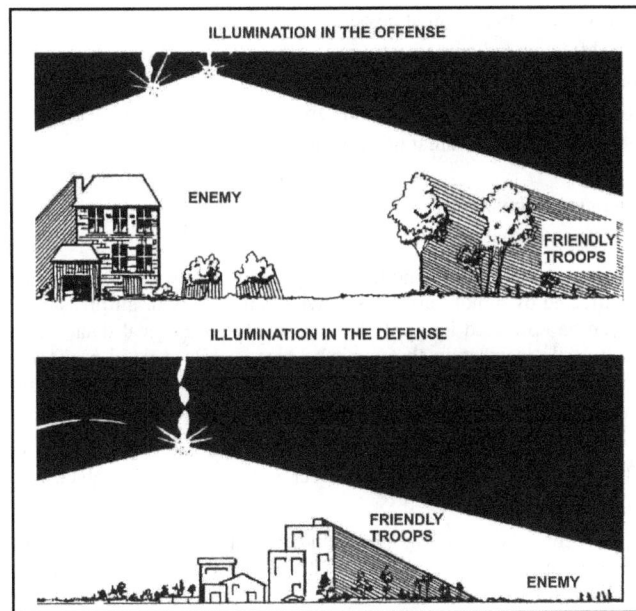

Figure 6-14. Use of illumination fires during urban operations

SECTION XII – MOUNTAIN OPERATIONS

6-195.   Infantry units are usually the most suitable force for this type of combat. Small-unit commanders often operate semi-independently. The most reliable sources of combat power for a small unit leader are often organic weapons found at the company and battalion.

6-196.   Mortars play a critical role in mountain operations. Their high-angle fire can seek out and destroy enemy forces that are almost invulnerable to other forms of fires. Heavy and medium mortars can move over most terrain to provide fire support for a commander. Light mortars can keep up with Infantry no matter what the terrain. Because ammunition is limited and usually difficult to resupply in the mountains, mortar leaders have to be especially vigilant about expenditures. Mortar leaders should advise their commander on how mortars can best support his operations, appropriate targets for mortars, methods of attack, location of firing positions, and expenditure of ammunition on a specific target.

6-197.   Use of meteorological data in the mountains is critical. Wind direction and speed frequently change. Range may be dramatically increased. Therefore, accuracy is decreased without frequent meteorological data updates.

EFFECTS OF MOUNTAINS ON MORTAR OPERATIONS

6-198.   Mortar fire can strike targets that low-angle fires cannot reach. These include targets on reverse slopes, in narrow ravines or trenches, and in forests or towns. Light mortar units can accompany Infantry anywhere they can go. Although having to be moved and resupplied by vehicles, heavy mortars can occupy firing positions well forward.

6-199.   Units deployed to a mountainous AO must understand the effects of the terrain and weather on operations. (See FM 3-97.6/FMFM 7-29 for details.) Some of the characteristics of mountains that affect mortar operations are—

- Rugged, compartmented terrain with steep slopes.
- Large AOs requiring dispersal of units.
- Limited infrastructure and road networks, limited areas to maneuver, and limited resupply routes.
- Isolated small unit actions.

- Difficulty in concentrating combat power.
- High altitude effect on helicopter support.
- Terrain that favors the defender.
- Weather that may span the entire spectrum from extreme cold with ice and snow to extreme heat.
- Heavy precipitation and the threat of flash floods.
- High winds.
- Large temperature fluctuations.
- Rapidly changing weather.

6-200. At high elevations, atmospheric conditions may significantly alter an indirect fire round's trajectory. The projectile may be affected by minor variations in wind, air density or air pressure, and air temperature from round to round. This can be corrected by applying current meteorological data and registration. Metrological data accounts for much of the correction that must be made while a valid registration mission helps ensure increased first round accuracy. Because of the rapid changes in weather, meteorological data should be frequently updated.

6-201. Registration missions should be conducted at an elevation close to that of a particular offensive mission. Because altitude difference can greatly affect accuracy, a large change in elevation requires the conduction of a new registration.

6-202. It is important to remember that a mortar round impacting 50 meters away from an intended target on fairly level or close to level terrain may have good effects. However, the same horizontal 50 meters in mountainous terrain may cause the round to impact significantly above or below the target. Due to a steep mountain slope, the impact of these rounds may render no effect at all as shown in Figure 6-15. Observers should be aware of this and consider creeping rounds for adjustments to increase the probability of target effects. Observers should also consider creeping adjustment rounds from a lower elevation up to a target because impacts over a ridgeline are difficult or impossible to observe.

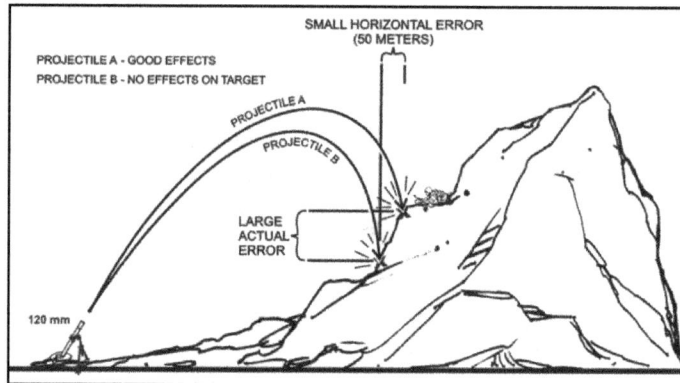

Figure 6-15. Effects of slope on hits

PREPARATION

6-203. To be successful, mortar units have to have accurate and timely information on the type of operations and environment that they can expect to encounter. Mortar unit leaders use this information to prepare their subordinates and equipment. This preparation falls into the general categories of physical preparation, training for the specific operational environment, and having the right equipment properly prepared.

PHYSICAL FITNESS

6-204. Every member of a unit must be in excellent physical condition. The extremes of operating in mountains demand even greater emphasis on being in the best physical shape possible. Leaders cannot function if they are not physically ready to keep up with their unit. Individual physical fitness is one key to successful operations in any combat environment, but especially in mountainous terrain or when faced with temperature extremes. Physically fit troops are better able to handle fatigue and stress created by the rigors of daily tasks. Mortarmen must also be trained to carry additional weight and lift heavy objects. Fatigue is a major cause of carelessness and complacency and is a major factor in an individual's risk of becoming a casualty. Fatigue rapidly degrades a troop's ability to think clearly and accomplish complex tasks, such as planning fires and conducting FDC operations. (See Chapter 9 for more details.)

TRAINING

6-205.   Mortar units should train for the conditions that they will face once deployed. Some units have the advantage of being able to contact their opposite number in-country and receiving information on the conditions and requirements of their future AO. All unit leaders should obtain the necessary security clearance to access this information. From the information gained from their contact with their opposite number in country, the mortar units should identify—

- Number of sections the unit will operate.
- Types of mortars.
- Number of firing positions to be occupied.
- Any in-theater augmentation of mortar weapons and equipment.
- Locations of the most dangerous positions.
- Types of missions fired.
- Type and availability of artillery support in the AO including counter.

6-206.   Based on the information above, a mortar leader can begin to plan and conduct training. Training includes—

- Becoming proficient on all mortar systems.
- Cross training mortar crews and FDC personnel.
- Certifying all indirect crewmen in FDC duties.
- Training attached riflemen as assistant gunners and ammunition bearers.
- Conducting missions with minimum mortar crews and FDCs.
- Operating and controlling fires for the planned number of mortars deployed.
- Using deployment to training centers to become proficient in controlling more than two mortar sections.
- Calculating fires in mountainous terrain, including vertical interval.

EQUIPMENT

6-207.   An incoming mortar unit usually prepares and ships their equipment well before the unit deploys. Some considerations when shipping equipment include—

- Breaking down and shipping material to the company or unit where the mortar unit will establish its fire position.
- Developing FDC packets with sufficient forms to last until the unit can order in-country.

OPERATIONAL CONSIDERATIONS

6-208.   Once in-country, the mortar unit has to be able to immediately take over and conduct missions. There may only be a brief transition period with the unit being relieved. The following are considerations for operations in mountainous terrain:

FIRES

6-209. Mortar units in the mountains conduct fire missions using the tactics and techniques discussed in this manual. (See FM 3-22.90 and FM 3-22.91 for more details regarding technical procedures.) Specific considerations for mountain operations can be categorized under—

Fire Direction Center Procedures and Types of Fires

6-210. Standard FDC procedures apply in mountain operations. However, the application of mortar tactics, techniques, and procedures may have to be modified to meet the special characteristics and conditions of mountain warfare. These special characteristics and conditions may include—

* Control and coordination of fires from often widely separated mortar units.
* Assignment of an appropriate mortar unit when multiple units are in range of the target.
* Frequency of the types of missions a mortar unit fires. For example, some units may fire the majority of their missions using the direct lay technique while others may use the FDC.
* Close proximity to targets to the mortar units and the use of the direct lay technique.
* Requirement to rapidly perform large deflection and elevation changes to fire multiple targets close to the firing unit.
* Requirement for minimum mortar crews and FDC personnel.
* Frequent updating of meteorological data because of rapidly changing conditions.
* Requirement to include target elevation in the call for fire.
* Bold elevation changes in order to adjust mortar fires on steep terrain.
* Enforcement of the priority of fires.
* Detection and adjustment of fires from multiple sources.
* Understanding the effects of altitude on the adjustment of rounds.
* Registering mortars at the same altitude as the anticipated targets.
* Steeps slopes and their effects on fires.
* Close coordination with CAS and close combat attack aircraft.

Ammunition

6-211. Ammunition and fuze settings are similar in mountains and more conventional AOs. However, specific ammunition and fuzing considerations for operations in mountains include—

* On rocky soil, HE with an impact fuze setting can generate secondary rock fragments.
* On terrain with large boulders, HE with a proximity fuze setting may cover a greater area than HE with an impact fuze.
* Snow may reduce the effect of ammunition with an impact fuze.
* The 81-mm M819 RP round is well-suited for the mountain fight due its mechanical time/super quick fuze.
* Units may receive all possible types of ammunition in the inventory. Because some types of ammunition data are not loaded into computers, tabular firing tables must be kept on hand for all ammunition.

Mortar Positions

6-212. Mortar units in mountains may be positioned within or outside perimeters and may be subject to enemy direct and indirect fires. Considerations to reduce the effect of enemy direct and indirect fires on the mortar position include—

* Prepare for 6400-mil operations.
* Protect the mortar firing point and FDC by digging in or building barriers and overhead cover for the FDC, personnel shelters, and ammunition storage areas. (See chapter 8 for more detail).
* If isolated from other units—
  * Attach rifle Infantry units.
  * Establish security.

- Assign defensive positions to mortar squads.
- Assign sectors of fire to dismounted and mounted direct fire weapons.
- Position obstacles and deploy M18 claymore mines.
- Be prepared to fire missions while under fire.
- Keep ready ammunition under cover.
- Mark close in targets with aiming posts and marking the sides of the mortar pit.

Mortar Gunnery

6-213. Mortar gunnery has to accommodate the unique conditions of mountains. These include—
- Anticipating poor visibility due to clouds, fog, or snow.
- Using remote sensors.
- Planning HE with proximity fuze setting on reverse slopes of hills and mountains.
- Planning frequent meteorological updates due to rapidly changing weather conditions.

Clearance of Fires

6-214. Clearance of fires can take a lot of time and reduce responsiveness. Units may be able to reduce the effects of clearance of fires procedures by establishing free-fire areas prior to missions.

Command and Control

6-215. Control of mortar units is difficult in mountains. Units are often separated by terrain features and cannot reinforce each other. It is usually a small unit fight with a leader using what weapons he has immediately available. Mission command/command and control considerations include—
- Spanning of control issues caused by assignment of additional mortar squads to the unit.
- Coordinating and controlling fires from widely separated mortar units.
- Masking effects of mountains or intervening hills on radio communications and visual signaling.
- Requiring directional antennas or retransmission stations to increase range.

Movement and Maneuver/Maneuver

6-216. Units need to be prepared for contact at all times. Units are especially vulnerable to attack in the mountains while conducting a road movement because roads channel their movement and the inability to maneuver off-road. Mortar units normally maneuver as part of a larger unit. They establish firing position on or close to the axis of advance. They can also maneuver along a separate axis to establish firing positions with an attached security element. If possible, the following methods should be used:
- Employ helicopters to move mortars to positions of advantage.
- Move heavy mortars forward by vehicle as far as possible and then establish a firing position. This position may also become the base of resupply for the mortar units with the maneuver element.
- If use of trailers is limited, carry mortar and ammunition in the vehicle.
- Establish and use procedures to counter ambushes, defeat roadblocks, and counter direct and indirect fires.
- Develop and use movement security including orientation of weapons, units assigned sectors, operations at the halt, and other actions.
- Practice immediate action drills, including near/far ambush and roadblock.
- Position units in defilade to increase survivability. However, beware of snow and rock slides in these positions.
- Know that on narrow mountain roads, turnaround locations for large vehicles and those pulling trailers may be scarce. Locate potential turnaround points during route reconnaissance.
- Plan for air reconnaissance of routes and positions.

PROTECTION

6-217. Mortar units are often located within perimeters and may be exposed to enemy direct and indirect fires. (See Chapter 8 for details regarding the protection of the mortar crew and mortar.) Operations in the mountains however, may require additional considerations, including—

- If necessary, build up mortar firing positions instead of digging down. This allows for a level position, reduces digging in rocky soil, and reduces the effects of precipitation. Soil-filled wire and fabric or metal containers, or other barrier materials may be used to build up mortar pit walls and protect the FDC.
- Understand there may be limited space to build supplementary positions.
- Camouflage the position. Have patrols take pictures at multiple angles from any surrounding high ground to determine effectiveness of the camouflage.
- Constantly improve protection for the firing position.
- Consider the danger of flash flooding in dry river beds or flood plains.
- Consider using open-column convoy techniques through mountain passes and other restrictive terrain.

SUSTAINMENT/LOGISTICS

6-218. Adequate sustainment/logistics in the mountains is difficult. The provision of sufficient mortar ammunition is a special concern of a mortar unit leader. Some of these considerations include—

- Using helicopter and airdrop resupply when appropriate.
- Planning for increased maintenance on vehicles and equipment due to the increased strain caused by terrain and weather.
- Planning for additional cold weather contingency items required for sustained unit operations.

6-219. Inspections of equipment and preventive maintenance are critical in mountain operations. Because of extremes in weather, equipment requires more inspection and maintenance to keep it operational. For example, fire missions in mountains are extremely hard on mortar baseplates.

6-220. Ammunition management is one of the most important tasks for a mortar platoon or section in a heavy mortar fight. Units should try to keep numerous types of all ammunition on hand at all times. A challenge is to maintain a sufficient amount of high-use ammunition on hand and in the supply system. Some considerations are as follows:

- Closely coordinating the supply of ammunition with company XO or first sergeant/company gunnery sergeant (Marine Corps).
- Maintaining a close relationship with ammunition personnel in the forward support company or brigade support battalion.
- Anticipating usage and accurately ordering ammunition.
- Keeping track of the amount, type, and lot numbers both on hand and on order.
- Ensuring proper storage of ammunition.
- Properly storing ammunition, using the following methods as needed:
  - When possible, using pallet material to keep ammunition off the ground.
  - Using material available to provide overhead cover.
  - Not storing all mortar ammunition in one location on the base.
- Having a plan to dispose of ammunition packing material.
- Having a plan to dispose of charge increments.
- Performing preventive maintenance checks and services on mortars after every mission, if possible.
- Identifying and reporting maintenance problems early.
- Developing procedures to accurately report rounds fired per mortar despite heavy usage.
- Borescoping and pulling over all weapons systems at least once every two months or every 500 rounds. This may be difficult because of the size of the AO.
- Training personnel to troubleshoot and fix problems.

INTELLIGENCE

6-221. Intelligence is critical in mountain operations. An enemy is usually familiar with the terrain and may receive reports from the local population. A mortar unit usually receives intelligence support from a company. Some points to consider include—

- Assuming your unit is under observation at all times.
- Increasing use of aerial reconnaissance and intelligence platforms and internal and external intelligence reports to compensate for reduced visibility and ground reconnaissance.
- Increasing emphasis on terrain considerations, such as use of defilade, in identifying enemy positions.

This page intentionally left blank.

Chapter 7

Special Considerations for a 60-mm Mortar Section

This chapter presents special considerations for the tactical employment of a 60-mm mortar section by Infantry, Ranger, and Marine Corps companies. It does not stand alone. It is dependent on the rest of this manual, FM 3-21.10/MCWP 3-11.1, and FMFM 6-4.

SECTION I – TEXT REFERENCES

7-1. Within this manual, selected topics are only briefly discussed and readers are referred to another publication for more detail. Mortar and other combat units use these tactics, techniques, and procedures in the same or very similar manner and a detailed discussion in this manual would be redundant. However, they are as important as the subjects discussed in detail. Table 7-1 consolidates the references to additional information.

Table 7-1. Guide for subjects referenced in text

Subject	References
Rates of fire	FM 3-22.91

SECTION II – LIGHT MORTARS ON THE BATTLEFIELD

7-2. Light mortars are the predominant mortar system fired and displaced while ground-mounted. However, a battalion commander may decide to use his medium mortars the same way. This is especially true for air assault operations. The tactics and techniques described below apply to light and medium mortars when used ground-mounted.

LIGHT MORTARS

7-3. The 60-mm mortar, M224, provides the mortar sections of Infantry, SBCT, and Ranger companies an effective, efficient, and flexible weapon. Rifle company commanders depend on these weapons to supply close fire support, suppression, smoke, and illumination. Light mortars are the most responsive and versatile sources of indirect fire support available. Their maneuverability, high rate of fire, low minimum-range restrictions, lethality, and proximity to commanders ensure the versatility, reliability, and responsiveness needed in light Infantry operations. Ammunition is light enough that sufficient amounts can usually be carried by the mortar section, HQ section, and rifle platoons.

7-4. Particularly during stability operations, field artillery units often conduct non-field artillery tasks, such as patrolling and manning checkpoints. This typically results in only a few howitzers or launchers being manned within a firing unit. Because of demands placed on a limited number of field artillery assets by counterfire, suppression, interdiction, and the employment of guided munitions, such as Excalibur, Infantry leaders must plan and train well to ensure that light mortar sections provide needed support in combat.

7-5. High-angle trajectories and multioption fuzes allow light mortars to effectively attack targets—
- In defilade on hilly, mountainous, or rolling terrain.
- Under jungle canopies.
- On marshy or snow-covered terrain.
- Behind buildings, on rooftops, and on top floors.

7-6. The short minimum range of the M224 makes the mortar well suited for close protective fires against an assaulting enemy, block-to-block fighting in cities, and combat over close terrain with restricted visibility.

7-7. A light mortar section is positioned between buildings, in confined areas, and on rough terrain. Light mortars are easy to conceal, can accompany raiding and counterattacking forces, can remain in position until the last moment, and can be moved with stealth. The location of a mortar section near rifle platoons makes communications by alternate means possible when conditions prevent radio contact with field artillery FDCs. The maneuverability of light mortars allows for sustained close fire support over the distances expected in light Infantry combat.

7-8. Commanders increase the effect of their light mortars by—
- Stressing the value of mortars to the close Infantry battle.
- Stressing the constant integration of mortar fire into a fire support plan.
- Allocating manpower to help move and secure mortars in rugged terrain.
- Training mortar squads to deliver responsive, accurate fires at all times.
- Considering timely resupply of mortar ammunition by including it in a sustainment/logistics plan.

ORGANIZATION

7-9. The organization of a 60-mm mortar section in the rifle company is based on a company's table of organization and equipment. A 60-mm mortar section is directly under the control of an Infantry and SBCT company commander. It is part of the weapons platoon in Ranger and Marine Corps rifle companies. (See Table 7-2 for the organization of both Army and Marine Corps light mortar sections.)

Table 7-2. Equipment and organization of Army and Marine Corps light mortar section

Personnel	Army	Marine
Section leader	1	1
Squad leaders	1	3
Assistant gunners	2	3
Ammunition bearers	2	3
Equipment	Army	Marine
M224 mortar	2	3
Binocular	2	3
M2 compass	2	3
LHMBC	2	3
Plotting board indirect fire	2	2
Radio set	1	1
Sight bore optical	1	1
Laser IR observation set	1	
Navigation set: satellite signals	1	
Computer system digital	1	

7-10. Army light mortar sections consist of two squads, each consisting of one mortar and its crew. The senior squad leader is a section leader. He is directly responsible to his company commander. There are no dedicated FDC personnel in Infantry mortar sections. The mortar section leader performs the duty of the FDC.

7-11. Marine Corps light mortar sections consist of three squads, each squad having one mortar and its crew. A section leader is a staff sergeant. He is directly responsible to a weapons platoon commander and is the dedicated FDC for the section.

7-12. A Ranger company's light mortar section has the same three-man squads as the other Infantry organizations. In addition, it has a separate section leader and a single FDC computer. FISTs in the Ranger battalion are assigned rather than attached. This fosters a close relationship between the mortar section leader and the FIST.

7-13. The equipment carried by a mortar section allows the section to perform all the functions of an indirect fire team. Each squad is equipped with a complete M224 and fire control equipment. A section leader has a boresight device and a radio.

7-14. To increase flexibility, commanders should consider cross-training Soldiers and Marines within rifle platoons to be ammunition bearers and assistant mortar gunners. Commanders can also train nonmortar personnel to employ the light mortar in its hand-held mode of operation.

RESPONSIBILITIES

7-15. In Army units, a section leader is also one of two mortar squad leaders and acts as the FDC, when required. A Marine Corps light mortar section leader has three mortar squads and also acts as the FDC, when required. All leaders of light mortar units have to be constantly aware of ammunition availability. (The responsibilities for the effective employment of light mortar sections are the same as those listed Chapter 2.)

EMPLOYMENT OPTIONS

7-16. A maneuver commander employs the mortar section based on his METT-TC/METT-T analysis. He has the following options when considering how to employ the 60-mm mortar section:

EMPLOY BY SECTION

7-17. When a commander employs mortars by section, the section operates from a single firing position under the control of a section leader. All mortars engage the same target. Mortars are emplaced based on their ability to fire from the position and availability of cover and concealment. A section leader passes fire commands to mortar squads by voice or over wire. To increase its responsiveness, a light mortar section operates from a position near the rifle platoons. It engages targets as quickly as possible, often using fire without an FDC. If fire with an FDC is used, one squad is designated by section TACSOP as the base squad.

7-18. Under extreme circumstances, a commander may choose to leave one of a section's mortars behind and have more ammunition carried for the remaining mortar. This could occur during operations in mountains, over deep snow, in jungle, or other extreme conditions or terrain. During assault climbs or infiltration attacks over rough terrain, the efforts of all six mortarmen may be needed just to get a single mortar and its ammunition into a firing position.

EMPLOY BY SQUAD

7-19. When a commander employs a mortar section by squad, he uses each squad as a separate firing unit. They may fire at the same target, but most often, they engage different targets. Employment by squad may take place during the initial phases of airborne, amphibious, or air assault operations, or while supporting other operational tasks, such as—

- Reinforcing an element conducting a combat patrol.
- Reinforcing the advance guard.
- Performing one-mortar illumination missions.
- Infiltrating the company along multiple routes.
- Supporting detachments left in contact.
- Displacing by bounds to give continuous support during movement by a company.

7-20. Employment by squad is the least desirable method. It should be used as a temporary measure when METT-TC/METT-T variables prevent mission accomplishment by section employment. By concentrating fires, a section can achieve a greater measure of destructive power. Employment of separate mortar squads lessens the destructive power achieved by firing as a section, but it does gain responsiveness to special situations. Employing by squads also reduces a mortar unit's ability to conduct coordinated illumination missions. Furthermore, squad employment increases the problems common to ammunition distribution and resupply, as well as fire control. Employment by squads can reduce a company commander's span of control problems if mortar squads are attached to platoons or a patrolling element.

Battalion Control of Company Mortars

7-21. A battalion commander has the option of detaching light mortar sections from rifle companies and physically consolidating them under the control of a battalion mortar platoon. This might be done when a battalion's objective is a compact, well-defined area that can be covered completely from one or two mortar firing locations. If all mortars are in range of targets, the same effect can be achieved by temporarily placing a company's mortars under the control of a battalion FDC.

7-22. Advantages of consolidating a battalion's mortars are—

- Fires can be massed and controlled by a single FDC.
- Ammunition resupply is much easier to control.
- Under-strength mortar squads can be consolidated and rested.
- Displacement and transportation can be more easily controlled.
- Security against an enemy ground attack is increased.

7-23. Disadvantages of consolidating a battalion's mortars are—

- Deprives rifle companies of organic mortar support to complement their direct fires and maneuver.
- Increases the chance that a large portion of a battalion's mortars will be destroyed by a single-enemy countermortar strike.
- Requires a larger firing position than normally needed.
- May limit target coverage and flexibility of fire support.
- Can cause a delay while mortar sections are consolidated, and again when they return to their parent company.

7-24. Consolidation of a battalion's mortars, like almost all nonstandard task organizations, is highly dependent on specific METT-TC/METT-T conditions. It has inherent advantages and carries with it inherent risks. It should not be used routinely, but only after a careful analysis of the situation and a commander's desired outcome.

Equipment Options

7-25. Based on a METT-TC/METT-T analysis, commanders may configure their light mortar units for the specific mission. This often involves weighing the advantages of increasing the speed of employment against the reduction of the overall capability and flexibility of the complete mortar. The mission, such as an air assault or airborne insertion, may require an immediate indirect fire capability however limited. Options include—

- Employing one mortar in the conventional mode with the other squad carrying additional ammunition and providing security. Marine Corps units can employ one or two light mortars in the conventional mode with the other squad(s) in support.
- Employing one or more mortars in the hand-held mode with the rest of the section carrying ammunition and providing security. This option may be considered if known, suspected, or likely targets are within the limited range of a hand-held mortar.

DISPLACEMENT

7-26. Based on scheme of maneuver and a company commander's guidance, a mortar section leader prepares a displacement plan as part of his fire plan. The displacement plan must contain detailed instructions on the type and amount of ammunition to be carried with the section. The company's plan must have provided details on the displacement of the section's bulk ammunition load. For example, rifle platoons may be tasked to carry mortar rounds and instructed on how to drop them off at the firing position. A section leader briefs the section on the displacement plan. He orients the section on potential targets using a map, compass, and prominent terrain features. After having received new information, the section leader updates the earlier orientation given to the section, when possible.

Offensive Operations

7-27. To support offensive operations, a displacement plan must permit rapid displacement and emplacement, while ensuring the use of immediate fire support. An enemy situation, the distance and terrain to be covered, and the need for continuous fire support determine the displacement method used. However, a mortar section may displace as a complete section. The section may occupy successive positions while the company continues to advance. It also may identify likely firing positions and continue to move with the company until required to fire. The commander may also decide to split the mortar section by placing one part, either still under company control or attached, behind the lead element and have the second part accompany the HQ section. Continuous orientation by all members of the section reduces the time to bring effective fire on an enemy.

DEFENSIVE OPERATIONS

7-28. A defensive displacement plan has the same needs as an offensive plan with some additions. Each member of a section should be shown the route to be used and the exact location of alternate and supplementary locations. Use of prestocked firing positions, pre-laid wire for communication, and predetermined firing data should be considered. Two methods to speed the emplacement of a mortar section during defense displacement are—

- A section leader reconnoiters subsequent firing positions and determines the locations of mortar baseplates. He places a tent peg or stake into the ground at the intended location. Attached to this peg is 5 meters of engineer tape and another peg. The section leader runs this tape out and uses his M2 compass to orient the tape in the direction of fire. He then stakes the tape down. Depending on the time of day when the position will be occupied and the tactical situation, chemical lights can be placed at the far end of the tape to aid the gunner. Upon arrival, a mortar crew emplaces the baseplate at one end of the tape, sets the mortar sight on 3200 mils, sights on the light or along the tape, refers the sight to the section's TACSOP deflection (normally 2800 mils), and places out the aiming posts. With practice, the mortar crew can emplace quickly during day or night.
- If possible, one mortar is carried to the firing location and emplaced using the M2 compass. The mortar crew places out an aiming post as if the mortar were going to occupy that position at that time. A stake is then driven into the ground at the rear of the baseplate, with a portion left visible. The mortar is moved to another position 25 to 30 meters away, and the procedure is repeated. The crew marks both the baseplate stakes and aiming posts with white engineer tape or chemical lights. It also checks mask and overhead clearance at each location.

RECONNAISSANCE AND POSITION SELECTION

7-29. Reconnaissance for mortars determines its use for mission accomplishment. Although ground and air reconnaissance can be used, a section leader normally performs a map reconnaissance. A detailed ground reconnaissance is the preferred method of locating positions for the mortar section, but lack of time and mobility may not allow it. A mortar section leader normally accompanies his commander on the leader's reconnaissance.

7-30. Advance party operations by a light mortar section are the exception rather than the rule. Size of the section and simplicity of a weapon make a rapid and efficient emplacement possible without an advance party. When a section is expecting to move, mainly at night, and enough time exists to reconnoiter and prepare a new position, the section leader does so. A set of direction and baseplate stakes, marked for easy identification, can help a crew in emplacement. Chemical lights of different colors can be useful, depending on the tactical situation. (For details on reconnaissance and position selection, see Chapter 6 of this manual.)

TYPES OF ENGAGEMENT

7-31. A light mortar section must be prepared to engage targets using either the conventional or hand-held mode. In the conventional mode, a mortar crew can operate with or without an FDC controlling fires. Although heavier, a light mortar in conventional mode can fire out to the full range of the ammunition while using either direct lay/alignment techniques or under control of the FDC. While much lighter and somewhat more responsive, the hand-held mode can only be used in the direct fire/alignment technique out to a maximum range of 1,340 meters.

7-32. Fire with an FDC increases the effect of a mortar section. A section leader sets up and operates an FDC when a mortar section occupies semi permanent positions or makes a long halt. An FDC influences the outcome of a battle by massing mortar fires, furnishing prearranged fires during reduced visibility, shifting fires, effecting time-on-target missions, lifting all fires, or furnishing fire support to other companies within range. Fire with an FDC may not always be possible. A mortar section can still be effective without using an FDC if members are well-trained in this method of fire.

7-33. Even though light Infantry companies can employ mortar without an FDC, they must not disregard the FDC method of employment. A section leader cross trains other members of the section in FDC procedures. He establishes and employs an FDC whenever possible.

COMMAND AND SUPPORT RELATIONSHIPS

7-34. A mortar section can fire in support of any of a company's platoons. A company commander sets priorities of fire and command relationships. He designates priority targets. Command relationships are limited to keeping a mortar section under a company commander's control or to attaching squads to rifle platoons. A company commander can attach one mortar squad to a platoon while keeping the remainder of the section under his control, such as when a platoon is sent out on a combat patrol.

SECTION III – SUPPORT DURING OFFENSIVE OPERATIONS

7-35. Light Infantry company offensive operations are characterized by dismounted movement, often over rugged terrain, and by rapidly changing situations. These operations require flexibility on the part of a mortar section. The value of a 60-mm mortar section in the offense does not lie in its volume of fire or its continuous fire support. A mortar section's best contribution to combat success is its immediate responsiveness to a company commander's orders, the speed at which it can be brought into action, and the effectiveness and accuracy of its multioption fuze-equipped rounds. Due to the limited ammunition and destruction power of each round, commanders must consider when and at what the mortar should be fired. The company mortar section should be used to engage targets that appear suddenly and cannot be immediately engaged by other indirect support. Once effective battalion mortar or field artillery fire is brought on the enemy, the company mortar section normally ceases fire to save ammunition. The commander must decide if increased fire is needed to destroy or neutralize the enemy. If so, he can direct the company mortar section to continue fire.

7-36. A lightweight M8 baseplate is used most often during offensive operations. In the attack or movement to contact, a larger M7 baseplate can be brought forward later. The smaller M8 baseplate is lighter by 11 pounds, which allows crews to carry three more rounds for each mortar. If a mortar squad is attached to a platoon conducting a combat patrol, a squad leader can choose to carry only the mortar cannon and the M8 baseplate. This is the lightest combination possible, weighing only 18 pounds. The mortar is then fired using the direct-lay mode.

7-37. A mortar section normally moves as a section within a company formation. The chance of enemy contact determines whether a commander chooses the traveling, traveling overwatch, or bounding overwatch technique of movement.

7-38. When a company is moving using the traveling or traveling overwatch technique, a mortar section moves either directly behind the company command group or directly behind a second rifle platoon in the line of march. A section leader monitors the company command radio net and continually orients section members to the terrain. At halts, he moves forward to coordinate with the company commander and the company FSO/FSC.

7-39. If a company is moving in bounding overwatch, a mortar section is usually positioned directly behind the command group, and it moves with that element. A section leader estimates the range to the lead elements of the bounding platoon, and he is prepared to provide fire support from his location or to move to a better position. The company commander may attach one mortar squad to each of two lead rifle platoons to assist them in overwatch.

7-40. Maintaining orientation is important for a mortar section when moving during limited visibility. During limited visibility, a company commander may move with the lead platoon. A mortar section then moves behind the last squad of this platoon rather than with the commander. During short halts, the mortar section spreads out in prone positions behind cover. During longer halts, mortars are set up, and a limited amount of ammunition is readied. Specified amounts of illumination ammunition (determined by TACSOP) can be carried ready-to-use.

AMMUNITION SUPPLY DURING OFFENSIVE OPERATIONS

7-41. A mortar section is the only indirect fire support asset that can accompany rifle platoons as they move to an objective and begin an assault. Planning considerations outlined in Chapter 3 apply to a 60-mm mortar section leader's planning. The amount and type of ammunition available are considered first when using a light mortar in the attack.

7-42. There is never enough ammunition, and it has to be rationed. A mortar section leader has to be always aware of his ammunition status. He has to prioritize usage and keep sufficient ammunition to accomplish his primary mission. He therefore has to advise his commander on the consequences of expending too much ammunition en route to the objective and thus not having enough for fires on the objective.

7-43. During maneuver to an objective, a mortar crew has to have sufficient ammunition immediately available to adjust to and engage the first target. This ammunition should be the amount carried by the crew. This provides the time required for more ammunition to be brought up and prepared. A section leader also has to estimate the number of rounds he will need at a given firing position so that he is not left with too much ammunition for his section to carry.

7-44. A company commander, with the recommendation by a mortar section leader, determines how much ammunition is carried and who carries it. A mortar section can carry only a limited amount of ammunition. Recent combat operations suggest that mortar units may slow or hinder maneuver due to the weight of ammunition carried by the crew. A commander should develop techniques and train Soldiers within maneuver units to carry, drop off, and recover mortar ammunition at firing points.

7-45. Each member of a rifle platoon and company HQ can carry one or two mortar rounds. This adds weight to the already heavy load of riflemen and machine gunners, but it also ensures that mortar ammunition is available. This method is hard to control if enemy opposition is intermittent but can be effective during a deliberate attack. As rifle platoons pass through or near proposed mortar firing position, they can drop their mortar rounds. A modification of this method was used in the Korean War when attacks were being made along or up steep ridge lines. Lead rifle platoons did not carry any mortar rounds. A mortar section moved second in the line of march, carrying as much ammunition as it could. Second and third rifle platoons, moving behind the mortars, carried one or two rounds on each man. When enemy contact was made, the leading platoon immediately began the assault, supported by the mortar section firing the ammunition it carried. As each succeeding rifle platoon passed the mortar position, it dropped its mortar rounds and joined the attack.

7-46. A rifle company can have a mortar section carry as much ammunition as possible and rely on vehicles, aircraft, or battalion-carrying parties to resupply ammunition. This method works best when the advance is along a road net or over trafficable terrain. Organic vehicles may be used, or captured enemy equipment may be pressed into service. A method that saves time and effort is to have mortar ammunition broken out of its boxes either at the ammunition transfer point or unit trains. Individual canisters can then be placed into color-coded aviator kit bags and stockpiled for movement forward by the available transportation means. Using a kit bag eases loading, unloading, and transferring the ammunition. About 15 rounds of ammunition can be carried in each kit bag, making a load that can be handled easily by two men or by one man in an emergency. In some areas of the world, labor service units provided by U.S. allies can carry ammunition. In lesser developed countries, indigenous pack animals may be available. If carrying parties or pack animals are used, a company XO and first sergeant/company gunnery sergeant must coordinate to ensure that guides and drivers/handlers are available and supervised.

SUPPORT DURING A MOVEMENT TO CONTACT

7-47. The displacement method chosen during a movement to contact depends on a company commander's evaluation of the chance of enemy contact, distance traveled, and terrain traversed. Mortars normally move as a section. If the terran does not allow good observation, it may be best to attach squads to the rifle platoons.

7-48. A commander may attach one of the mortar squads to a lead platoon. This allows quick response to enemy contact by the lead element, but it hampers the massing of fires by the section. When a company is acting as an advance guard and has a dedicated battery in DS, a company commander keeps the mortar section under his control. A section leader monitors the company command net and makes sure the section is in range of anticipated targets. The mortar section can supplement the fires of the dedicated battery by covering other priority targets as they become visible. In the movement to contact, light mortars are effective when firing HE and WP for suppression or WP for screening and obscuration.

7-49. A mortar section carries only a limited amount of ammunition during a movement to contact. The disadvantage is offset by their ability to bring immediate fire on the enemy. During World War II, a mortar section was most effective in the movement to contact when it followed close behind lead elements, opened fire quickly, had effective first rounds, and fired about three or four rounds for each target. When an enemy offers intermittent resistance, a section is best used by attaching a mortar squad to forward platoons. This uses the quick response of mortars to its fullest. If there is a greater resistance, mortars are kept under a company commander's control and moved 75 to 100 meters behind lead platoons. This provides quick response while making concentration of fire easier.

7-50. Communication between a lead platoon (that can see targets) and a mortar section is critical. There are several effective methods that have been used in combat to aid such communications:

- An FO for a lead platoon can be operating under predesignated control and be on the mortar section radio net. He can thus contact the light mortar section directly. However, the FO has to change frequencies to use other fire assets. Alternatively the FO of the lead platoon can be under decentralized control and use the fires assets most appropriate for the target. This last method requires an experienced FO.

- A mortar section leader can monitor the radio frequency of the lead platoon. If enemy resistance is encountered, mortars immediately stop and conduct a hip shoot, firing the adjusting round forward of the friendly lead elements. This requires close monitoring of the lead platoon's location by the section leader who acts as the FDC. The platoon sends corrections to the mortars by radio. This method is used when the company commander expects the enemy resistance to be great. The mortar section is protected from the initial enemy fires by remaining slightly to the rear, yet staying close enough to fire quickly.

- A mortar section can move behind the company command group until the lead element makes contact with the enemy. The section leader then leads the section forward to a position where they can fire using either direct alignment or direct lay. The company commander directs the section leader by voice command, arm-and-hand signals, radio, or messenger.

SUPPORT DURING A HASTY ATTACK

7-51. In a hasty attack, a commander aggressively develops the situation and uses immediate fires and maneuver to maintain momentum.

7-52. Targets engaged by a mortar section are mainly targets of opportunity, although a commander preplans targets, when possible. A company commander may keep the mortar section under his control. Alternatively, the commander may attach one or all mortar squads to rifle platoons. This provides immediate but limited indirect fire support to the platoon in what may be a platoon fight but prevents the commander from quickly supporting the decisive effort with indirect fires. In either event, the section leader uses his judgment and initiative, based on a FRAGO or the absence of orders, to determine how best to support the company maneuver. He employs the section aggressively to support the assault elements as they close with an enemy.

7-53. Once an objective is seized, a mortar section is brought forward to a position from which to support the entire company. The mortar section prepares to fire against enemy counterattack. The section leader acts decisively, using his best judgment and initiative to accomplish the commander's intent. The mortar section plays a key role in the defense against a counterattack. During the period after the seizure of the objective and before the assault force has reorganized, consolidated, and planned other fires, the company mortar section is the most responsive indirect fire support means available. The section leader displaces the section forward to support the company, establishes fire control and communications, computes data and prepares to fire the section FPF, evaluates existing ammunition stocks, redistributes ammunition, coordinates resupply requests, and makes sure his squads prepare hasty defensive positions. He must do this with little guidance from the company commander.

SUPPORT DURING A DELIBERATE ATTACK

7-54. A deliberate attack is characterized by detailed planning, both for maneuver elements and fires. A commander uses a light mortar section to supplement scheduled fires of heavier indirect fire weapons. The flexibility of light mortar is best suited for use against targets of opportunity encountered during an attack and for immediate screening missions. It also has the smallest RED of any indirect fire support system available to an Infantry platoon. It can therefore be used on an objective after other systems such as a 155-mm howitzer and 120-mm mortar have to shift to other targets, and before the Infantry's direct fire weapons begin their fires on the objective.

7-55. Light mortars are included in preparation fires when ammunition, positioning, and an enemy situation permit. A commander keeps in mind that mortar ammunition fired early can be hard to replace later. Mortars should provide fires on an objective to support a final assault, especially if supporting artillery is 155 mm. This allows indirect fire suppression of an enemy until assaulting forces close to within about 60-65 meters (with a 10-percent probability of friendly casualties) or 100-175 meters (with a 0.1-percent probability of friendly casualties), depending on range. Assaulting forces can get closer to an enemy under the cover of small caliber mortar fire than would be possible with fires from light or medium artillery.

7-56. During a deliberate attack against a fortified position, a mortar section is best employed with the company's support element. Although 60-mm HE fires will not penetrate a properly constructed fortification with overhead cover, they force the enemy to remain inside his positions, limiting his observation. High explosive fires inflict casualties on troops in open trenches. By firing WP, a mortar section obscures enemy observation from adjacent positions and assists the assault element in gaining a foothold. After the assault element has made an entry into the fortified position, a mortar section moves forward with the support element. Follow-on elements from the company carry mortar ammunition as they move forward and through the support position.

7-57. During urban operations, a light mortar section is employed with a company's support element. The section provides rifle platoons the firepower and obscuration needed to isolate a building or strongpoint while assault and security elements move forward to gain an initial foothold.

7-58. A 60-mm mortar is effective against enemy positions on urbanized terrain. Its high rate of fire and short minimum range allow a mortar section to mass fire on specific enemy positions in the restricted confines of city fighting. It attacks targets behind buildings that cannot be hit by low-angle artillery fire. A mortar section obscures, neutralizes, suppresses, or illuminates targets. A multioption fuze increases a mortar round's effectiveness, but the HE round, even employing the delay fuze setting, can penetrate only the upper floors of light buildings.

SECTION IV – SUPPORT DURING DEFENSIVE OPERATIONS

7-59. A 60-mm mortar section provides a company commander with organic indirect fire support that must be integrated into a company's overall defensive fire plan to be effective. A 60-mm fire is also closely coordinated with other fires assets such as the battalion 81-mm or 120-mm mortars and Army BCT or Marine Infantry regiment and higher artillery support.

7-60. A company mortar section is employed as a section during defensive operations with priority of fires to a designated rifle platoon. The mortar section is assigned an FPF, which is integrated into the company's defensive fire plan to augment fires of heavier weapons.

7-61. A light mortar section should be emplaced in a defilade position near the company CP. It may collocate with a company reserve or rearmost rifle platoon. Wire communications may be established through a company CP with each rifle platoon and OPs. The section's second telephone can be connected to a wire line laid to the platoon having the priority of fires. This provides alternate communications if a primary wire is cut by artillery fire. Positions are dug in, and overhead cover is provided for both ammunition and crew. Positions are camouflaged and wire lines are buried.

7-62. A section leader acts as an FDC and closely coordinates with a FIST/FiST chief and company commander to ensure effective integration of a section's fires. A section leader locates and, if time permits, prepares an observation post (OP) where he can control the fires of the section himself, if wire communication is lost. He monitors the company command radio net and can change to a platoon frequency or the FIST/FiST frequency, depending on the company commander's guidance.

7-63. A mortar section's fires are not normally included in a defender's counterpreparation fires. Battalion mortars and field artillery should be used for this role. A company mortar section can be used to engage targets of opportunity, especially at night, or targets in close defilade positions. A light mortar section is used to fire as an immediate response to enemy direct fire weapons or against enemy mortars firing from positions near friendly lines. It is better to engage small enemy probes, breach teams, or reconnaissance patrols with indirect fire from the mortar section than to disclose the locations of friendly machine gun, squad automatic weapon, or rifle positions.

7-64. Once an enemy attacks, a company mortar section fires to break up their formations and destroy their forces. Enemy elements assaulting friendly positions and enemy crew-served weapons locations are primary targets. Fires from a 60-mm mortar are effective against enemy forces that have closed with friendly elements. A mortar section can still engage these targets by using near-surface burst and proximity-fuze settings or rounds fired directly onto dug-in friendly positions. This type mortar fire is effective against an enemy infantry outside while not harming friendly personnel inside a well-constructed bunker with overhead cover. A mortar section, firing from the reserve platoon's position, can support a counterattack or limit an enemy penetration. If a rifle company is counterattacking, a mortar section supports with fire from planned positions.

7-65. For planning, an Army 60-mm mortar section can fire an FPF that is about 70 meters wide and 35 meters deep, while a Marine Corps section can fire an FPF that is about 105 meter wide by 35 meter deep. Final protective fires are normally fired using impact or near-surface burst fuze settings. A mortar section has a single FPF assigned. Because of the lightweight and small bursting radius of a mortar round, single mortar FPFs have limited effectiveness. A commander may decide not to have an FPF and may assign a priority target to the section or individual squads. A mortar section's FPF should be carefully integrated into the defensive fire plan of a company. It is most effective when a mortar section's FPF supplements the FPF of a battalion mortar platoon and supporting field artillery. The accuracy and short minimum range of an M224 mean that the FPF can be close to friendly positions. (The M224 firing charge 0 has a maximum range probable error of only 3 meters.) Mortar FPFs are always within small-arms range of friendly positions.

7-66. A company commander must consider a section's ammunition status, the resupply rate, and the tactical situation when designating how much ammunition to keep in reserve for the FPF. The company TACSOP should set guidelines regarding the amount of ammunition to be fired at any one target. This is important since ammunition stockpiled can be expended rapidly. The company TACSOP clearly states who has the authority to call for the FPF and under what conditions.

7-67. A mortar section is used to engage the following:

- Dismounted enemy infantry, especially when it is covered from direct fire or concealed.
- Enemy armored vehicles, using HE rounds with proximity fuze settings. This causes the crew to button up, reducing effectiveness of a vehicle while separating it from any accompanying dismounted infantry.
- Enemy long-range, direct-fire weapons that support the attack. The section engages these using a mixture of WP and HE rounds to suppress and screen.
- Assaulting enemy forces, using close defensive fires and FPF.
- Enemy mortars, especially light and medium mortars, with a combination of proximity and near-surface burst fuze settings.
- Enemy forces trying to breach friendly wire or mine obstacles.
- Targets during limited visibility with either white light or IR illumination. The small size and limited burn time of a 60-mm illumination round make it more suitable for point illumination rather than area.
- Reduce enemy observation and disrupt ATGM fires with smoke. It can also be used to mark targets for air strikes. The round has a limited incendiary and casualty-producing effect.

SUPPORT DURING RETROGRADE OPERATIONS

7-68. A mortar section leader coordinates closely with a company commander and an FSO to ensure that he understands a mortar section's role in a company retrograde fire support plan. Factors influencing the mission, employment, and movement of a 60-mm mortar section are as follows:

- Whether the withdrawal will be conducted under pressure.
- Whether detachments left in contact, security forces, or the entire withdrawing force is to be supported.
- Whether smoke screening is needed. The screen produced by the M224 mortar WP round is not as effective as that of heavier mortars and field artillery. The mortar section should be used to obscure selected, critical areas or to add to the screen produced by other elements. It can be effective when used to screen the withdrawal of small elements, such as OPs.
- Whether ammunition and transportation assets are available to support the mortar section. If ammunition can be stockpiled at progressively rearward positions and vehicles available can assist in section displacement, the 60-mm mortar section can maintain almost continuous fires as the company withdraws. Communication to control the displacement of the mortar section must be positive and timely.
- The displacement schedule of the battalion mortars and supporting field artillery. If possible, the 60-mm mortar section should not displace at the same time as the battalion mortars.

7-69. During retrograde, a mortar section is normally employed as a single element, but a commander may want to split the section, depending on his needs. If there are detachments left in contact, a mortar can be attached to a detachment left in contact commander. A single squad is then used to continue the normal fires of the section and to aid a detachment left in contact in breaking contact, if needed.

SUPPORT DURING A RELIEF IN PLACE

7-70. A company mortar section is the last element to be relieved. It stays in position, ready to fire, until all the maneuver elements are relieved. A section leader passes all target lists and FPF information to the relieving section. Ammunition, prestocked in a defensive location, is transferred to the relieving section. Baseplates and aiming posts can be transferred, especially if the section being relieved has well-prepared defensive positions. A relieving mortar section's base mortar can be laid parallel with mortars of the relieved section by sight-to-sight reciprocal lay. Wire lines should be transferred to the relieving section.

7-71. A mortar section may be required to continue firing missions associated with normal battlefield activity during relief in place. If so, two section leaders coordinate to ensure a smooth transition of responsibility. The section leader of the relieved section should conduct a daylight reconnaissance of the route back to the company assembly area, as well as the section's location in the assembly area.

SECTION V – RATES OF FIRE

7-72. A 60-mm mortar section can quickly fire large amounts of ammunition. An M224 can fire 120 rounds in four minutes—a three-man crew may have 15 to 20 rounds in the air before the first-round impacts. The high rate of fire is due to the simplicity of the mortar and its lightweight ammunition. The cooling fins at the base of the mortar allow a high rate of fire to be maintained for long periods.

7-73. In the past, mortar crews, trying to produce and maintain a high rate of fire, have used a two-man loading method. This method should not be used; it increases the chances of double-loading the mortar and causing an in-bore premature detonation. A single loader can fire almost as fast with less chance of double-loading. If a high rate of fire is required and ammunition is available, a squad leader can assist the ammunition bearer in preparing rounds. With practice, they can establish a smooth flow of rounds. (See FM 3-22.91 for details.)

SECTION VI – LOAD-CARRYING TECHNIQUES

7-74. A load carried by a 60-mm mortar section has a direct effect on a section's ability to traverse terrain at the rate needed to move with other elements of a rifle company.

7-75. Since a mortar section is most effective when it is close to the point of enemy contact (although not under direct fire), a company commander and a section leader must monitor a section's load and keep it at the minimum required for the mission and tactical situation. Section members should carry only their minimum combat load to carry the mortar and enough ammunition. If transportation for a section's existence load is not available, the amount of ammunition and firepower of the section is reduced.

7-76. An M224 can be broken down into parts and hand carried. This, plus flexibility in the choice of baseplates, allows a section leader to tailor a section's load to a specific mission and terrain.

7-77. If a company conducts an administrative road march, the section leader should request or coordinate to have mortars and ammunition moved either by battalion or company vehicles. This conserves the strength of section members, allows members to carry their entire existence load, and provides the maximum protection to the ammunition, which can be kept in its packing boxes. A mortar section should move in the march column near the vehicle carrying the mortars. Care must be taken in transporting mortars to ensure that nothing is lost or damaged, especially the sights. A section member can be detailed to ride with the mortars to ensure mortars are safe and delivered to the correct location.

7-78. If a company conducts a tactical foot march or if vehicular transport is not available, mortars should be carried using the three-man carry. A section leader and squad leader carry the radio, telephones, aiming posts, sight units, boresight, LHMBC, and plotting boards. They relieve the gunner and assistant gunner of their loads from time to time, allowing them to rest. Ammunition can either be carried on battalion vehicles or distributed among a crew members and rifle platoons. To ease the strain, loads should be rotated often.

7-79. When a mortar crew accompanies a patrol or performs an airborne or air assault insertion, it may carry only the cannon with the M8 baseplate attached. This is the lightest combination possible (18 pounds), allowing the easiest portability. It requires that the mortar be employed in the direct-fire or direct-lay mode.

SECTION VII – LOAD-CARRYING DEVICES

7-80. Heavy loads of equipment and ammunition carried by a mortar section can quickly exhaust troops moving over rugged terrain unless loads are distributed evenly and load-carrying equipment is properly used. Individual rounds should be kept in their cylindrical packing container to protect both fuze and propellant charges from exposure and possible damage. A mortarman also has to carry his individual weapon, ammunition, and protective and personal equipment. Mortar ammunition containers can be strapped to an individual's equipment. Section leaders should try to find ways to reduce fatigue when transporting additional mortar ammunition. Some possible means for doing so are as follows:

INDIVIDUAL LOAD-CARRYING EQUIPMENT

7-81. A modular lightweight load-carrying equipment pack can carry an individual's combat load as well as additional mortar ammunition. Additional 60-mm mortar rounds can be carried inside a pack or outside pockets of other members of the unit, not just the mortar crews. Mortar ammunition carried in these packs should be packed on top of all other items in the top portion of the pack so they can be offloaded quickly and easily when required.

STANDARD ARMY LITTERS

7-82. For carrying mortar ammunition short distances, a standard Army litter can be used. A detail of two-to-four men can carry significant amounts of mortar ammunition over rough terrain by lashing it to a litter and using universal slings to distribute a load. Using a sling frees hands to carry weapons or negotiate obstacles. This method is useful in circumstances where an ammunition resupply vehicle can approach near a mortar section location, but large amounts of ammunition must still be carried the last few yards. Carrying the ammunition in one or two trips by using a litter reduces the time that a carrying party is exposed to enemy observation or fire. To avoid violating the Law of Land Warfare and jeopardizing the noncombatant status of medical personnel, they should not be used to move ammunition.

LIGHTWEIGHT LITTERS

7-83. Rapidly employable compact and flexible confined space extraction litters can also be used to move mortar ammunition and equipment. Other lightweight litters can also be used to transport ammunition. The number of men required to move ammunition using these litters is a function of the type and condition of the terrain, travel distance, and the number of rounds transported.

Chapter 8

Mortar Firing
Survivability Techniques and Defense

Mortar units are vulnerable to enemy attack as they fight alongside Infantry rifle companies. Because of mortar units' lethality, they are often targeted by an enemy with direct fire, indirect fire, and assault. Mortar units must be able to defend themselves while continuing to provide fires. This chapter covers threats mortar units may face and techniques to reduce their vulnerability to enemy attack. It discusses the construction of mortar firing positions and other techniques to increase survivability, as well as tactics to defend a mortar position against enemy close assault.

SECTION I – TEXT REFERENCES

8-1.   Within this manual, selected topics are only briefly discussed and readers are referred to another publication for more detail. Mortar and other combat units use these tactics, techniques, and procedures in the same or similar manner and a detailed discussion in this manual would be redundant. However, they are as important as the subjects discussed in detail. Table 8-1 consolidates the references to additional information.

Table 8-1. Guide for subjects referenced in text

Subject	References
Passive and active air defense measures	FM 3-21.9/MCWP 3-14/MCWP 3-14.1
Constructing protective bunkers	FM 5-103
	FM 5-34/MCRP 3-17A
	GTA 90-01-011
Levels of protection	FM 5-103
Employment of machine guns	FM 3-22.68/MCWP 3-15.1

SECTION II – THREATS TO MORTAR SURVIVABILITY

8-2.   A mortar platoon leader must consider a number of threats. The greatest dangers to mortars are—

ENEMY COUNTERFIRE

8-3.   Mortar units may encounter intense enemy counterfire intended to reduce their support of friendly forces. Target acquisition radar, along with ground and air reconnaissance (both manned and unmanned), sound ranging, radio direction-finding, and other methods are all used to locate mortar units. Faced with counterfire threat, a mortar leader must understand that—

- Friendly mortars may be the first priority for enemy artillery, mortar, rocket, and direct fires.
- Skilled enemy observers can accurately locate friendly mortar positions using laser range-finders or simple map reading.
- Enemy countermortar radars are accurate with a small location error.
- Enemy radio intercept/direction finding can rapidly and accurately locate radio transmitters.

8-4. Many potential adversaries worldwide have effective artillery, rocket, and heavy mortar assets. Foreign nations are also developing, or have developed, precision guided mortar, artillery and air delivered munitions, such as the Krasnopol laser-guided artillery round. Because of their size, range, and high-angle fire, mortars are the most likely indirect fire weapons to be used against U.S. mortars.

8-5. The doctrine used by many potential adversaries calls for the use of both indirect and direct fire before an attack. U.S. mortar units are specifically targeted. As part of the battalion, they may receive heavy counterfire. Some enemy attacks have delivered up to 450 rounds on a company position as part of a 30-minute preparatory fire. In addition to HE fragmentation rounds, some enemy weapons fire rounds that include—

- Incendiary rounds filled with thermite canisters in a WP matrix. When these rounds burst, they produce some fragmentation and dense smoke from the WP. The thermite canisters scatter and burn intensely, causing fires in exposed ammunition and fuel.
- Enhanced blast warheads, which are powerful but have little fragmentation. They are used to suppress and disrupt U.S. tracked mortars, which are protected from fragments by their mortar carriers, and to crush field fortifications.
- Sub-projectile warheads, which explode above the ground and scatter thousands of small, finned anti-personnel flechettes.

GROUND ATTACK

8-6. When mortars support offensive operations, the greatest ground threat is chance contact with enemy forces that have been bypassed or purposely left behind, or from enemy irregular forces (partisans, guerrillas, insurgents). When mortars support defensive operations, the greatest threats are enemy reconnaissance and main forces but a significant threat may be posed by terrorist, guerrilla, or insurgent forces.

8-7. Enemy reconnaissance teams may encounter mortars by chance contact or can be given the mission to locate U.S. mortar positions. Once reconnaissance teams encounter mortar locations, they may attack or report their locations for destruction by indirect fire or by enemy ground forces. If mortars are located where enemy penetrations occur, they can be attacked by virtue of the enemy's momentum.

AIR ATTACK

8-8. Enemy aircraft pose a threat to mortars due to the difficulty in concealing mortar firing positions from aerial observation. Armed helicopters pose a major threat because of their stand-off acquisition ability. Many armies in the world now have UASs specifically used for reconnaissance and attack.

8-9. A mortar platoon must conceal itself from enemy aircraft through passive air defense measures. (See FM 3-21.9/MCWP 3-14/MCWP 3-14.1 for details on these measures.)

8-10. A mortar platoon usually does not engage in active air defense unless directly attacked by enemy aircraft, and only then according to air defense rules and procedures found in the air defense TACSOP. Individual small-arms weapons and machine guns provide a limited self-defense capability against enemy aircraft. (See FM 3-21.9/MCWP 3-14/MCWP 3-14.1 for techniques used to defend small units against enemy air attack.)

SECTION III – PROTECTION AGAINST ENEMY COUNTERFIRE

8-11. Choosing tactically sound mortar positions in defilade and using concealed reverse-slope positions are effective techniques against enemy counterfire. Defilade is protection from fire provided by an obstacle such as a hill, ridge, or bank. It is important to mortars because of the difference in the trajectories of field guns, howitzers, rocket launchers, and mortars (Figure 8-1).

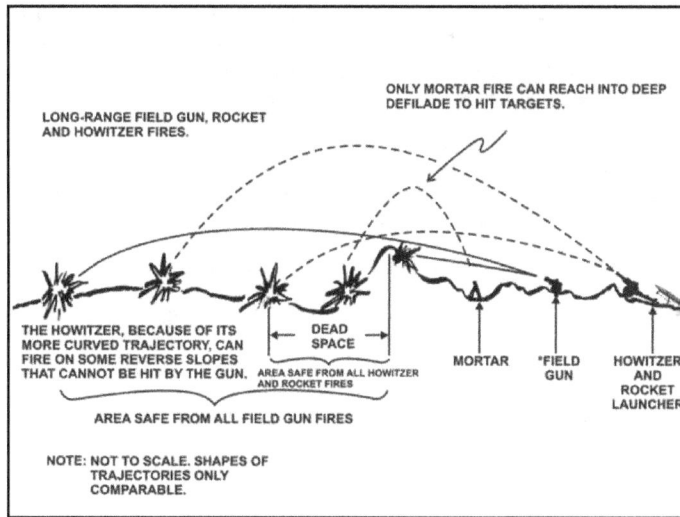

Figure 8-1. Examples of trajectories and dead space

8-12. Establishing a mortar firing position within the dead space created by a hill mass or building does not eliminate an enemy's ability to locate the unit. It does make it difficult for an enemy to place effective counterfire on the U.S. position.

8-13. The flatter trajectory of enemy field guns, howitzers, and rocket launchers creates a dead space behind large hill masses and tall buildings. U.S. mortars can occupy positions in this area and be almost impervious to counterfire. Because of their trajectory and range, U.S. mortars can fire out of defilade against most targets in the battalion or company area. Even deep defilade only partly reduces the maximum range of a mortar (Figure 8-2). Defilade protects mortar positions from field gun and low angle howitzer fires but not from enemy mortar fires and artillery high angle fire. However, to shoot into the dead space, enemy mortars must be moved close to friendly positions, making them vulnerable to U.S. counterfire.

8-14. Defilade provides excellent protection from enemy indirect fire. However, a mortar leader must not think that it provides absolute protection. He must understand that he is opposed by thinking enemies who have their own methods to seek and destroy friendly fire assets, even when they are in good defilade positions.

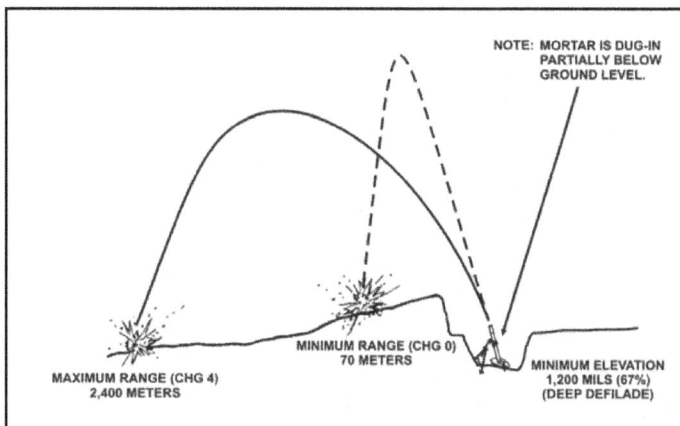

Figure 8-2. Example of range coverage from defilade

8-15. A geometric formula can determine the estimated extent of dead space using the cotangent of the angle of fall for the weapon firing (Figure 8-3). For mortar fires, the cotangent of fall can be extracted from tabular firing tables. Although enemy mortars do not have exactly the same trajectory as U.S. mortars, the information in the U.S. firing tables can be used as a rough approximation until more accurate information is available.

8-16. The average angle of fall of low-angle howitzer fire is about 25 degrees, which equates to a cotangent of the angle of fall of about 2.0. Therefore, the dead space is about two times the height of the defilade. If a mortar position is chosen that has a minimum safe elevation of 900 mils, that position is safe from 122-mm and 152-mm howitzer rounds fired directly over the hill mass or ledge. The angle of fall of field guns is even lower and their dead space is much greater.

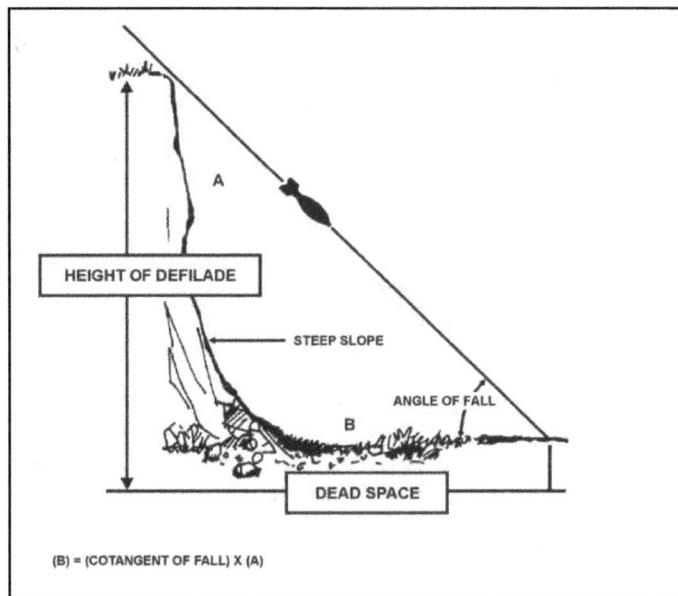

Figure 8-3. Geometric relationships

Note. On today's battlefield, an enemy may be equipped with weapons other than those from the old Warsaw Pact nations. Many developed countries have sold modern weapons to other countries and these weapons may be used by U.S. enemies. Although examples and discussions refer to weapons that were current when the Soviet Union was in existence, a mortar leader should be prepared to encounter other systems with different capabilities.

8-17. On flat terrain, defilade may be hard to find. On rolling or slightly broken terrain, it can usually be located. Defilade is easily located in mountainous terrain and built-up areas. Large buildings create large areas of dead space that can extend over several streets. Dead space created by a large building is about three times the height of the building for howitzers and about one-half the building height for mortar fires. (These distances are only guidelines and assume counterfires from directly to the front. Counterfires from the oblique and flank will have less dead space.) The actual size of the dead space depends on the weapon, round, charge, range combination, and elevation difference between the weapon and target.

Note. If an enemy fires artillery or rockets at an elevation of 800 mils, the dead space behind each building is about equal to the height of the building.

8-18. If U.S. mortars are close to a tall mass construction building and firing at near maximum elevation, they are virtually impervious to frontal fires from the BM-21 multiple rocket system, one of the world's most effective counterfire weapons. The BM-21 has a maximum firing elevation of about 885 mils. If the mortar position is within a building's dead space, incoming rounds from that direction either will strike the building or pass over the mortars to strike behind them (Figure 8-4). U.S. mortars should be positioned as close to buildings as possible while still maintaining clearance to fire over them.

8-19. Mortars should not be positioned close to buildings that have a large surface area made of glass because of the secondary fragment hazard. Short buildings close to the mortar position on any side do not provide much dead space in which to position mortars, but they will stop fragments from that side. If the open area the mortar is firing from is small and the adjacent walls can stop fragments, incoming rounds have to be almost a direct hit to be effective.

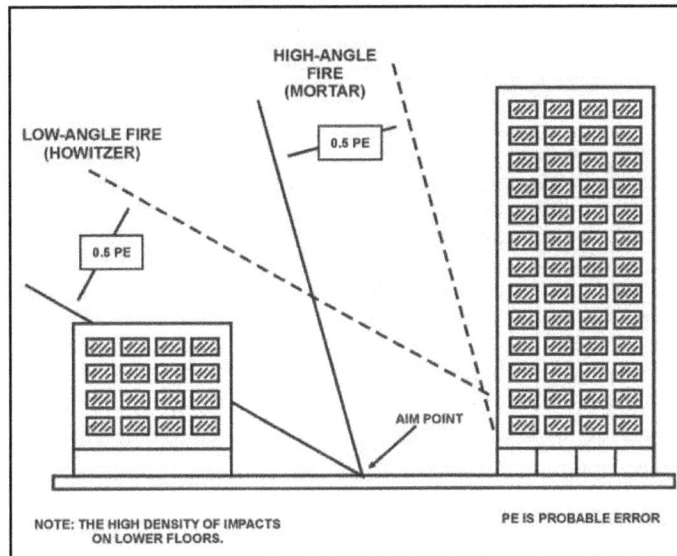

Figure 8-4. Expected locations of impact from high and low angles of fire

SECTION IV – PROTECTED POSITIONS

8-20. Mortar units may occupy a firing position only long enough to fire a few missions before displacing or they may occupy it for several days or longer. Sometimes, mortar units occupy semi-permanent firing positions, especially during counterinsurgency and stability operations. All mortar squads should seek protected positions and continue improvements as long as they occupy them. Preparing protected mortar firing positions can take much time, labor, and material. If completely accomplished by hand, it is slow and fatiguing. If construction materials and engineer equipment are available, protective positions can be built more quickly, which results in more rested and responsive mortar crews. Prefabricated protection materials and field expedient materials can also be used to build mortar positions, personnel and ammunition shelters, and FDC shelters.

8-21. This section discusses basic protection criteria and includes sample protected mortar and FDC positions. The examples are specific to mortars, but do not go into detail on material and construction methods. Specific information on construction materials and methods are covered in GTA 90-01-011.

CONSIDERATIONS AND GUIDELINES

8-22. Positions should be constructed with sidewalls and overhead cover. Sidewalls are walls or barriers that stop fragments and reduce blast effects from near-miss impacts of rockets, artillery, and mortar rounds. They should be of minimal height, protect against the fragmentation and blast from near hits, and support the overhead cover. Overhead cover protects personnel from direct impacts of indirect fires. The basic concept is to provide a pre-detonation layer and a shielding layer over the personnel being protected. The pre-detonation layer causes a point-detonating fuze of the incoming round to function and detonate the round before it can penetrate inside the position. The shielding layer absorbs the resulting fragments. Overhead cover has to be adequately supported and only large enough to protect essential operations.

8-23. Entrances should also be constructed to shield fragmentation and blast from entering the position. This can be accomplished by building a barrier in front of an entrance or by building an entrance with a 90-degree angle.

8-24. Considerable time and material is required to protect positions against large caliber rounds, especially those with delay fuzes. Mortar leaders have to prioritize the amount of time devoted to building positions and their other priorities.

8-25. Mortar positions must be protected against enemy rocket, mortar, and artillery counterfire by either digging into the earth or building up protective positions. The following are two examples of the effectiveness of protection against indirect fire:

- In 1976, the German Infantry School fired artillery and mortars, with the intensity set by Soviet doctrine, on various field positions in which Infantrymen were represented by mannequins. Results showed that troops laying prone in the open would suffer 100 percent casualties. Those in open fighting positions without overhead cover would suffer 30 percent casualties. However, troops dug-in with overhead cover would expect fewer than 10 percent casualties, mostly by direct hits.
- During the entire month of February 1968, an average 1,100 rounds of enemy indirect fire fell daily on the Marine Corps' combat base at Khe Sanh, South Vietnam. This fire included 82-mm and 120-mm mortars, 100-mm and 130-mm field guns, 122-mm and 152-mm howitzers, and 122-mm rockets. The Marines reported that this fire had little effect once they had prepared proper field fortifications. One rifle company reported that from 350 to 500 82-mm mortar rounds hit its position within two hours with only moderate damage.

8-26. From this combat experience against common weapons and from tests conducted by the Army, the following guidelines for protection levels have been developed:

- A minimum of 18 inches of packed earth is required to protect a position from fragmentation. This is not enough to protect against direct hits or near-misses.
- A pre-detonation layer and a shielding layer consisting of three layers of well-compacted sandbags protects against a direct hit from an 82-mm mortar round with a point detonating fuze.
- One layer of pre-detonation layer and a shielding layer consisting of eight layers of well-compacted sandbags can protect against a direct hit from a 120-mm mortar round with a point detonating fuze.
- Considerable construction time and materials are required to protect a bunker against a direct hit by a 120-mm mortar round with a delay fuze. Heavy bunkers with timber supports and carefully constructed shielding material can minimize the damage done by a direct hit. They can also protect the occupants from fragments and near-misses.
- Without concrete or steel, no field fortifications can be built to withstand a direct hit from a 122-mm rocket or a 152-mm HE round. Even dud 152-mm rounds will penetrate about 4 feet of solid earth. However, properly constructed bunkers will protect against fragments and near-misses. (See FM 5-103 and FM 5-34/MCRP 3-17A for more details.)

GROUND-MOUNTED MORTAR POSITIONS

8-27. Mortar units must be able to continue to fire missions while under direct and indirect fire enemy fire. They must be able to defend their position and contribute to the defense of the larger unit of which they are a part.

PROTECTION CRITERIA

8-28. A commander determines the amount of protection required and balances mission accomplishment, protection, time, and the resources available. No matter what type or level of position his units build, they should meet the following criteria:

- Allow crews to engage planned targets, especially priority targets, as well as cover an enemy's most likely avenues of approach. This may require establishing a position capable of firing within a 6400-mil fan out to the full range of a weapon.
- Provide adequate space to prepare ammunition while making deflection and elevation changes.

- Protect crews from direct small arms fire, airbursts, and rounds impacting nearby.
- Expose minimum open area to enemy indirect fires while still allowing effective operations.
- Store and protect ready ammunition from airbursts and rounds impacting nearby.
- Provide crews the ability to defend positions and to contribute to defense of the unit.
- Provide shielded entry and exit points from positions.
- Provide protected routes between adjacent mortar positions, the FDC, and reserve ammunition storage areas.
- Protect the crew, weapon, equipment, and ammunition from inclement weather and flooding.
- Provide communications between the mortar crew, HQ, observers, and the FDC.
- Protect the FDC from airbursts and rounds impacting nearby.
- Protect the FDC from inclement weather.
- Provide adequate light, heat, facilities and space within the FDC for continuous operations.
- Provide camouflage and concealment.

LEVELS OF PROTECTION

8-29. Mortar positions can be protected in a variety of ways. The best positions are protected by both defilade and camouflage. When natural defilade is not available, positions must be protected by fortifications. The amount of protection is based on the threat. Under general war conditions, mortar units may have to protect themselves against sophisticated detection devices, such as UASs and counter-mortar radars, and firepower equivalent to our own. During other operations the threat may not be as high but the position always has to protect the mortar and crew from powerful direct and indirect fire weapons. (See FM 5-103 for more details.)

8-30. The following are thicknesses of dry soil required to stop the effects of selected direct and indirect fire weapons:

- Direct fire, 7.62-mm at 100 yards: 20 inches.
- Direct fire, 37-mm at 400 yards: 60 inches.
- Direct fire, rocket-propelled, grenade-shaped charge: 78 inches.
- Indirect fire, 82-mm, fragmentation and blast exploding 50 feet away: 10 inches.
- Indirect fire, 152-mm, fragmentation and blast exploding 50 feet away: 20 inches.

TYPES OF PROTECTION

8-31. There is no single standard mortar firing position. The amount and availability of engineer support and the availability of prefabricated materials determines the type of position that can be built. Terrain and soil conditions may require the unit to build up walls and barriers instead of digging them down. Any structurally sound position that meets the established criteria is adequate. All positions must be continually improved and maintained.

> *Note.* The dimensions in the figures below for the construction of mortar and FDC positions are guidelines only. Leaders should determine the location, dimensions, and the materials used to construct these positions based on the terrain, enemy, and METT-TC/METT-T considerations.

8-32. The types of protection are—

Standard Ground Mounted Dug-In Mortar Positions

8-33. The standard ground-mounted, dug-in mortar position has the following three stages of construction (Figure 8-5):

- Basic mortar pit.
- Basic mortar pit with added personnel shelters.
- Basic mortar pit with personnel shelters and ammunition bunkers.

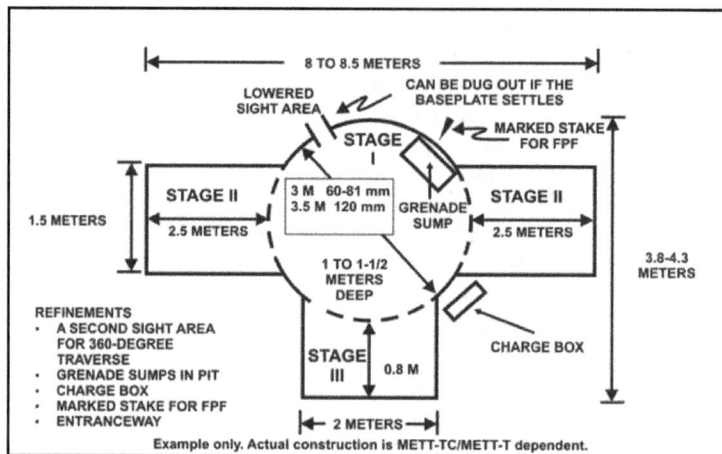

Figure 8-5. Mortar position (three stages of construction)

8-34. A dug-in position for 81-mm/60-mm mortars is the same as for 120-mm mortars with only slight changes in dimensions. A standard mortar position must be constructed with a flat bottom. It can be constructed totally below, partly above, or completely above ground, depending on the time and material available and the composition of the ground at the intended position. A below-ground position normally offers the best protection.

Stage I

8-35. After a leader selects a general location, a crew marks the exact baseplate position and begins construction. A mortar pit for 81-mm/60-mm mortars should be approximately 3 meters wide and a maximum of 1½ meters deep. Mortar pit for a 120-mm mortar should be about 4 meters wide. The important thing is for the width of a mortar pit to allow operations to be conducted while minimizing the exposed area. All walls or parapets above ground should be at least 1 meter thick for protection against small-arms fire and shell fragments. Soil-filled wire and fabric or metal containers, sandbags, logs, 55-gallon drums, dirt-filled ammunition boxes, timber, or other materials can be used. A gunner must be able to see the aiming posts or the distant aiming point through all deflection and elevation settings. Construction for a heavy mortar pit is the same, except the pit diameter is 3½ meters.

Stage II

8-36. When time allows, protection should be increased by constructing personnel shelters with overhead cover. Personnel shelters should be constructed perpendicular to the principal direction of fire with firing ports positioned as determined by assigned small-arms sectors of fire. Shelters should be built at the same depth (1½ meters) as the pit, and 1½ meters wide, and 2½ meters long on opposite sides of the pit with a minimum of ½ meter of overhead cover. There should be a blast barrier of at least two sandbags in thickness separating personnel shelters from the mortar pit. Firing ports can be made using wooden ammunition boxes with the bottoms knocked out or improvised with available materials. Personnel should use sandbags to adjust the opening to the smallest usable size. Corrugated metal culvert halves covered with earth make good personnel shelters (Figure 8-6). Whatever design is selected, it should never support the weight of the overhead cover on sandbags. Timber or some other structurally sound material should be used.

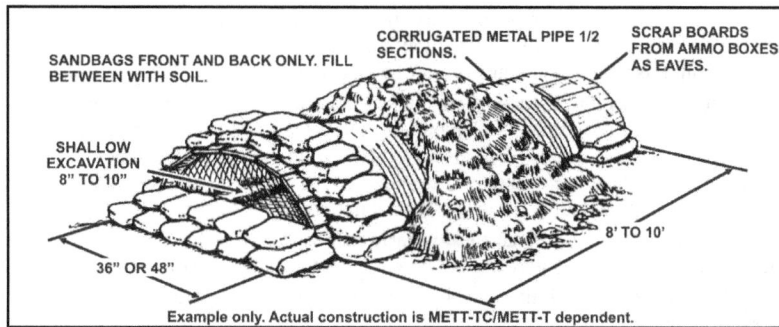

Figure 8-6. Corrugated metal culvert halves used as personnel shelter

Stage III

8-37. As position improvement continues, bunkers should be constructed for ready ammunition. A bunker is approximately 2 meters wide, 1 ammunition box (length) deep, and 2 ammunition boxes (stacked on their sides) high. Bunkers are divided into four sections separated by the ammunition boxes stacked on their sides (Figure 8-7). Ammunition boxes can be used for tonnage to protect ammunition from moisture. Support stringers are placed across the stacked boxes to provide a base on which to place additional dirt-filled ammunition boxes for the top. Boxes are filled with dirt to increase stability and add protection. A canvas tarpaulin or plastic sheet is placed on the top of the ammunition boxes and covered with dirt and sandbags to form at least an 18-inch layer over the bunker. A tarpaulin should drape over the opening to a bunker to protect ammunition. Sandbags on top add stability and protection while reducing the danger of wooden splinters.

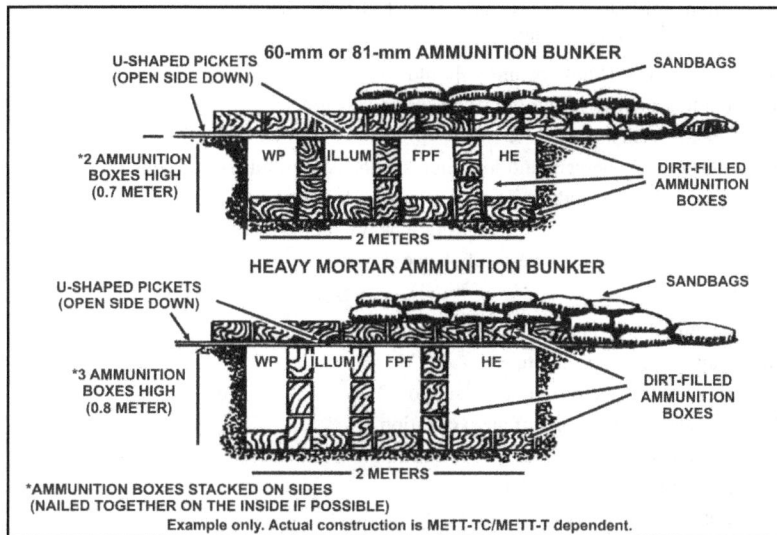

Figure 8-7. Ammunition storage area (front view)

8-38. Once a mortar position is completed to Stage III, a crew should—

- Add another sight area to allow 360-degree traverse.
- Dig grenade sumps (at least one) in the circular pit. They are dug against the wall of the pit, using the trench-style pit as shown in FM 3-21.75.
- Add an entry with a 90-degree blast baffle. This can enter either the circular pit or one of the personnel shelters. Eventually, it should connect with a crawl trench toward the FDC.

- Dig a hole outside the circular pit, near the ammunition bunker, for placing excess charges until disposal. Personnel should place an empty ammunition box in this hole; a cover will protect excess charges from flash fires. Sandbags should be placed on the box lid when not placing charges into it.
- For a gunner's quick reference, place stakes around the rim of the circular pit or mark the sides corresponding to priority targets. Personnel should also mark a stake corresponding to the FPF with a distinctive mark. These stakes are also useful for illumination targets since precise lay of the mortar is not required. Their use makes mortars more responsive in countering enemy direct and indirect fires. Stakes should be put in securely and not disturbed.
- Install alternate wire lines from the mortar positions to the FDC and tag the alternate and primary lines. All communications wire should be buried at least 4 inches below ground.
- Sandbag the base of the aiming posts without disturbing them. This protects them from being blown over by enemy fire.
- Continue to improve the position by providing overhead cover for ammunition handlers to prepare rounds for firing.

8-39. A Stage III ground-mounted mortar position takes from 30 to 40 man-hours if dug by hand, depending on the type soil and the tools used. If engineer equipment is used to make the initial pit and bunkers, this time can be shortened. The amount of material required depends on the depth of the excavation and the type of material used. (See FM 5-34/MCRP 3-17A and GTA 90-01-011 for more details.)

8-40. As time permits, personnel should add sandbag layers to increase protection. These sandbags must be properly supported. Poorly supported overweight bunkers can collapse under enemy fire, killing or injuring personnel inside.

Fire Direction Center Bunkers

8-41. There is no standard FDC bunker design. (See FM 5-103 for several versions.) Figures 8-8 through 8-10 show various bunker designs and standards.

8-42. When constructing FDC bunkers, units should—
- Construct to proper engineering standards and ensure adequate shoring material is used.
- Dig down as much as possible.
- Fill sandbags to 75 percent and interlock sandbags for double-wall construction and corners.
- Rivet excavations in sandy soil and use wire and fabric containers when possible.
- Inspect the safety of bunkers daily, after a heavy rain, and after receiving enemy fires.
- Maintain, repair, and improve positions continuously.
- Camouflage positions.

8-43. When constructing FDC bunkers, never—
- Fail to supervise construction.
- Use sand or sandbags for structural support.
- Drive vehicles within 6 feet of an excavation.
- Overfill sandbags.
- Omit lateral bracing on stringers.
- Take shortcuts in construction safety.
- Build above ground unless absolutely necessary.

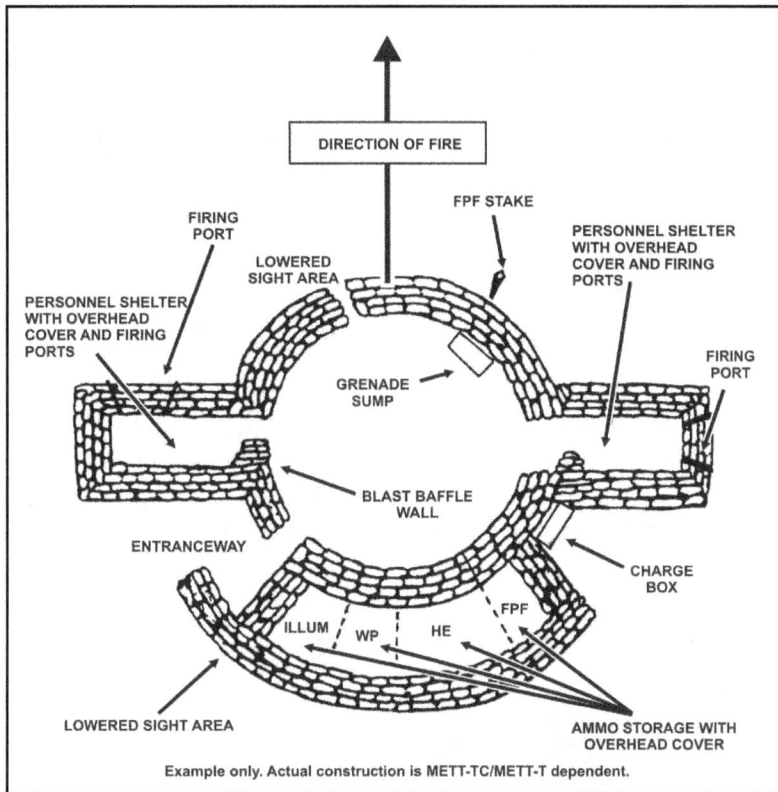

Figure 8-8. Completed ground-mounted mortar position (overhead view) with refinements

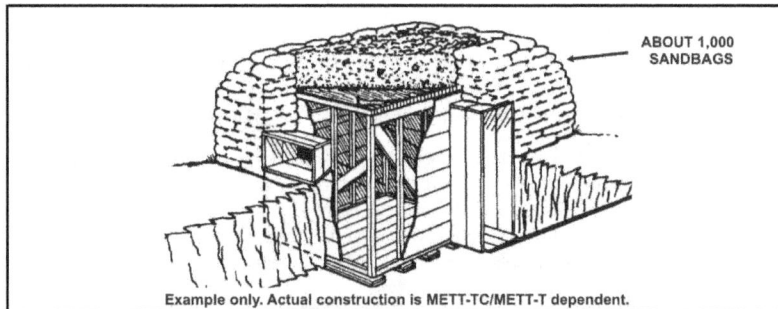

Figure 8-9. Cutaway view of a standard bunker

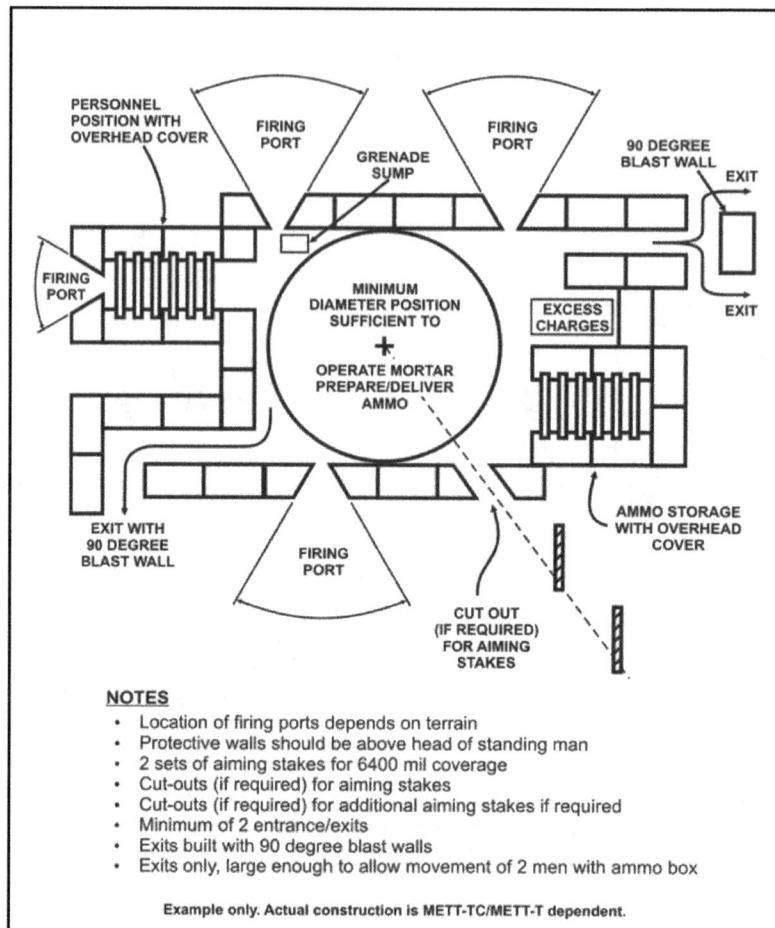

NOTES
- Location of firing ports depends on terrain
- Protective walls should be above head of standing man
- 2 sets of aiming stakes for 6400 mil coverage
- Cut-outs (if required) for aiming stakes
- Cut-outs (if required) for additional aiming stakes if required
- Minimum of 2 entrance/exits
- Exits built with 90 degree blast walls
- Exits only, large enough to allow movement of 2 men with ammo box

Example only. Actual construction is METT-TC/METT-T dependent.

Figure 8-10. Fortified mortar position using soil-filled wire and fabric containers

Protection Using Prefabricated Protection Materials

8-44. Prefabricated barrier material is increasingly available and has some important advantages over more traditional material. Side and overhead cover built with sandbags can provide sufficient protection but are labor intensive and require constant maintenance. Prefabricated materials such as wire and fabric containers, metal containers, and modular reinforced concrete walls are commonly used to build walls and barriers in semi-permanent positions. Reinforced concrete or other types of semi-permanent shelters can be constructed to house an FDC.

8-45. The three general construction stages listed in the construction of the standard dug-in position should also be used in the construction of positions using pre-fabricated materials.

Wire and Fabric Container

8-46. Wire and fabric container (Figure 8-11) sections consist of a series of large, linked, self-supporting cells. Tests have shown that a 2-foot thickness is adequate to stop all fragments from 60-mm mortar through 122-mm rocket and 155-mm artillery rounds. Each cell consists of collapsible wire mesh lined with fabric. Cells can expand from a compact, folded storage configuration. Advantages are that they provide a rigid vertical wall and can be transported collapsed, and upon arrival expanded and filled.

Figure 8-11. Wire and fabric container revetment

8-47. Wire and fabric containers come in a variety of sizes. The sizes that are probably best suited in the construction of mortar fighting positions are the 2- or 4½-feet-high versions. The national stock number for this version is 5680-99-968-1764 (beige) and 5680-99-001-9397 (green). Wire and fabric container cells provide excellent all-around protection but they are not designed to provide overhead cover. Other construction materials must be used as stringers and then covered with a protective layer of overburden so that the final position provides not only protection from nearby ground bursts, but also protection from proximity bursts and plunging fires. Wire and fabric barriers must be arranged so that not only is the position protected, but the members of a mortar crew can defend the position against ground assault.

8-48. Each shipment of wire and fabric container cells comes with detailed guidance for construction. It is important to follow these instructions as closely as possible to ensure that the position is stable, long-lasting and requires minimal maintenance. During site selection and construction personnel should—

- Select a site with a level, firm surface with good drainage to support the structure.
- Place containers in the desired location and orientation before expanding them.
- Fill containers with a dry mixture of sand and gravel.

Reinforced Concrete, Corrugated Metal Bin, or Timber Shelters

8-49. Personnel bunkers made of reinforced concrete, corrugated metal revetment material, or timber can be built either above or below ground. They offer excellent protection against direct and indirect fire and, if properly constructed with appropriate collective protection equipment, they provide protection against chemical and biological agents. A type of highly protective reinforced-concrete bunker has been used successfully in Iraq and Afghanistan (Figure 8-12). This bunker is generally constructed with reinforced concrete sections with Jersey barriers placed across each end. Additionally, in some situations standard 20-foot-long International Standards Organization/Milan containers can be adapted to use as personnel shelters, either covered with sandbags or dug into the earth.

Figure 8-12. Example improvised bunker using concrete culvert sections

MOUNTED MORTAR POSITIONS

8-50. Even though tracked mortar carriers provide protection against small-arms weapons and most shell fragments, they can be penetrated by heavy shellfire. As with ground-mounted mortars, it is best to select firing positions with natural defilade. If that is not available, mortar carriers should be dug-in or have protective barriers erected around them.

8-51. A protective position for a tracked mortar carrier is too large to be dug by hand; engineer equipment is normally required. Some work with hand tools is needed to finish the position. As an alternative, wire and fabric containers can be used to construct revetments into which the vehicle can be driven.

8-52. Bulldozers, Stryker engineer support vehicles, deployable universal earth movers, or other vehicles can build a hasty fighting position for a mortar carrier. A tracked mortar carrier requires a position that is approximately 20 feet long (with entrance ways at one end), 10 feet wide, and 6 feet deep. A Stryker mortar carrier requires a position to be 25 feet long, 13 feet wide and 11 feet deep. The carriers must be able to move into the position. The spoil should be spread out to avoid a distinct hump of fresh dirt, and the floor of the position should be level (Figure 8-13).

8-53. As time permits, this hasty firing position can be improved. The sides can be widened slightly to allow movement around the track to perform maintenance. An ammunition bunker can be dug into one side of the position to store additional ammunition. In loose, sandy soil, the sides of the position should be reverted to prevent a cave-in.

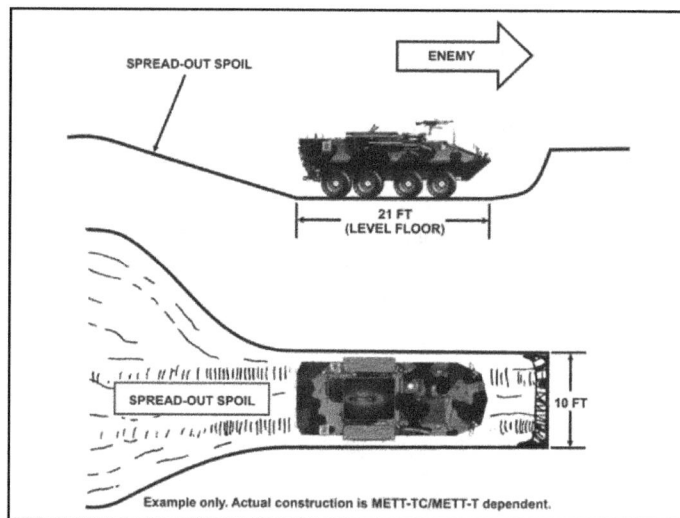

Figure 8-13. Hasty mortar vehicle

Note. Figure 8-13 includes the Marine Corps light armored vehicle-mortar.

POSITIONS IN A STRONGPOINT OR FORWARD OPERATING BASE

8-54. A strongpoint is a battle position fortified as strongly as possible to withstand direct assaults by dismounted Infantry supported by heavy indirect fire. Mortars in a strongpoint must continue to provide close and continuous fires, even when under attack. All mortar positions should include overhead cover for personnel and ammunition. An FDC must be protected by earth and overhead cover. Ammunition storage areas, communications trenches, and wire lines must all be protected.

8-55. Even if an enemy masses fires against a strongpoint, mortars can survive and continue to fight if they are properly dug-in.

ADDITIONAL INDIVIDUAL PROTECTION

8-56. In addition to building protective positions, mortar leaders can increase the individual protection of platoon members by—
- Wearing proper eye protection.
- Wearing individual body armor and flame retardant uniforms.
- Wearing the appropriate CBRN individual protective equipment.
- Training personnel in buddy aid and as combat life saver.
- Wearing hearing protection.
- Properly storing and disposing of excess propellant charges.
- Properly storing prepared ammunition in covered containers.

SECTION V – OTHER SURVIVABILITY TECHNIQUES

8-57. To support a commander's intent for mortar fires, a mortar section must survive an enemy's efforts to eliminate it. Survival requires mortars to avoid detection as long as possible, confuse an enemy as to their true location, and to defend themselves against enemy attacks.

SHOOT-AND-HIDE POSITIONS

8-58. Shoot positions are positions from which mortars fire. Hide positions are located in a covered and concealed area and are occupied by mortar crews when not firing. The use of shoot-and-hide positions is an effective technique when covered and concealed firing positions are not available or when enemy counterfire is anticipated. For example, if the only place mortars can shoot from is on a roadway, a hide position adjacent to the road and under some trees, the position could be occupied by the crew until receipt of a fire mission. Baseplates can be left in the shoot position, or stakes can be used to mark positions. Aiming posts and the aiming circle may be left set up. Units with an MFCS can be particularly effective using this technique.

CAMOUFLAGE

8-59. Camouflaging a position is accomplished during all stages of construction. Erecting camouflage netting, when available, should be accomplished before beginning construction to conceal the work effort.

FIRING LOWEST CHARGE AND ELEVATION

8-60. Firing the lowest charge and elevation reduces the chance of mortar rounds being detected by radar because of reduced trajectory and time in flight. Also, responsiveness of fires is increased by reducing time of flight. Target effects must be considered since lower trajectories also mean less lethal area coverage.

FREQUENT DISPLACEMENT

8-61. Frequent displacement enhances survivability from enemy counterfire but can also degrade the ability of mortars to provide immediate massed fires. To aid continuous fire support, employment and displacement by section and squad may be needed. The timing and number of moves are critical to survival and should be based on commander's guidance, the tactical situation, and enemy target acquisition and counterfire threat. Frequent displacement reduces the time available to properly prepare positions and increases crew fatigue.

OFFSET REGISTRATION

8-62. Offset registration reduces the vulnerability of the primary position when one mortar fires adjustment rounds from offset locations. It also increases control problems and relies on radio communications to transmit firing data.

ROVING MORTAR

8-63. A roving mortar can conduct registrations and fire missions from a number of supplementary positions. This assists in concealing a platoon's primary position and in confusing the enemy as to the number of mortar sections or tubes employed. A platoon vacates these supplementary firing positions upon completion of a specific mission.

REDUCING THE NUMBER OF ADJUSTING ROUNDS

8-64. Platoons can increase accuracy and reduce adjusting rounds in several ways. All reduce the threat from enemy target acquisition. A few of the means are—

- Position-location devices such as a GPS or position azimuth determining system.
- Registrations (abbreviated, regular).
- Computation of meteorological data corrections.
- Hasty survey from known points to eliminate map errors.
- Use of friendly artillery radar to accurately locate firing position (coordinate through FSO/FSC).

8-65. Although these techniques reduce vulnerability, increase effectiveness of fires, and conserve ammunition, they may require support from artillery (survey teams, radar, meteorological data).

WIRE COMMUNICATIONS

8-66. Platoons can use wire in a static situation and, when time allows, wire is recommended for all positions. It provides reliable communications while reducing the electronic signature that results from using radios. However, emplacing wire takes time and can be cut by enemy artillery, unless it is dug in.

MASSING FIRES

8-67. Massing fires of several sections is a technique to overload enemy target acquisition means. It can also reduce the number of volleys needed on one target. Massing mortar fires can be difficult to control and may require increased radio communications. When possible, sections should mass mortar fires by firing time-on-target missions.

TERRAIN MORTAR POSITIONING

8-68. To increase survivability on the battlefield, a mortar unit must take full advantage of the natural cover and concealment afforded by the terrain and existing vegetation. This method is standard procedure for mortar units with operational automated fire direction systems. Units without these systems or operating under degraded fire direction conditions use terrain mortar positioning. (See Chapter 7 for details.)

SECTION VI – GROUND DEFENSE PLAN

8-69. Platoon leaders ensure that a mortar platoon does everything possible for its own security. Regardless of where a mortar platoon, section, or squad is located, defense of the position against a ground attack must be planned, organized, and implemented.

COORDINATION AND SECURITY PLAN

8-70. When there is a high threat of enemy ground attack, a mortar unit may have additional personnel to assist in the defense. A mortar unit can be positioned near a reserve company or near other friendly forces that can assist in providing security. If a mortar platoon is positioned near a friendly unit, it should be fully integrated into the defense. In this way, a unit will be able to tailor security measures to assist the mortar unit. Coordination includes—

- Location of primary, alternate, and supplementary firing positions.
- Designation of individual sectors of fire.

- Identification of dead space between units and how to cover it with fire.
- The use of visual and audible signals.
- Location of OPs.
- Location and types of obstacles and how to cover them with fire.
- Patrols to be conducted to include size, type, time of departure and return, and routes.

8-71. Mortar units may be positioned inside perimeters that are defended by other U.S. forces or host country armed forces. A mortar unit leader must coordinate with the base defense CP to determine his unit's responsibilities. He must, however, understand that the protection of his unit is his responsibility and establish procedures for close-in defense and security.

DEFENSE PLAN

8-72. A mortar platoon leader's defense plan includes the following tasks that are accomplished based on priority of work:

- Establishing local security.
- Positioning and laying mortars.
- Establishing the FDC.
- Clearing mask and overhead obstructions.
- Improving mortar positions (continuous).
- Establishing sectors of fire for individual weapons.
- Emplacing obstacles such as protective wire and tangle foot.
- Emplacing command-detonated claymore mines.

SECURITY MEASURES

8-73. A mortar leader establishes security for his unit so that the enemy cannot observe or surprise the platoon. He considers the company TACSOP, the orders received from his commander, the enemy situation, and terrain and visibility conditions.

8-74. Observation posts are situated to provide early warning along enemy avenues of approach. They should be covered and concealed and have covered and concealed routes to and from them. If available, the platoon employs sensors to provide early warning.

8-75. The mortar platoon leader establishes security within the platoon's firing positions. This is accomplished by—

- Establishing positions that avoid enemy avenues of approach.
- Enforcing noise and light discipline.
- Minimizing electronic transmissions.
- Assigning sectors of observation and fire.
- Placing machine guns along most likely enemy approaches.
- Tying in with adjacent squads and other units, if applicable.
- Positioning OPs.
- Emplacing obstacles.
- Conducting stand-to.

8-76. A mortar platoon leader must designate a set number of men to be alert at all times. The number will vary with the enemy situation, terrain, and visibility. Normally, at least one-fourth of the platoon should be alert at all times. When an attack is expected, the entire platoon is alert.

POSITIONING OF MORTAR SQUADS

8-77. When positioning mortars, a mortar unit leader ensures that mortars can provide effective indirect fire support. Normally, mortar firing positions are also the positions from which squads defend. If time is available, squads can prepare alternate and supplementary positions. A platoon leader gives each squad primary and secondary sectors of fire, and a squad leader gives each individual primary and secondary sectors of fire. Sectors of fire should be planned so that adjacent sectors of fire are overlapping. All available machine guns and close combat munitions should be included in the defense plan. Machine gun positions and sectors of fire should cover likely Infantry avenues of approach and fire across the platoon's front. Machine gun sectors of fire should overlap. Each machine gun should be given primary and secondary sectors of fire. (See FM 3-22.68/MCWP 3-15.1 for details.)

OBSTACLES AND MINES

8-78. When time permits, a platoon improves the security of a mortar position by emplacing protective wire and claymore mines. The placement of obstacles and mines must be coordinated with the senior commander at a defensive position.

CONDUCT OF THE DEFENSE

8-79. By understanding the type of missions that a mortar platoon can be expected to perform and by knowing when and how the platoon may be attacked, a platoon leader can tailor his defense based on resources and the threat. During the defense, a platoon leader must—

* Continue to provide responsive indirect fire support even while defending the mortar position.
* Supervise to ensure that security is maintained.
* Control and direct fire.
* Move troops within the position to counter enemy efforts.
* Monitor ammunition resupply and equipment replacement.
* Reorganize and reestablish the defense during lulls in battle.

Chapter 9
Sustainment/Logistics

Sustainment/logistics is essential for the operation of mortar units. Without mortar ammunition and other supplies, mortar units cannot accomplish their mission. This chapter discusses the aspects of sustainment/logistics that affect battalion mortars and company mortars. Sustainment/logistics includes the areas of administration and logistics that keep mortarmen mobile, fed, armed, clothed, maintained, and supplied for combat operations. Sustainment/logistics procedures are the same for mortar units as any other combat unit. They differ primarily in the types and bulk of ammunition required. Such supplies are coordinated and distributed through field and combat trains.

SECTION I – TEXT REFERENCES

9-1. Within this manual, selected topics are only briefly discussed and readers are referred to another publication for more detail. Mortar and other combat units use these tactics, techniques, and procedures in the same or very similar manner and a detailed discussion in this manual would be redundant. However, they are as important as the subjects discussed in detail. Table 9-1 consolidates the references to additional information.

Table 9-1. Guide for subjects referenced in text

Subject	References
Medical evacuation	FM 3-21.10/MCWP 3-11.1

SECTION II – PLANNING CONSIDERATIONS

9-2. Planning sustainment/logistics operations is primarily a company- and battalion-level responsibility. While a company commander and XO plan the operation, a mortar leader is responsible for his unit's execution of the plan. During planning, a mortar leader recommends the number and mix of mortar ammunition required for the mission and he also provides input. Since a mortar unit is usually separated from a HQ and HQ company and has unique ammunition requirements, mortar leadership, especially a section leader and platoon sergeant, is heavily involved in its sustainment/logistics operations. A platoon sergeant or section leader executes the sustainment/logistics plan at squad and vehicle level.

SUSTAINMENT/LOGISTICS PLAN

9-3. Planning considerations include the development of the sustainment/logistics plan that is based on the operational requirements. The sustainment/logistics plan addresses—
- Types of support.
- Quantities, especially types and mix of mortar ammunition required for the mission.
- Type of targets and threats.
- Terrain and weather.
- Time and location.
- Requirements.
- Resupply techniques.

INDIVIDUAL RESPONSIBILITIES

9-4. Individual sustainment/logistics responsibilities within a mortar unit include—
- A platoon/section leader has overall responsibility for his unit's sustainment/logistics. He is specifically responsible for its planning and providing input into a company's plan.

- A platoon sergeant or company mortar section leader is a unit's main sustainment/logistics operator. He executes his unit's logistical plan based on platoon and company TACSOPs.

SECTION III – AMMUNITION SUPPLY RATES

9-5. The critical factor in the ability of a mortar unit to support a commander's scheme of maneuver and to accomplish its mission is the availability of mortar ammunition. The expenditure of mortar ammunition must be managed based on tactical priorities and ammunition availability. Tactical commanders manage and control expenditures by the use of ammunition allocations. Unit basic loads should be reviewed prior to a deployment to ensure that an adequate amount and type of ammunition is on hand for anticipated usage.

REQUIRED SUPPLY RATE

9-6. A battalion or squadron operations officer in coordination with a mortar platoon leader and platoon sergeant estimates the type and amount of mortar ammunition needed for a particular combat operation. He then submits these RSRs to a BCT or Marine Infantry regiment HQ. A mortar platoon leader assists an operations officer in determining the RSRs. He uses historical records, rate-of-fire computations, or a combination of both. Once an RSR is determined, it is used to plan the transportation requirements for moving a mortar platoon's ammunition from an ammunition transfer point to a firing location.

CONTROLLED SUPPLY RATE

9-7. Due to rapidly changing combat situations and problems that may arise in the logistical system, the actual available supply rate of mortar ammunition can be less than the RSR. If so, action must be taken to control expenditures. Each tactical commander, down to battalion level, announces a CSR of mortar ammunition, expressed in rounds (by type) per mortar per day. A mortar platoon or section leader considers the CSR during his planning and execution of fires. A CSR cannot be exceeded except in emergencies and then only by the permission of the next higher commander. It is more combat effective to limit the number of mortar missions fired, firing enough rounds for each mission, than to ration rounds.

SECTION IV – SUPPORT AND REQUESTING SUPPLIES

9-8. Battalion and company sustainment/logistics support is located in their trains. Trains are groupings of sustainment/logistics vehicles, equipment, and personnel; they are divided into combat and field trains. Unit combat trains are forward and coordinate the sustainment/logistics effort while unit field trains receive, organize, and distribute supplies. Mortar units request supplies through their company XO or first sergeant/company gunnery sergeant. These requests are sent forward and logistics packages (LOGPACs) are assembled, moved forward, and distributed. A mortar platoon sergeant, HQ and HQ's company and line first sergeants meet the vehicles carrying LOGPACs at the logistic release point and lead them to the platoon and section positions.

BATTALION TRAINS

9-9. Battalion field trains are where most of a battalion's bulk-loaded ammunition, fuel, food, and other supplies are kept until delivered forward by LOGPAC to a company. A battalion combat trains CP receives supply requests from a company, consolidates them, and forwards them. A battalion combat trains consist of a CP, a battalion aid station, maintenance personnel and equipment, and vehicles loaded with the rest of the battalion's combat load and fuel.

COMPANY TRAINS

9-10. Company trains are the focal point for company sustainment/logistics operations. The first sergeant/company gunnery sergeant or XO positions the trains and supervises sustainment/logistics operations. It is the most forward sustainment/logistics element, and provides essential medical treatment and critical resupply support. The size and composition of company trains vary depending upon the tactical situation. Trains may consist of nothing more than planned locations on the ground during fast-paced offensive operations, or they may contain two-to-five tactical vehicles during resupply operations.

REQUESTS FOR SUPPORT AND ROUTINE SUPPLIES

9-11. Requesting support and routine supplies is a simple matter for a mortar unit. A heavy mortar platoon sergeant or company mortar section leader submits requests, by hand or electronically via voice radio or FBCB2 to the company CP. A company XO or first sergeant transmits mortar unit requirements through a supply sergeant to a battalion logistics staff officer who directs a support platoon leader to ship supplies.

9-12. Maintenance and recovery support are requested the same way as supplies. An XO or first sergeant/company gunnery sergeant directs a company's maintenance assets to a platoon.

9-13. During an operation, support is limited to medical and maintenance activities. Emergency resupply is performed by a first sergeant/company gunnery sergeant. He continuously monitors the company command net and the FBCB2 and sends medical and maintenance support forward to a mortar unit when required. He informs combat trains on a continuing basis.

SECTION V – RESUPPLY

9-14. This section covers classes of supply, miscellaneous items, resupply operations and techniques, LOGPACs, and in- and out-position supply techniques. There are few supply items held at a company and battalion, and most resupply originates in a BCT support area. Therefore, accurate and timely requests for supply, maintenance, and other sustainment/logistics functions are essential to maintain a mortar unit and its ability to accomplish its mission.

BASIC LOADS

9-15. A commander normally prescribes a standard amount of supplies to be kept on hand, called a basic load. It is the amount of supplies necessary to sustain operations until resupply. The most common basic loads are Class I (rations and water), Class II (clothing, especially mission-oriented protective posture equipment), Class III (petroleum, oils, and lubricants), and IV (protection supplies, especially sandbags and concertina wire), and Class IX (repair parts, especially batteries), and Class V (ammunition). The type and amount of the required basic load is in a unit's TACSOP. Mortar leaders are especially concerned about ammunition and its availability. Ammunition supplies depend on the RSR and the length of time before resupply. It is limited by what can be transported, but not necessarily in a single lift. Ammunition basic loads for a mortar unit should be examined in detail by a mortar platoon leader, reviewed by an operations staff officer and logistics staff officer, and approved by a battalion commander. Likewise, basic loads for company mortar sections are reviewed by a section leader and approved by a company commander. Basic loads are divided into the combat load (carried on a mortar unit's vehicles or personnel) and the bulk load (carried in a battalion field trains). Planning factors for Marine Corps units are contained in Marine Corps Order 8010.1.

9-16. When mortar units are located in firing positions for more than a short period, they may be able to build up stockades of ammunition far in excess of what could be carried as a basic load in the traditional sense. Leaders at all levels must manage ammunition closely. Both too little and too much can present problems for a unit.

9-17. The composition of a particular Class V basic load is METT-TC/METT-T dependent. Class V basic loads for mortars are constantly modified by a battalion commander based on that battalion's situation.

9-18. Combat experiences in World War II and Korea have shown that an on-board mix of 70 percent HE, 20 percent WP or smoke, and 10 percent illumination ammunition is the most flexible. These percentages may need to be modified for stability and other operations because of the ROE and other factors. These percentages must also be modified by a commander based on the available supply rate and the mission.

9-19. There is not always enough ammunition on-hand and there may be times when amounts of ammunition delivered to the mortars will be controlled. This is known as CSR and is designed to limit rounds per weapon per day. CSRs are imposed for two reasons— to conserve ammunition and to avoid an ammunition shortage for a designated tactical operation.

9-20. During fire support planning, consideration is given to ammunition requirements. This makes it essential for a mortar platoon leader or platoon sergeant to be present to advise what types and amounts of ammunition will be required. For example, if a mission is to be an illuminated attack at night, then additional illumination rounds must be brought forward to the mortar sites. If a mission is defense (day or night), sufficient HE and WP rounds must be on site. In either situation, a mortar platoon leader contacts supported commanders and advises them of any ammunition constraints.

9-21. Mortar ammunition is heavy, bulky, and takes time to break down and load onto vehicles or distributing it to personnel to carry. Mortar leaders should plan adequate time and resources to conduct these tasks. Table 9-2 provides data on mortar ammunition weights and dimensions.

Table 9-2. Weights and dimensions of selected mortar ammunition

Ammunition	Weight of Individual Round (LBS)	Number per Container	Container Weight (LBS)	Dimensions (L x W x H Approx.) (In)
60-mm M720 HE	3.75	16	116	15x13x20
60-mm M721 ILLUM	3.76	16	116	15x13x20
60-mm M722 Smoke	3.75	16	116	15x13x20
81-mm M821A2 HE	9.42	3	53.6	23x14x6
81-mm M853A1 ILLUM	9.43	3	58	30x14x6
81-mm M819 Smoke	10.8	3	63	30x14x6
120-mm M934 HE	31.2	2	96	12x6x32
120-mm M983 ILLUM	31.2	2	97	12x6x32
120-mm M929 Smoke	31.2	2	96	12x6x32

OTHER CLASSES OF SUPPLY

9-22. A company commander is responsible for ensuring that his mortar unit has sufficient supplies of commonly used items. These are normally requested in bulk and divided into platoon-sized shipments.

CLASS I: RATIONS AND WATER

9-23. A company XO or first sergeant/company gunnery sergeant orders rations (Class I) for a mortar unit based on its strength. Hot meals are prepared at a central location (battalion field trains) and trucked forward to a logistical release point. A mortar platoon sergeant or platoon representative meets the vehicle and guides it to the feeding location. Field feeding of hot meals and the delivery of meals, ready to eat can be accomplished in the following two ways:

- Food is brought to mortarmen at their position. To maintain readiness, a feeding plan is necessary. Usually, half of the unit eats while the other half maintains security and preparedness to fire.
- Crews are moved some distance away, usually several hundred meters, to where the food is served. In such cases, a feeding plan is critical to provide continuous support. Normally, no more than a third to one-half of the crews should be away from their positions at one time.

CLASS II: CLOTHING AND INDIVIDUAL EQUIPMENT

9-24. Unclassified maps are a Class II supply item and are requested the same as other supplies. Unclassified maps are obtained by a battalion logistics staff officer based on requirements established by a intelligence staff officer. They are distributed either through battalion supply channels or from an intelligence staff officer to the company HQ.

CLASS III: PETROLEUM, OIL, AND LUBRICANTS

9-25. Petroleum, oil, and lubricants (Class III) are delivered to a mortar platoon by battalion fuel trucks. The trucks are part of a battalion support platoon. Trucks deliver both fuel and required package products, such as engine oil, grease, and antifreeze. When this is done, mortars, with ammunition, should be ground-mounted or a platoon must accept the loss of firepower. A driver and vehicle commander should accompany the vehicle to the refuel point. The rest of the crew mans the firing positions.

9-26. When displacing, a platoon should be able to top off its vehicles from a manned logistic release point while en route to a new firing position.

CLASS IV: CONSTRUCTION AND ENGINEERING MATERIALS

9-27. Sandbags, wire and fabric containers, metal containers, timber material, and other barrier material fall into supply Class IV and are issued as needed or as required. It requires a lot of material to adequately protect a position, and leaders should refer to the appropriate manuals for required material and construction methods.

CLASS IX: REPAIR PARTS

9-28. Crew-replaceable items are requested through a company XO or first sergeant/company gunnery sergeant for company and battalion mortar platoons. Repair parts are usually brought forward with Class I, III, and V resupply. Other repair parts required by company and battalion maintenance are either on hand, in a company's prescribed load list, or requested as required. Mortar platoons can carry some of the repair parts in their carriers, such as light bulbs, firing pins, and other crew-replaceable, expendable parts.

9-29. Batteries, other than vehicle batteries and rechargeable batteries, are controlled by a communications section. Like ammunition, each platoon keeps a basic load of batteries, by type, on hand. Replacement batteries are requested and are delivered along with other supplies. The stockade, use, and reordering of batteries has become most important with the fielding of more modern devices such as CBRN alarms and night vision devices.

RESUPPLY OPERATIONS

9-30. Resupply operations can be described as routine, immediate, and prestock. Each method is developed in a company TACSOP and rehearsed in training. The actual method selected will depend on the METT-TC/METT-T conditions.

9-31. Routine resupply operations are the regular resupply of Classes I (rations and water), III (petroleum, oils, and lubricants), V (ammunition), and IX (repair parts) items; mail; and any other items requested. Routine resupply normally takes place daily. Periods of limited visibility are often the best times to resupply. Class III should be resupplied at every opportunity. The LOGPAC technique is a simple, efficient way to accomplish routine resupply operations. A company team and battalion TACSOPs specify the exact composition and march order of the LOGPAC. A LOGPAC is a centrally organized resupply convoy originating at battalion field trains. LOGPACs should contain all anticipated supplies required to sustain a mortar unit for a specified time (usually 24 hours or until the next scheduled LOGPAC operation).

9-32. Company supply sergeants/police sergeants assemble a LOGPAC under the supervision of a support platoon leader or HQ and HQ's company commander in battalion field trains located in the BCT/RCT support area. Replacements and individuals released from a hospital are brought to a company on LOGPAC vehicles. Once a company LOGPAC is prepared for movement, a supply sergeant/police sergeant moves it as part of the task force resupply convoy led by a support platoon leader. In emergencies, a LOGPAC can be dispatched individually to meet a first sergeant/company police sergeant at a logistic release point.

9-33. A task force LOGPAC convoy is met at a battalion logistic release point by representatives from the combat trains and unit maintenance collection point (UMCP), company first sergeants/company gunnery sergeant, and the platoon sergeant from the mortar platoon. The first sergeant/company gunnery sergeant—

- Turns in routine reports to combat trains representatives.
- Turns in parts requisitions and the deadline status to a UMCP representative.

- Picks up routine correspondence.
- Awaits the LOGPAC.

9-34. A platoon sergeant or his representative meets the LOGPAC and guides the LOGPAC to a platoon resupply point.

RESUPPLY TECHNIQUES

9-35. A first sergeant/company gunnery sergeant establishes a mortar platoon's resupply point using the in-position (tailgate), out-of-position (service station), or prepositioning technique. A commander, or XO if delegated, decides on the technique to be employed and informs the first sergeant/company gunnery sergeant. The first sergeant/company gunnery sergeant briefs each LOGPAC vehicle driver on the resupply technique to be used. He also notifies the mortar platoon that it is ready. The commander directs the platoon to conduct resupply based on the tactical situation. Any of these techniques can be used for resupply, but the in-position (tailgate) technique is the most common and preferred for a mortar unit because of the amount of ammunition to be transferred. However, sometimes the mortar platoon may have a more urgent need for resupply that cannot wait for a routine LOGPAC and immediate resupply must be used.

IN-POSITION RESUPPLY

9-36. In-position resupply is a technique of bringing supplies directly to the mortar position. Resupply vehicles drive to each mortar carrier or position to refuel and deliver ammunition.

OUT-OF-POSITION RESUPPLY

9-37. This resupply technique is the least preferred method, but there are times when it is unavoidable. It is used when an enemy situation or the terrain prevents movement of thin-skinned supply vehicles forward to a platoon's position.

9-38. When this method is used, individual vehicles move back to, or through, a centrally located rearm and refuel point. Based on the enemy situation, one vehicle per platoon, section, or even an entire platoon pull out of their positions, resupply, and return to their position. In this method—

- Mortar vehicles enter the resupply point following one-way traffic flow.
- Only vehicles requiring immediate unit or higher maintenance stop in the maintenance holding area before conducting resupply.
- Those wounded-in-action, killed-in-action, and enemy prisoners-of-war have not already been evacuated; they are removed from platoon vehicles when they stop at a refuel or rearm point.
- Vehicles rearm and refuel moving through each point.
- Crews rotate individually to feed, pick up mail, pick up supplies, and refill or exchange water cans.
- When all vehicles have completed resupply, they move to the holding area where a platoon leader or platoon sergeant conducts a pre-combat inspection (time permitting).

Note. A medical evacuation vehicle is positioned an equal distance from refueling and rearming points. This decreases the distance traveled by litter teams and provides safety from fire or explosion for the casualties.

9-39. Before sending vehicles for resupply, heavy mortars from a combined arms battalion may be ground mounted. This is done when a mission requires all mortars be prepared to fire. However, ground-mounted mortars lose their automatic fire direction capability and must follow the procedures for degraded fire direction operations. If a platoon is required to displace before the return of vehicles, ground-mounted mortars and partial crews are cross-loaded on the remaining vehicles and moved to the next position. Personnel sent back for resupply are briefed on the most likely contingency. They use the platoon displacement plan or FBCB2 to determine the location of the vehicle.

9-40. Trainload is a modified version of out-of-position resupply. With this method, a platoon sends a portion of its vehicles back to the supply point, loads them up, and then returns to resupply the rest of the platoon.

9-41. When translating is the desired method, a platoon ground-mounts its mortars (if mounted), and sends a man or two from each mortar with an empty carrier. With this method, all mortars can still fire with only minimum degradation due to missing personnel.

PRE-POSITIONING

9-42. Units may preposition supplies on or near the point of planned use. This permits a mortar unit to move into a position and have ammunition. Class V supplies are often prepositioned for a mortar platoon, especially in the defense. The location and amount of prepositioned ammunition must be carefully planned and each mortar squad leader informed. A platoon leader must verify the locations of the propositioning sites during his reconnaissance and rehearsals. When propositioning supplies, the following must be considered:

- Covered and protected positions are needed for propositioned ammunition. If sufficient trailers are available, they can be used to preposition ammunition. Mortar carriers/prime movers can tow them from the preposition site to the next position.
- Propositioning frees cargo vehicles to return and bring more ammunition forward.
- A mortar platoon cannot guard preposition sites and, therefore, risks the capture or destruction of prepositioned ammunition.
- Propositioned ammunition must be far enough away from vehicles and individual fighting positions so its destruction will not cause friendly vehicle damage or personnel casualties, yet close enough to be loaded by hand.
- Prepositioned ammunition must be removed from its protective packing before it can be loaded or fired. This takes time and creates large amounts of residue. Prying and cutting tools are needed to quickly open large amounts of ammunition boxes.

9-43. The decision to use the preposition technique is normally made at battalion level. When a position that has been prestocked is occupied, the prestocked supplies are to be used first. Depending on the situation, this means that a mortar platoon immediately tops off the vehicle fuel tanks and fills up the on-board ammunition racks. Any remaining ammunition from the prestock supply is fired before any of the on-board ammunition is fired.

IMMEDIATE RESUPPLY

9-44. Occasionally, a mortar platoon may have an urgent need for resupply that it cannot wait for a routine LOGPAC (normally a result of combat). Emergency resupply can involve any type of supplies, but ammunition and fuel are the most common. Battalion combat trains normally keep some mortar ammunition up-loaded and ready to move to a mortar platoon. Emergency resupply is often conducted while in contact with an enemy. Heavy combat may generate a need for ammunition several times in the course of a day. A mortar platoon sergeant and company mortar section leader must track ammunition expenditures, understand the amount of time required for resupply, and request ammunition in time to prevent on-hand ammunition stocks affecting their unit's operations.

AERIAL RESUPPLY

9-45. Aerial resupply is a fast method to resupply mortar units, especially those in isolated positions. If available, helicopters can carry internal or external ammunition loads directly to a firing position. Ammunition may be prepared and marked in accordance with a TACSOP on pallets, if available, for delivery by sling-load. The location of a sling-load should be identified for planned or emergency resupply.

SECTION VI – MAINTENANCE

9-46. Maintenance includes inspecting, testing, servicing, repairing, requisitioning, recovering, and evacuating vehicles and equipment. An operator performs a key role in ensuring that vehicles, weapons, and equipment are maintained and operational by conducting preventive checks and services. Leaders ensure that operators are assigned to and perform preventive checks and services on each piece of equipment assigned to a unit. Maintenance at the mortar unit level consists of thorough preventive maintenance checks and services and reporting of maintenance problems to the company. Mortar units have equipment, especially weapons and electronic systems, which may have to be evacuated and repaired at the BCT or higher level. Accurate reporting of problems can therefore speed the repair and return of mission essential equipment.

UNIT MAINTENANCE COLLECTION POINT

9-47. A company XO and first sergeant organize company combat trains and usually consist of the UMCP. The UMCP is normally located near the combat trains or collocated with the combat trains for security, and should be on a main axis or supply route. The UMCP is manned by elements of a forward support company from a brigade support battalion. The UMCP provides vehicle and equipment evacuation, and maintenance support to a field maintenance support teams. Field maintenance support teams evacuate vehicles and equipment to the UMCP that cannot be repaired within two hours. Normally, vehicles or equipment evacuated to the UMCP that cannot be towed or repaired within 4-6 hours, are further evacuated to field trains, brigade support battalion/combat logistics battalion, or higher level support unit.

MAINTENANCE REPAIR FLOW

9-48. Company maintenance functions begin with preventive maintenance checks and services, daily crew responsibility, and crew level preparation of the appropriate equipment inspection and maintenance forms. These forms are the primary means through which a company obtains maintenance support or repair parts. The forms follow a pathway from crew level to a BCT/RCT support area and back. Per unit TACSOP, a company XO or first sergeant/company gunnery sergeant supervises the flow of these critical maintenance documents and parts. The flow of reporting and repairing equipment includes the following:

- Squad leaders or vehicle commanders collect the maintenance forms each day and send them via FBCB2 or give them to the platoon sergeant or company mortar section leader, who consolidates the forms for their platoon or company mortar section.
- The platoon sergeant/section forwards an electronic version or gives a hard copy of the forms to the XO or first sergeant/company gunnery sergeant, who reviews and verifies problems and deficiencies and requests parts needed for maintenance and repairs. The electronic versions of the forms are consolidated at company level and then transmitted to the battalion and its supporting combat repair team. During the next LOGPAC operation, the completed hard copy forms are returned to the combat repair team to document completion of the repair.
- In the BCT/RCT support area, the required repair parts are packaged for delivery during the next scheduled resupply or through emergency resupply means.
- The individuals or vehicle crew conducts initial maintenance, repair, and recovery actions on site. Once it is determined that the crew cannot repair or recover the vehicle or equipment, the platoon contacts the XO or first sergeant/company gunnery sergeant. If additional assistance is needed, the combat repair team assesses the damaged or broken equipment and makes necessary repairs to return the piece of equipment to fully mission-capable or mission-capable status, if appropriate.

SECTION VII – MEDICAL SUPPORT

9-49. This section covers medical support for company and battalion mortar platoons, evacuation of casualties, priority of evacuation, and reporting casualties. Procedures are the same as for any Infantry unit except that company mortar sections do not usually have a medic attached.

COMPANY MORTARS

9-50. Infantry companies are provided combat medics/corpsmen on the basis of one per rifle platoon and one senior combat medic/corpsmen for each company HQ. An evacuation section with an ambulance may be attached. Company mortar platoons receive medical support from the company HQ or from a rifle platoon, depending on the situation. Casualties are transported in empty supply vehicles or by requesting ambulance support from the company HQ.

BATTALION MORTARS

9-51. A battalion mortar platoon is assigned a combat medic/corpsmen. The mortar platoon requests evacuation, on an administrative/logistics net, directly from the battalion aid station, located with the combat trains. Casualties can be backhauled on returning supply vehicles.

EVACUATION

9-52. The evacuation of casualties is the same for any Infantry unit. (See FM 3-21.10/MCWP 3-11.1 for details.)

SECTION VIII – INDIVIDUAL PERFORMANCE

9-53. This section discusses methods for sustaining the mortar section's performance during prolonged combat. In any conflict, combat operations are continuous and are at a high pace. Mortar platoons and sections must fight without stopping for long periods. Under these conditions performance of a unit suffers. A mortar leader uses several methods to conserve and prolong his unit's combat effectiveness.

STRESS IN COMBAT

9-54. The confusion, stress, and lethality of the modern battlefield place a burden on the Infantryman's endurance, courage, perseverance, and ability to perform in combat. Mortarmen conducting combat operations must perform complex collective and individual tasks without adequate sleep and under stress. Stress in combat is caused by the following:

- **Fear.** All experience the fear of death or being wounded, or the fear of failing in the eyes of one's comrades.
- **Limited visibility and low-light levels.** Smoke, darkness, fog, rain, snow, ice, and glare make it hard to see. The extended wear of night vision goggles, protective masks, or laser protective lenses causes stress.
- **Disrupted wake/sleep cycle.** Performance suffers during normal sleeping hours due to the disruption of the normal schedule.
- **Decisionmaking.** Mental stress results from making vital decisions with little time and insufficient information. It is increased during times of great confusion and exposure to danger.
- **Physical fatigue.** Working the muscles faster than they can be supplied with oxygen and fuel can cause individuals to function poorly without rest.
- **Physical discomfort.** Extreme cold, heat, wet, or thirst adds greatly to the level of individual stress.

FATIGUE

9-55. As sustained operations continue, all individuals begin to show effects of general fatigue and lack of sleep. Unless this is counteracted, mortar performance declines rapidly. Mortar sections can conduct sustained operations for 24 to 48 hours, extending 72 hours when required. Extensive training and standardization, plus cohesion and esprit de corps, allow limited sustained operations beyond 72 hours. All units experience serious degradation of combat effectiveness that quickly rises after 72 hours. A rule of thumb is to expect 25 percent degradation in performance for every 24 hours without sleep. Under the extreme demands of combat, units historically have conducted sustained operations for a maximum of 120 hours. The result was a total deterioration of combat effectiveness. Operations in mission-oriented protective posture, level four cause faster degradation of combat effectiveness. Leaders should consider the following effects of fatigue on mortar units:

- Though essential for endurance, sheer determination cannot offset the cumulative effects of sustained sleep loss. A unit that is subjected to extensive sustained operations requires a long period of rest and recuperation to regain combat effectiveness.
- Platoon and section leaders plan fires, integrate communications and plans, establish positions, and coordinate tactics. They show the effects of lack of sleep faster than the members of mortar squads.
- An FDC performs mentally demanding and complex tasks. Its ability to continue performing these tasks degrades severely over a period. For example, adjusting multiple missions can become difficult, and firing calculations are likely to be wrong as well as slow. Self-initiated tasks are especially likely to be forgotten.

CONTINUOUS OPERATIONS

9-56. Continuous operations cause a slower, but no less serious, degradation of combat effectiveness. Whether a task is degraded by loss of sleep depends on many interacting and sometimes counteracting factors. Complicated tasks are more stimulating to the brain and require more training to master. A simple task requires less training to do but can be boring. A high level of alertness is required to perform a task well after sleep loss. The following factors are interactive:

- **Task complexity or ambiguity.** FDC computer operators perform the most complex tasks and are usually the first to show the effects of sleep loss. Simpler, clearer tasks are less affected by sleep loss; complicated or ambiguous tasks will suffer from fatigue and loss of sleep. This applies to both physical and mental tasks.
- **State of alertness.** Combat operations are conducted at such a fast pace that a high state of arousal is maintained. However, even the most alert individuals are susceptible to crashing. This commonly occurs early during combat after as little as 24 hours of intense stress and sleeplessness. The body abruptly stops producing the high levels of adrenaline needed to sustain the initial activity. The result can be severe drowsiness, leading to near unconsciousness. Mortarmen, alert and aroused for 24 hours during the marshaling, loading, and insertion phase of an operation, can be overcome by intense fatigue, which starts after dawn of the first day of combat.
- **Level of training.** Extensive training delays the degradation of a task caused from lack of sleep. Training does not prevent lack of sleep from eventually affecting the performance of a task, but repetitive, stressful, realistic training can delay and moderate these effects.
- **Physical training.** Good physical training prepares the individual for sustained operations. It also allows him to recover quicker after a short rest than someone who is in poor physical condition. A good diet and healthful life style prepares the mortarman to cope with the physical stress of sustained operations.

TECHNIQUES TO SUSTAIN OPERATIONS

9-57. To maintain effectiveness, mortarmen must overcome adverse conditions. The rate of performance degradation must be slowed. The methods mortar leader can use to slow degradation and to prepare to fight sustained operations are—

- **Prepare individuals.** Preventive measures are often more effective for keeping groups healthy and active. They include improving or maintaining good physical condition, balanced nutrition, good personal hygiene, and immunizations.
- **Provide good leadership.**
- **Set high standards.**
- **Develop individual and unit confidence.**
- **Establish good communication channels.** In combat, knowledge of the situation and the status of both enemy and friendly units sustain men.
- **Cross train.** Extensive cross training in the mortar platoon provides flexibility. Critical tasks, such as FDC and aiming circle operations, must be cross trained.
- **Develop coping skills.** All members must experience and learn to cope with adverse factors, especially stress and lack of sleep.
- **Develop good physical fitness.** Whether moving heavy weapons, carrying large loads, or digging, physically fit mortarmen can use their strength reserves to recover after only a brief rest.
- **Build stamina.** Each member must develop aerobic fitness to work more and withstand the stress of sustained operations.
- **Practice pacing while extending physical limits.** All must be trained to pace themselves to work at their maximum range without degradation.
- **Foster a spirit and attitude of winning.** In combat, winning depends on skill and dedication. Especially in sustained operations, a mortarman who is dedicated demonstrates the extra strength needed to win.
- **Foster cohesion, esprit, morale, and commitment.**
- **Guarantee and encourage the free exercise of an individual's faith.**

TECHNIQUES TO SUSTAIN COMBAT PERFORMANCE

9-58. The following techniques can be used to sustain combat performance:
- Share physical and mental burdens among all members of the unit.
- Rotate boring tasks often.
- Share tasks by assigning two or more men to perform them.
- Cross-check all FDC calculations, sight settings, and map coordinates among other members of the unit.
- Avoid using strong artificial stimulants. The use of amphetamines or other strong stimulants has risks that outweigh the benefits.
- Learn to recognize signs of serious performance degradation in others. The least affected crewmen must perform the most important combat tasks.
- Learn to recognize signs of serious degradation in oneself. Leadership requires thinking, judging, calculating, determining, recognizing, distinguishing, and decision-making. These abilities degrade quickly in sustained operations.

UNIT SLEEP PLAN

9-59. A mortar unit leader must ensure his platoon can conduct both sustained and continuous operations. The only way a platoon can conduct continuous operations over long periods is to ensure all personnel get enough rest.

9-60. Platoon and section leaders must devise and enforce a work-rest-sleep plan for their unit. Squad leaders must enforce this plan, which must include provisions for all to obtain sleep. The plan should allow individuals at least four hours of sleep each 24 hours, preferably uninterrupted and ideally between 2400 and 0600. Priority for sleep should go to FDC personnel, drivers, and others whose judgment and decision making are critical to mission accomplishment. Even with an average of four hours of sleep a night, individual performance will gradually degrade.

9-61. Twelve-hour shifts are the most effective. Rotating shifts are difficult for most to adjust to and should be avoided, if possible.

9-62. The quality of sleep is important. Four hours of sleep in a protected, comfortable position at a comfortable temperature are much more helpful than a longer but more uncomfortable period.

9-63. The effects of sleep deprivation are cumulative. If three troops do their part of a task at 50 percent effectiveness, the chances that the whole task will be accomplished correctly are less than 50 percent. In fact, it is about 12 percent ($.5 \times .5 \times .5 = .125$). Army studies on the effects of individual sleep deprivation on artillery FDC and mortar crews show that seven hours of sleep for each man a day can maintain effectiveness indefinitely. Five to six hours of sleep a day can maintain acceptable performance for 10 to 15 days. Four hours of sleep for each day can maintain acceptable performance for only two to three days. Less than three hours of sleep a day is almost the same as not sleeping at all.

DUTY MORTAR

9-64. One method for allowing mortar crews to rest, which has proven useful in combat, is the designation of a duty mortar. One mortar crew is designated for answering all initial calls for fire. This crew remains awake near its mortar during the entire tour of duty. The other crews can sleep without having anyone awake to respond immediately to fire missions. All mortars in the section must be laid on the priority target if one has been designated. A minimum amount of ammunition is prepared to fire the priority mission. Local security must still be established, and the FDC must have at least two people awake, a radiotelephone operator and an FDC computer. An easily initiated and effective signal for the whole mortar section to wake up and join in the fire mission must also be established. This may have to be a runner, since history has shown that exhausted mortar crews will not wake up, even when the mortar next to them begins to fire. After several days of sleep deprivation, the body will not respond to the sounds of outgoing fire.

This page intentionally left blank.

Glossary

Acronym	Definition
AO	area of operations
ATGM	antitank guided missile
BCT	brigade combat team
CAS	close air support
CBRN	chemical, biological, radiological, and nuclear
CFL	coordinated fire line
CP	command post
CSR	controlled supply rate
DS	direct support
FBCB2	Force XXI battle command, brigade, and below
FDC	fire direction center
FIST	fire support team
FiST	fire support team (Marine Corps)
FM	frequency modulation; field manual
FMFM	Fleet Marine Force Manual
FO	forward observer
FPF	final protective fire
FRAGO	fragmentary order
FSC	fire support coordinator (Marine Corps)
FSCC	fire support coordination center (Marine Corps)
FSCL	fire support coordination line
FSCM	fire support coordinating measure
FSO	fire support officer
GPS	Global Positioning System
GS	general support
HE	high explosive
HQ	headquarters
IR	infrared
JMEM	Joint Munitions Effectiveness Manual
LHMBC	light handheld mortar ballistic computer
LOGPAC	logistics package

MCWP	Marine Corps Warfighting Publication
MCRP	Marine Corps Reference Publication
METT-T	mission, enemy, terrain and weather, troops and support available- time available (Marine Corps)
METT-TC	mission, enemy, terrain and weather, troops and support available- time available, and civil considerations (Army)
MFCS	mortar fire control system
NBC reports	nuclear, biological, and chemical reports
OP	observation post
OPCON	operational control
OPORD	operation order
RCT	regimental combat team (Marine Corps)
RED	risk-estimate distance
ROE	rules of engagement
RP	red phosphorous
RPG	rocket-propelled grenade
RSR	required supply rate
SA	situational awareness
SBCT	Stryker Brigade Combat Team
TACSOP	tactical standing operating procedure
TLP	troop-leading procedure
UAS	unmanned aircraft system
UMCP	unit maintenance collection point
WARNO	warning order (Army)
WARNORD	warning order (Marine Corps)
WP	white phosphorous
XO	executive officer

References

SOURCES USED
These are the sources quoted or paraphrased in this publication.

FM 1-02, *Operational Terms and Graphics*, 21 September 2004.

JP 3-02, *Amphibious Operations*, 10 August 2009.

JP 3-09, *Joint Fire Support*, 30 June 2010.

JP 3-09.3, *Close Air Support*, 8 July 2009.

DOCUMENTS NEEDED
These documents must be available to the intended user of this publication.

ARMY FORMS
DA Forms are available on the APD web site (www.apd.army.mil).

DA Form 2028, *Recommended Changes to Publications and Blank Forms*, February 1974.

ARMY FIELD MANUALS
FM 3-0, *Operations*, 27 February 2008.

FM 3-06.11, *Combined Arms Operations in Urban Terrain*, 28 February 2002.

FM 3-09.12, *Tactics, Techniques, and Procedures for Field Artillery Target Acquisition*, 21 June 2002.

FM 3-09.31, *Tactics, Techniques, and Procedures for Fire Support for the Combined Arms Commander*, 1 October 2002.

FM 3-09.32, *JFIRE Multi-Service Tactics, Techniques, and Procedures for the Joint Application of Firepower*, 20 December 2007.

FM 3-11.4, *Multiservice Tactics, Techniques, and Procedures for Nuclear, Biological, and Chemical (NBC) Protection*, 2 June 2003.

FM 3-21.8, *The Infantry Rifle Platoon and Squad*, 28 March 2007.

FM 3-21.9, *The SBCT Infantry Rifle Platoon and Squad*, 2 December 2002.

FM 3-21.10, *The Infantry Rifle Company*, 27 July 2006.

FM 3-21.20, *The Infantry Battalion*, 13 December 2006.

FM 3-21.75, *The Warrior Ethos and Soldier Combat Skills*, 28 January 2008.

FM 3-21.91, *Tactical Employment of Antiarmor Platoons and Companies*, 26 November 2002.

FM 3-22.68, *Crew Served Weapons*, 21 July 2006.

FM 3-22.90, *Mortars*, 7 December 2007.

FM 3-22.91, *Mortar Fire Direction Center Procedures*, 17 July 2008.

FM 3-97.6, *Mountain Operations*, 28 November 2000.

FM 4-0, *Sustainment*, 30 April 2009.

FM 4-20.197, *Multiservice Helicopter Sling Load: Basic Operations and Equipment*, 20 July 2006.

FM 4-20.198, *Multiservice Helicopter Sling Load: Single-Point Load Rigging Procedures*, 20 February 2009.

FM 5-0, *The Operations Process*, 26 March 2010.

FM 5-34, *Engineer Field Data*, 19 July 2005.

FM 5-103, *Survivability*, 10 June 1985.

FM 6-20, *Fire Support in the Airland Battle*, 17 May 1988.

FM 6-20-20, *Tactics, Techniques, and Procedures for Fire Support at Battalion Task Force and Below*, 27 December 1991.

FM 6-30, *Tactics, Techniques, and Procedures for Observed Fire*, 16 July 1991.

Fleet Marine Force Manual

FMFM 6-4, *Marine Rifle Company/Platoon*, 17 February 1978.

Graphical Training Aids

GTA 90-01-011, 5th Edition, *Joint Forward Operations Base (JFOB) Survivability and Protective Construction Handbook*, 1 October 2009.

Marine Corps Publications

Marine Corps Order 8010.1E, *Class V(W) Planning Factors for Fleet Marine Force Combat Operations*, 15 April 1997.

MCDP 1-0, *Marine Corps Operations*, 27 September 2001.

MCRP 3-16.1A, *Tactics, Techniques, and Procedures for Field Artillery Target Acquisition*, 21 June 2002.

MCRP 3-16C, *Tactics, Techniques, and Procedures for Fire Support for the Combined Arms Commander*, 1 October 2002.

MCRP 3-16.6A, *JFIRE Multi-service Tactics, Techniques, and Procedures for the Joint Application of Firepower*, 20 December 2007.

MCRP 3-17A, *Engineer Field Data*, 19 July 2005.

MCRP 4-11.3E VOL I, *Multiservice Helicopter Sling Load: Basic Operations and Equipment*, 10 April 1997.

MCRP 4-11.3E VOL II, *Multiservice Helicopter Sling Load: Single-Point Load Rigging Procedures*, 20 February 2009.

MCRP 5-12A, *Operational Terms and Graphics*, 21 September 2004.

MCWP 3-11.1, *Marine Rifle Company/Platoon*, 17 February 1978.

MCWP 3-11.2, *Marine Rifle Squad*, 27 November 2002.

MCWP 3-11.4, *Helicopterborne Operations*, 16 August 2004.

MCWP 3-14, *Employment of the Light Armored Reconnaissance Battalion*, 17 September 2009.

MCWP 3-14.1, *Light Armored Vehicle -25 Gunnery and Employment*, 17 December 1997.

MCWP 3-15.1, *Machine Guns and Machine Gun Gunnery*, 1 September 1996.

MCWP 3-16, *Fire Support Coordination in the Ground Combat Element*, 28 November 2001.

MCWP 3-16.6, *Supporting Arms Observer, Spotter, and Controller*, 15 October 1998.

MCWP 3-35.3, *Military Operations on Urbanized Terrain (MOUT)*, 26 April 1998.

MCWP 3-37.2, *Multiservice Tactics, Techniques, and Procedures for Nuclear. Biological, and Chemical (NBC) Protection*, 2 June 2003.

MCWP 5-1, *Marine Corps Planning Process*, 24 August 2010.

Joint Publications

JP 1-02, *Department of Defense Dictionary of Military and Associated Terms*, 8 November 2010.

Other Publications

STANAG 2934, ED. 3, *Artillery Procedures – AARTYP -1(B)*.

WEBSITES

Some of the documents and individual and collective tasks referred to in this publication may be accessed at one the following Army websites:

Army Knowledge Online, https://akocomm.us.army.mil/usapa/doctrine/index.html

StrykerNet, https://strykernet.army mil

Digital Training Management System, https://dtms.army mil/DTMS

Reimer Doctrine and Training Digital Library, http://www.train.army mil

Marine Corps Doctrine Website, https://www.doctrine.usmc.mil/main.asp

Index

M

Marine Corps 81-mm and 60-mm mortar units, 1-16

massed fire, 4-2

mines, 4-13, 6-8, 6-9, 6-36, 8-17, 8-18

mission accomplishment, 2-1, 3-15, 6-6, 6-16, 7-3, 7-5, 8-6, 9-11

mission execution, 2-11

mortar fire control system, 1-17, 1-18, 1

mortar fires, 1-3
close support, 1-3
counterfire, 1-3, 1-4, 1-6, 5-3, 5-6, 5-9, 5-14, 6-3, 6-4, 6-17, 6-18, 6-20, 7-1, 8-1, 8-2, 8-3, 8-4, 8-6, 8-15
deception fires, 1-3
harassment fires, 1-3
interdiction fires, 1-3, 5-5, 5-9, 5-10

mortar platoon leader, 2-3, 2-4, 2-7, 2-10, 3-7, 3-12, 3-15, 3-17, 3-21, 3-24, 5-2, 5-3, 5-4, 5-8, 5-9, 6-6, 6-7, 6-9, 6-14, 6-20, 8-1, 8-17, 9-2, 9-3, 9-4

mortar squad leader, 2-6, 9-7

mortar tactical missions, 3-4

mortar unit leader(s), 2-1, 2-2, 2-7, 2-11, 2-12, 3-1, 3-2, 3-5, 3-6, 3-15, 3-17, 3-21, 5-2, 5-3, 5-8, 5-12, 5-13, 5-14, 6-1, 6-4, 6-11, 6-12, 6-13, 6-16, 6-20, 6-35, 6-37, 8-4, 8-17, 9-11

mountainous terrain, 6-1, 6-33, 6-34, 6-35, 8-4

N

no-fire area, 3-10

O

offensive operations, 4-13, 5-1, 5-2, 5-4, 5-18, 6-12, 7-5, 7-6, 8-2, 9-3
attacks, 5-2

exploitation and pursuit, 5-3
linkup, 3-4, 3-10, 5-4
movement to contact, 5-1, 5-2, 5-4, 5-20, 7-6, 7-7, 7-8
raids and ambushes, 5-4
reconnaissance in force, 5-4

operational control, 1-9, 3-3, 1

P

passage of lines, 5-18

planned fires, 1-5, 3-17, 3-24

platoon commander, 1-16, 1-18, 2-2, 7-2

platoon leaders, ix, 2-1, 3-21, 5-4

platoon sergeant, 1-16, 2-3, 2-4, 2-5, 2-6, 2-11, 6-5, 6-10, 9-1, 9-2, 9-3, 9-4, 9-5, 9-6, 9-7, 9-8

precombat inspections, 2-8
equipment, 2-8
mortar unit personnel, 2-8
supplies, 2-9
vehicles, 2-9

priorities of fire, 3-2, 3-3, 3-5, 3-6, 3-7, 6-6, 7-6

priority of missions, 3-3

priority targets, 3-11, 3-12

prisoners of war, 1-19, 2-10, 5-3, 5-14, 9-6

R

reconnaissance mortar units, 1-18

relief in place, 5-19

resupply operations, 9-3, 9-5

risk, x, 1-6, 1-7, 2-4, 5-6, 5-13, 5-19, 5-20, 6-34, 1

S

security measures, 8-17

security operations, 5-18

smoke mission, 4-9, 4-10, 4-11, 4-12

sniper, 3-13, 5-10, 5-11, 5-12, 5-13, 5-14, 6-24

stand-off attacks, x, 5-11, 5-12, 5-14

support relationships, x, 2-2, 3-3, 3-4, 3-6, 3-15
Army, 3-4
Marine Corps, 3-6

surface-to-surface attack, 3-9

sustainment/logistics, 2-10, 6-3, 6-4, 6-37, 9-1
planning, 1-7, 1-8, 1-12, 2-1, 2-2, 2-4, 2-7, 3-1, 3-2, 3-3, 3-11, 3-14, 3-15, 3-16, 3-20, 3-21, 3-24, 4-1, 4-2, 4-4, 4-5, 4-9, 4-10, 5-2, 5-3, 5-4, 5-8, 5-12, 5-14, 5-18, 5-20, 6-5, 6-12, 6-23, 6-24, 6-26, 6-31, 6-34, 7-7, 7-9, 7-10, 9-1, 9-2, 9-4

T

target area coverage, 6-6

target effects, 3-11, 4-1, 4-7, 4-9, 6-33

target types, 3-11
opportunity, 3-11
planned, 3-11

threats, 1-2
air attack, 8-2
electronic-warfare, 2-13
enemy counterfire, 8-1
ground attack, 8-2
irregular, 1-2
traditional, 1-2

troop commander, 2-2

U

UAS, 5-14, 6-5, 6-24, 8-2, 1

urban operations, 3-17, 6-30, 6-31, 6-32, 7-9

V

vulnerability, 4-2, 5-3, 6-18, 8-1, 8-15, 8-16

W

wounded-in-action, 9-6

ATTP 3-21.90
(FM 7-90)
MCWP 3-15.2
4 April 2011

By order of the Secretary of the Army:

GEORGE W. CASEY, JR.
General, United States Army
Chief of Staff

Official:

[signature: Joyce E. Morrow]

JOYCE E. MORROW
Administrative Assistant to the
Secretary of the Army
1106906

DISTRIBUTION:

Active Army, Army National Guard, and U.S. Army Reserve: To be distributed in accordance with the initial distribution number (IDN) 110801, requirements for ATTP 3-21.90.

BY DIRECTION OF THE COMMANDANT
OF THE MARINE CORPS

[signature: George J. Flynn]

GEORGE J. FLYNN
Lieutenant General, U.S. Marine Corps
Deputy Commandant for Combat Development
and Integration

PCN: 143 000092 00

9 781780 399591